JAMESTOWN LITERATURE PROGRAM
Growth in Comprehension & Appreciation

Reading & Understanding

Nonfiction

LEVEL I

About the Cover and the Artist

The design on the cover of this book is a quilt called The Great Divide, *created by quilt artist Esther Parkhurst of Los Angeles, California. Esther has lectured and exhibited extensively, and her work is included in over ninety corporate and private art collections in the United States and Japan.*

Books in the Program

Short Stories, Level I	*Cat. No. 861*		Short Stories, Level II	*Cat. No. 881*
Hardcover Edition	*Cat. No. 861H*		Hardcover Edition	*Cat. No. 881H*
Teacher's Guide	*Cat. No. 871*		Teacher's Guide	*Cat. No. 891*
Nonfiction, Level I	*Cat. No. 862*		Nonfiction, Level II	*Cat. No. 882*
Hardcover Edition	*Cat. No. 862H*		Hardcover Edition	*Cat. No. 882H*
Teacher's Guide	*Cat. No. 872*		Teacher's Guide	*Cat. No. 892*
Plays, Level I	*Cat. No. 863*		Plays, Level II	*Cat. No. 883*
Hardcover Edition	*Cat. No. 863H*		Hardcover Edition	*Cat. No. 883H*
Teacher's Guide	*Cat. No. 873*		Teacher's Guide	*Cat. No. 893*
Poems, Level I	*Cat. No. 864*		Poems, Level II	*Cat. No. 884*
Hardcover Edition	*Cat. No. 864H*		Hardcover Edition	*Cat. No. 884H*
Teacher's Guide	*Cat. No. 874*		Teacher's Guide	*Cat. No. 894*

JAMESTOWN LITERATURE PROGRAM
Growth in Comprehension & Appreciation

Reading & Understanding
Nonfiction

LEVEL I

Jamestown Publishers
Providence, Rhode Island

JAMESTOWN LITERATURE PROGRAM
Growth in Comprehension & Appreciation
Reading & Understanding Nonfiction
LEVEL I

Catalog No. 862
Catalog No. 862H, Hardcover Edition

Developed by
Jamestown Editorial Group
and
Helena Frost Associates, Gaynor Ellis, Editor

Cover and Text Design: Deborah Hulsey Christie
Photo Research: Helena Frost Associates

Illustrations:
Chapter 5, James Thurber

Photographs:
Chapter 1, National Archives
Chapter 2, Susan B. Anthony: The Granger Collection
Chapter 2, parade: Library of Congress
Chapter 3, Brian Berry/Yale School of Music
Chapter 4, Museum of the City of New York
Chapter 6, Australian Tourist Commission
Chapter 7, Kendall Young Library, Webster City, Iowa
Chapter 8, The New York Public Library
Chapter 9, Anne Frank: AP/Wide World Photos
Chapter 9, concentration camp: H. Armstrong Roberts
Chapter 10, Culver Pictures
Chapter 11, Laura Ingalls Wilder: Harper & Row
Chapter 11, Panama-Pacific International Exposition:
Culver Pictures
Chapter 12, Library of Congress
Chapter 13, Robert Kelley, Life Magazine © Time Inc.
Chapter 14, AP/Wide World Photos

Printed in the United States of America

2   3   4   5   6   RM   98   97   96   95   94

ISBN 0-89061-487-3
ISBN 0-89061-690-6, Hardcover Edition

Acknowledgments

Acknowledgment is gratefully made to the following individuals and publishers for permission to reprint the selections in this book.

"The United States *vs.* Susan B. Anthony" (pp. 145–161) from *Women of Courage* by Margaret Truman. Copyright © 1972 by Margaret Truman Daniel. Reprinted by permission of William Morrow & Company, Inc.

"Homecoming for a Jazz Musician" (pp. 56–67) from *Willie and Dwike: An American Profile* by William Zinsser. Copyright © 1984 by William K. Zinsser. Reprinted by permission of the author.

"Keeping Up with the Joneses, Jr." by Phyllis McGinley. From *Sixpence in Her Shoe* by Phyllis McGinley. Copyright © 1960, 1962, 1963, 1964 by Phyllis McGinley. Reprinted by permission of Macmillan Publishing Company.

"The Dog That Bit People" by James Thurber. From *My Life and Hard Times,* published by Harper & Row, Publishers, Inc. Copyright © 1933, 1961 by James Thurber.

"That Astounding Creator—Nature" by Jean George. Copyright © 1964 by The Reader's Digest Association, Inc. Reprinted by permission from the January 1964 *Reader's Digest.*

"Not Built with Mortal Hands" ("The Man with No Hands") by MacKinlay Kantor. Copyright © 1952 by The Hearst Company.

"The Icing of the Cream" by Becky Rupp. First published in the August 1986 issue of *Country Journal,* Harrisburg, PA.

"Life in Hiding" by Anne Frank. Excerpts from *Anne Frank: The Diary of a Young Girl* by Anne Frank. Copyright © 1952 by Otto H. Frank.

Reprinted by permission of Doubleday & Company, Inc. and Vallentine, Mitchell & Company, Ltd. (for Canadian rights).

"The President Visits Panama" by Theodore Roosevelt. Excerpts from *Theodore Roosevelt's Letters to His Children* by Theodore Roosevelt. Copyright © 1919 by Charles Scribner's Sons; copyright © renewed 1947 by Edith K. Carow Roosevelt. Reprinted by permission of Charles Scribner's Sons.

"A Letter Home" by Laura Ingalls Wilder. Excerpt from *West from Home: Letters of Laura Ingalls Wilder to Almanzo Wilder, San Francisco, 1915* by Laura Ingalls Wilder. Copyright © 1974 by Roger Lea McBride. Reprinted by permission of Harper & Row, Publishers, Inc.

"Plymouth Rock and the Pilgrims" by Mark Twain. From *Mark Twain Speaking*, published by Iowa University Press, 1976. Reprinted by permission of Harper & Row, Publishers, Inc.

"I Have a Dream" by Martin Luther King, Jr. Copyright © 1963 by Martin Luther King, Jr. Reprinted by permission of Joan Daves.

"Choice: A Tribute to Dr. Martin Luther King, Jr." by Alice Walker. Copyright © 1983 by Alice Walker. From *In Search of Our Mothers' Gardens* by Alice Walker. Reprinted by permission of Harcourt Brace Jovanovich, Inc.

Contents

To the Student

When you read newspaper articles, history books, instructional articles, and biographies you are reading nonfiction. The story of Babe Ruth's life, the story of the sinking of the *Titanic*, and an account of a soldier's experiences in Vietnam are all examples of nonfiction. Nonfiction is literature that discusses real people and events, rather than imaginary ones.

Good nonfiction is certainly as interesting as fiction. And much nonfiction is written in story form or contains stories within it. Many people like nonfiction because they enjoy reading about things that really happened or because they like reading other people's ideas and opinions. Nonfiction tells you what is happening in your town, city, or country. It keeps you up-to-date on the trends in fashion, music, and art. In nonfiction writers argue, describe places and people, and try to persuade you to do certain things or think in certain ways. They give you glimpses into the ways in which other people live. Through nonfiction, you can visit any place in the world and learn what other people think about, wish for, and feel.

Much of the writing you do is nonfiction. When you write a book report or a research paper, you are writing nonfiction. By studying the works of outstanding nonfiction writers, you can learn techniques to improve your own writing.

Each chapter in this book contains one nonfiction selection and a lesson that teaches skills that will help you to interpret that selection. Those skills will also help you to get the most out of nonfiction you read on your own in the future. Each selection is preceded by an introduction to the selection and to the author. Often, knowing an author's background helps you to understand his or her writings better.

The last feature of the book is a glossary that includes all the literary terms introduced in the book. As you read, you will find several literary terms underlined in each chapter. The first time a term appears in the text, it is underlined and defined. In the glossary, a page reference following each term indicates where the term first appears.

Autobiography and Biography

A Slave Learns to Read and Write
FREDERICK DOUGLASS

Use of Language

The United States vs. Susan B. Anthony
MARGARET TRUMAN

How a Biographer Interprets Facts

Homecoming for a Jazz Musician
WILLIAM ZINSSER

Character Development

2

*A*ll the selections in this book have one thing in common: they fit into a category of writing called nonfiction. Nonfiction is prose writing that gives factual information about real people, places, and events. Nonfiction writing covers a wide variety of subjects. News and feature articles in newspapers and magazines are nonfiction. Many books in libraries and in bookstores are also nonfiction. Nonfiction books include reference works such as encyclopedias and atlases, as well as books about such topics as travel, history, and science.

Among the most popular forms of nonfiction are autobiographies and biographies. The selections in Unit One represent those two types of nonfiction writing. An autobiography is the story of a person's life written by that person. A biography is the story of a person's life written by another person. Both words come from the Greek roots *bio*, meaning "life," and *graph*, meaning "writing." The prefix *auto-* means "self." So biography is "life writing" while autobiography is "self life writing."

In a biography or an autobiography, the person whose life story is being told is called the subject. In an autobiography, the subject and the author are the same person.

You might think that biographers or people writing their autobiographies do not need to use much imagination because they are simply writing about facts. That is not true. Writers of biographies and autobiographies start with facts, but they must use their imaginations to bring those facts to life. If the authors did not do so, their writing would not spark your interest.

The three people about whom you will read in Unit One each met and overcame challenges in their lives. A straightforward retelling of those challenges might not be as interesting as the ways in which each author has chosen to reveal them. In Unit One you will study some of the ways in which writers of biographies and autobiographies create vivid and appealing works.

Chapter 1

Selection   *A Slave Learns to Read and Write*
Excerpt from
**Narrative of the Life of Frederick Douglass,
An American Slave**

FREDERICK DOUGLASS

Lesson   *Use of Language*

About the Selection

Frederick Douglass published his autobiography in 1845 when he was about twenty-eight years old. People usually do not write their autobiographies until they are much older. Douglass's autobiography, however, describes only his early life, when he was a slave.

Douglass was born into slavery on a Maryland plantation about 1817. He did not know his exact birthdate and only learned his approximate age through a casual remark by his owner. Before Douglass was a year old, he was separated from his mother. She was sent to another farm belonging to the same slave-owning family. The separation of a slave mother from her child was a common practice at the time. Douglass's mother died when he was seven. He had seen her only four or five times in his life.

During his first twenty-one years, Douglass was passed back and forth between different members of the same slave-owning family. Sometimes he lived on their rural plantations and sometimes in the city of Baltimore. His treatment was better or worse depending on which of the various masters he had.

On September 3, 1838, at the age of twenty-one, Frederick Douglass successfully escaped from slavery. When he reached New York City, he married Anna Murray, a free black woman whom he had met in Baltimore. Together, they went to New Bedford, Massachusetts, where for four years Douglass worked as a day laborer. His life changed greatly, however, when he attended a convention of the Massachusetts Anti-Slavery Society in 1841. The Society had been organized by abolitionists—people who wanted to do away with slavery. When the leaders of the convention discovered that Douglass was a former slave, they asked him to speak about slavery. His speech was so powerful that the society immediately hired him to lecture about abolition.

Douglass's self-confidence and his superb command of language caused some people to doubt that he had grown up in slavery. They simply could not believe that a former slave could have achieved his level of education. So Douglass wrote his autobiography, *Narrative of the Life of Frederick Douglass, An American Slave,* to prove that he had in fact been a slave.

Shortly after the book was published, Douglass went on a lecture tour of Great Britain and Ireland. He returned to the United States with enough earnings to buy his freedom from his former master. (Under United States law, an escaped slave could be returned to his former owner even after years of freedom.)

Soon after his return to the United States, Douglass founded an abolitionist newspaper, *The North Star,* in Rochester, New York. It was the first newspaper in the United States to be owned by a black man. Even while he was editing and writing, Douglass still made public appearances. He spoke in support of abolition. He also helped the growing woman's rights movement and became a leader of the Underground Railroad in Rochester. The Underground Railroad was a system for helping escaped slaves reach freedom in Canada.

When the Civil War began in 1861, Douglass volunteered to help recruit blacks for the Union Army. After the war, he served in various government positions and was appointed ambassador to Haiti. He continued to lecture and write until his death on February 20, 1895.

Besides the *Narrative of the Life of Frederick Douglass,* Douglass wrote two other autobiographical works. *My Bondage and My Freedom* expands on his experiences in slavery and covers the years from 1841, where the *Narrative* leaves off, to 1855. *Life and Times of Frederick Douglass* summarizes his earlier experiences and includes the events of his life to 1881.

In the excerpt from the *Narrative* that you will read, Douglass describes experiences that he had when he was about seven or eight years old. At that time he was sent from a rural plantation to Baltimore to be a house servant to Mr. and Mrs. Hugh Auld. His job was to look after the Aulds' young son Thomas. Like most slaves, Douglass did not know how to read or write, but he had a quick, eager mind. When Mrs. Auld began to teach him to read, he proved to be a good student.

Lesson Preview

The lesson that follows "A Slave Learns to Read and Write" focuses on the author's use of language. Usually when you read nonfiction, you pay a great deal of attention to what the author is saying. Equally important, however, is *how* the author uses language. Frederick Douglass's autobiography has been praised for its clear and elegant writing. For a man who taught himself to read and write, Douglass learned to use language remarkably well. He used his skill as a writer not only to describe scenes from his life but also to reveal his feelings about those events.

The questions that follow will help you learn how Douglass uses language. As you read, think about how you would answer these questions.

1 Does Douglass's language seem to be informal or formal? Does it sound as if he is actually talking to you?

2 Which scenes are easiest for you to picture? What makes them vivid?

3 What are Douglass's feelings about the incidents he describes? How can you tell what he is feeling?

Vocabulary

Here are some difficult words that appear in the selection that follows. Study the words and their definitions, as well as the sentences that show how the words are used. This will help you get the most from your reading.

servility cringing submissiveness. *The overbearing foreman expected obedient servility from all the factory employees.*

impudent disrespectful; rude. *The student was kept after school because of the impudent remarks he had made to his teacher.*

tranquil peaceful; calm. *Early in the morning the stillness of the ocean is quiet and tranquil.*

invaluable priceless. *These ancient manuscripts are an invaluable source of information about the past.*

shunned avoided. *We shunned his company because he was always so rude and unfriendly.*

odium hatred and contempt. *The odium attached to a criminal record makes it difficult for some parolees to find jobs.*

emaciated very thin. *The emaciated stray dog finally began to gain weight after we fed it regularly.*

offal garbage; refuse. *Careless farmers often feed their pigs offal instead of considering the animals' nutritional needs.*

depravity wickedness; corruption. *The political depravity of the candidate made me decide to vote for his opponent.*

indispensable absolutely necessary. *Flour is an indispensable ingredient in bread.*

denunciation public condemnation. *The council's public denunciation of the mayor forced him to resign in disgrace.*

A Slave Learns to Read and Write

Excerpt from

Narrative of the Life of Frederick Douglass, An American Slave

FREDERICK DOUGLASS

At about the age of seven or eight, Frederick Douglass was sent from a rural plantation to serve a new master and mistress in Baltimore. In the excerpt from his autobiography that follows, Douglass describes several incidents that helped shape his life.

My new mistress proved to be all she appeared when I first met her at the door,—a woman of the kindest heart and finest feelings. She had never had a slave under her control previously to myself, and prior to her marriage she had been dependent upon her own industry for a living. She was by trade a weaver; and by constant application to her business, she had been in a good degree preserved from the blighting and dehumanizing effects of slavery. I was utterly astonished at her goodness. I scarcely knew how to behave towards her. She was entirely unlike any other white woman I had ever seen. I could not approach her as I was accustomed to approach other white ladies. My early instruction was all out of place. The crouching servility, usually so acceptable a quality in a slave, did not answer when manifested toward her. Her favor was not gained by it; she seemed to be disturbed by it. She did not deem it impudent or unmannerly for a slave to look her in the face. The meanest slave was put fully at ease in her presence, and none left without feeling better for having seen her. Her face was made of heavenly smiles, and her voice of tranquil music.

But, alas! this kind heart had but a short time to remain such. The fatal poison of irresponsible power was already in her hands, and soon commenced its infernal work. That cheerful eye, under the influence of slavery, soon became red with rage; that voice, made all of sweet accord, changed to one of harsh and horrid discord; and that angelic face gave place to that of a demon.

Very soon after I went to live with Mr. and Mrs. Auld, she very kindly commenced to teach me the A, B, C. After I had learned this, she assisted me in learning to spell words of three or four letters. Just at this point of my progress, Mr. Auld found out what was going on, and at once forbade Mrs. Auld to instruct me further, telling her, among other things, that it was unlawful,[1] as well as unsafe, to teach a slave to read. To use his own words, further, he said, "If you give a nigger an inch, he will take an ell.[2] A nigger should know nothing but to obey his master—to do as he is told to do. Learning would *spoil* the best nigger in the world. Now," said he, "if you teach that nigger (speaking of myself) how to read, there would be no keeping him. It would forever unfit him to be a slave. He would at once become unmanageable, and of no value to his master. As to himself, it could do him no good, but a great deal of harm. It would make him discontented and unhappy." These words sank deep into my heart, stirred up sentiments within that lay slumbering, and called into existence, an entirely new train of thought. It was a new and special revelation, explaining dark and mysterious things, with which my youthful understanding had struggled, but struggled in vain. I now understood what had been to me a most perplexing difficulty—to wit,

1. Strict laws in the South made it a crime for slaves to learn to read and write.
2. **ell:** a unit of measurement equal to forty-five inches.

the white man's power to enslave the black man. It was a grand achievement, and I prized it highly. From that moment, I understood the pathway from slavery to freedom. It was just what I wanted, and I got it at a time when I the least expected it. Whilst I was saddened by the thought of losing the aid of my kind mistress, I was gladdened by the invaluable instruction which, by the merest accident, I had gained from my master. Though conscious of the difficulty of learning without a teacher, I set out with high hope, and a fixed purpose, at whatever cost of trouble, to learn how to read. The very decided manner with which he spoke, and strove to impress his wife with the evil consequences of giving me instruction, served to convince me that he was deeply sensible of the truths he was uttering. It gave me the best assurance that I might rely with the utmost confidence on the results which, he said, would flow from teaching me to read. What he most dreaded, that I most desired. What he most loved, that I most hated. That which to him was a great evil, to be carefully shunned, was to me a great good, to be diligently sought; and the argument which he so warmly urged, against my learning to read, only served to inspire me with a desire and determination to learn. In learning to read, I owe almost as much to the bitter opposition of my master, as to the kindly aid of my mistress. I acknowledge the benefit of both.

I had resided but a short time in Baltimore before I observed a marked difference, in the treatment of slaves, from that which I had witnessed in the country. A city slave is almost a freeman, compared with a slave on the plantation. He is much better fed and clothed, and enjoys privileges altogether unknown to the slave on the plantation. There is a vestige of decency, a sense of shame, that does much to curb and check those outbreaks of atrocious cruelty so commonly enacted upon the plantation. He is a desperate slaveholder, who will shock the humanity of his nonslaveholding neighbors with the cries of his lacerated slave. Few are willing to incur the odium attaching to the reputation of being a cruel master; and above all things, they would not be known as not giving a slave enough to eat. Every city slaveholder is anxious to have it known of him, that he feeds his slaves well; and it is due to them to say, that most of them do give their slaves enough to eat. There are, however, some painful exceptions to this rule. Directly opposite to us, on Philpot Street, lived Mr. Thomas Hamilton. He owned two slaves. Their names were Henrietta and Mary. Henrietta was about twenty-two years of age, Mary was about fourteen; and of all the mangled and emaciated creatures I ever looked upon, these two were the most so. His heart must be harder than stone, that could look upon these unmoved. The head, neck, and shoulders of Mary were literally cut to pieces. I have frequently felt her head, and found it nearly covered with festering sores, caused by the lash of her cruel mistress. I do not know that her master ever whipped her, but I have been an eyewitness to the cruelty of Mrs. Hamilton. I used to be in Mr. Hamilton's house nearly every day. Mrs. Hamilton used to sit in a large chair in the middle of the room, with a heavy cowskin always by her side, and scarce an hour passed during the day but was marked by the blood of one of these slaves. The girls seldom passed her without her saying, "Move faster, you *black gip!*" [3] at the same time giving them a blow with the cowskin over the head or shoulders, often drawing the blood. She would then say, "Take that, you *black gip!*"—continuing, "If you don't move faster, I'll move you!" Added to the cruel lashings to which these slaves were subjected, they were kept nearly half-starved. They seldom knew what it was to eat a full meal. I have seen Mary contending with the pigs for the offal thrown into the street. So much was Mary kicked and cut to pieces, that she was oftener called *"pecked"* than by her name.

I lived in Master Hugh's family about seven years. During this time, I succeeded in learning to read and write. In accomplishing this, I was compelled to resort to various stratagems. I had no regular teacher. My mistress, who had kindly commenced to instruct me, had, in compliance with the advice and direction of her husband, not only ceased to instruct, but had set her face against my being instructed by anyone else. It is due, however, to my mistress to say of her, that she did not adopt this

3. **gip:** expression of anger, impatience, contempt.

course of treatment immediately. She at first lacked the depravity indispensable to shutting me up in mental darkness. It was at least necessary for her to have some training in the exercise of irresponsible power, to make her equal to the task of treating me as though I were a brute.

My mistress was, as I have said, a kind and tender-hearted woman; and in the simplicity of her soul she commenced, when I first went to live with her, to treat me as she supposed one human being ought to treat another. In entering upon the duties of a slaveholder, she did not seem to perceive that I sustained to her the relation of a mere chattel,[4] and that for her to treat me as a human being was not only wrong, but dangerously so. Slavery proved as injurious to her as it did to me. When I went there, she was a pious, warm, and tender-hearted woman. There was no sorrow or suffering for which she had not a tear. She had bread for the hungry, clothes for the naked, and comfort for every mourner that came within her reach. Slavery soon proved its ability to divest her of these heavenly qualities. Under its influence, the tender heart became stone, and the lamblike disposition gave way to one of tiger-like fierceness. The first step in her downward course was in her ceasing to instruct me. She now commenced to practice her husband's precepts. She finally became even more violent in her opposition than her husband himself. She was not satisfied with simply doing as well as he had commanded; she seemed anxious to do better. Nothing seemed to make her more angry than to see me with a newspaper. She seemed to think that here lay the danger. I have had her rush at me with a face made all up of fury, and snatch from me a newspaper, in a manner that fully revealed her apprehension. She was an apt woman; and a little experience soon demonstrated, to her satisfaction, that education and slavery were incompatible with each other.

From this time I was most narrowly watched. If I was in a separate room any considerable length of time, I was sure to be suspected of having a book, and was at once called to give an account of myself. All this, however, was too late. The first step had been taken. Mistress, in

4. **chattel:** personal property other than land.

teaching me the alphabet, had given me the *inch,* and no precaution could prevent me from taking the *ell.*

The plan which I adopted, and the one by which I was most successful, was that of making friends of all the little white boys whom I met in the street. As many of these as I could, I converted into teachers. With their kindly aid, obtained at different times and in different places, I finally succeeded in learning to read. When I was sent on errands, I always took my book with me, and by going one part of my errand quickly, I found time to get a lesson before my return. I used also to carry bread with me, enough of which was always in the house, and to which I was always welcome; for I was much better off in this regard than many of the poor white children in our neighborhood. This bread I used to bestow upon the hungry little urchins, who, in return, would give me that more valuable bread of knowledge. I am strongly tempted to give the names of two or three of those little boys, as a testimonial of the gratitude and affection I bear them; but prudence forbids;—not that it would injure me, but it might embarrass them; for it is almost an unpardonable offense to teach slaves to read in this Christian country. It is enough to say of the dear little fellows, that they lived on Philpot Street, very near Durgin and Bailey's ship-yard. I used to talk this matter of slavery over with them. I would sometimes say to them, I wished I could be as free as they would be when they got to be men. "You will be free as soon as you are twenty-one, *but I am a slave for life!* Have not I as good a right to be free as you have?" These words used to trouble them; they would express for me the liveliest sympathy, and console me with the hope that something would occur by which I might be free.

I was now about twelve years old, and the thought of being a *slave for life* began to bear heavily upon my heart. Just about this time, I got hold of a book entitled "The Columbian Orator." Every opportunity I got, I used to read this book. Among much of other interesting matter, I found in it a dialogue between a master and his slave. The slave was represented as having run away from his master three times. The dialogue represented the conversation which took place between them, when the slave was retaken the third time. In this dialogue, the whole argument in behalf of slavery was brought forward by the master, all of which was disposed of by the slave. The slave was made to say some very smart as well as impressive things in reply to his master—things which had the desired though unexpected effect; for the conversation resulted in the voluntary emancipation of the slave on the part of the master.

In the same book, I met with one of Sheridan's mighty speeches on and in behalf of Catholic emancipation.[5] These were choice documents to me. I read them over and over again with unabated interest. They gave tongue to interesting thoughts of my own soul, which had frequently flashed through my mind, and died away for want of utterance. The moral which I gained from the dialogue was the power of truth over the conscience of even a slaveholder. What I got from Sheridan was a bold denunciation of slavery, and a powerful vindication of human rights. The reading of these documents enabled me to utter my thoughts, and to meet the arguments brought forward to sustain slavery; but while they relieved me of one difficulty, they brought on another even more painful than the one of which I was relieved. The more I read, the more I was lead to abhor and detest my enslavers. I could regard them in no other light than a band of successful robbers, who had left their homes, and gone to Africa, and stolen us from our homes, and in a strange land reduced us to slavery. I loathed them as being the meanest as well as the most wicked of men. As I read and contemplated the subject, behold! that very discontentment which Master Hugh had predicted would follow my learning to read had already come, to torment and sting my soul to unutterable anguish. As I writhed under it, I would at times feel that learning to read had been a curse rather than a blessing. It had given me a view of my wretched condition, without the remedy. It opened my eyes to the horrible pit, but to no ladder upon which to get out. In moments of agony, I envied my fellow-slaves for their stupidity. I have

---

5. **Richard Brinsley Sheridan (1751–1816):** an Irish-born playwright and member of the British Parliament. He supported equality for Catholics in Ireland at a time when Britain ruled Ireland, denying Irish Catholics basic political rights.

Use of Language

often wished myself a beast. I preferred the condition of the meanest reptile to my own. Any thing, no matter what, to get rid of thinking! It was this everlasting thinking of my condition that tormented me. There was no getting rid of it. It was pressed upon me by every object within sight or hearing, animate or inanimate. The silver trump of freedom had roused my soul to eternal wakefulness. Freedom now appeared, to disappear no more forever. It was heard in every sound, and seen in every thing. It was ever present to torment me with a sense of my wretched condition. I saw nothing without seeing it, I heard nothing without hearing it, and felt nothing without feeling it. It looked from every star, it smiled in every calm, breathed in every wind, and moved in every storm.

I often found myself regretting my own existence, and wishing myself dead; and but for the hope of being free, I have no doubt but that I should have killed myself, or done something for which I should have been killed. While in this state of mind, I was eager to hear anyone speak of slavery. I was a ready listener. Every little while, I could hear something about the abolitionists. It was some time before I found what the word meant. It was always used in such connections as to make it an interesting word to me. If a slave ran away and succeeded in getting clear, or if a slave killed his master, set fire to a barn, or did anything very wrong in the mind of a slaveholder, it was spoken of as the fruit of *abolition.* Hearing the word in this connection very often, I set about learning what it meant. The dictionary afforded me little or no help. I found it was "the act of abolishing;" but then I did not know what was to be abolished. Here I was perplexed. I did not dare to ask anyone about its meaning, for I was satisfied that it was something they wanted me to know very little about. After a patient waiting, I got one of our city papers, containing an account of the number of petitions from the north, praying for the abolition of slavery in the District of Columbia, and of the slave trade between the States. From this time I understood the words *abolition* and *abolitionists,* and always drew near when that word was spoken, expecting to hear something of importance to myself and fellow-slaves. The light broke in upon me by degrees. I went one day down on the wharf of Mr. Waters; and seeing two Irishmen unloading a scow[6] of stone, I went, unasked, and helped them. When we had finished, one of them came to me and asked me if I were a slave. I told him I was. He asked, "Are ye a slave for life?" I told him that I was. The good Irishman seemed to be deeply affected by the statement. He said to the other that it was a pity so fine a little fellow as myself should be a slave for life. He said it was a shame to hold me. They both advised me to run away to the north; that I should find friends there, and that I should be free. I pretended not to be interested in what they said, and treated them as if I did not understand them; for I feared they might be treacherous. White men have been known to encourage slaves to escape, and then, to get the reward, catch them and return them to their masters. I was afraid that these seemingly good men might use me so; but I nevertheless remembered their advice, and from that time I resolved to run away. I looked forward to a time at which it would be safe for me to escape. I was too young to think of doing so immediately; besides, I wished to learn how to write, as I might have occasion to write my own pass. I consoled myself with the hope that I should one day find a good chance. Meanwhile, I would learn to write.

The idea as to how I might learn to write was suggested to me by being in Durgin and Bailey's shipyard, and frequently seeing the ship carpenters, after hewing, and getting a piece of timber ready for use, write on the timber the name of that part of the ship for which it was intended. When a piece of timber was intended for the larboard[7] side, it would be marked thus—"L." When a piece was for the starboard[8] side, it would be marked thus—"S." A piece for the larboard side forward, would be marked thus—"L.F." When a piece was for starboard side forward, it would be marked thus—"S.F." For larboard aft, it would be marked thus—"L.A." For starboard aft, it would be marked thus—"S.A." I soon learned the names of these letters, and for what they were

---

6. **scow:** large, flat-bottomed boat with square ends.
7. **larboard:** left side of a ship looking forward.
8. **starboard:** right side of a ship looking forward.

Use of Language

intended when placed upon a piece of timber in the shipyard. I immediately commenced copying them, and in a short time was able to make the four letters named. After that, when I met with any boy who I knew could write, I would tell him I could write as well as he. The next word would be, "I don't believe you. Let me see you try it." I would then make the letters which I had been so fortunate as to learn, and ask him to beat that. In this way I got a good many lessons in writing, which it is quite possible I should never have gotten in any other way. During this time, my copybook was the board fence, brick wall, and pavement; my pen and ink was a lump of chalk. With these, I learned mainly how to write. I then commenced and continued copying the Italics[9] in Webster's Spelling Book, until I could make them all without looking on the book. By this time, my little Master Thomas had gone to school, and learned how to write, and had written over a number of copy-books. These had been brought home, and shown to some of our near neighbors, and then laid aside. My mistress used to go to class meeting at the Wilk Street meeting-house every Monday afternoon, and leave me to take care of the house. When left thus, I used to spend the time in writing in the spaces left in Master Thomas's copybook, copying what he had written. I continued to do this until I could write a hand very similar to that of Master Thomas. Thus, after a long, tedious effort for years, I finally succeeded in learning how to write.

9. Italics: style of printing in which the letters are slanted.

Reviewing the Selection

Answer each of the following questions without looking back at the selection.

Recalling Facts

1. Mrs. Auld stopped teaching Frederick Douglass because
   ☐ a. she did not have time.
   ☐ b. her husband forbade it.
   ☐ c. she felt that he did not appreciate it.
   ☐ d. her own son needed her attention.

Understanding Main Ideas

2. Which sentence best expresses the main idea of the selection?
   ☐ a. Plantation slaves had a hard life.
   ☐ b. Mrs. Auld changed greatly after her marriage.
   ☐ c. Some masters were more cruel than others.
   ☐ d. Douglass was determined to learn to read and write.

Placing Events in Order

3. After Mrs. Auld stopped teaching Frederick,
   ☐ a. her husband found out about the lessons.
   ☐ b. Frederick was sent back to the plantation.
   ☐ c. Frederick decided to work on the docks.
   ☐ d. Frederick asked the white boys to teach him.

Finding Supporting Details

4. One example of cruelty to slaves was
   ☐ a. Mrs. Hamilton's treatment of her two slaves.
   ☐ b. Mr. Auld's whipping Frederick.
   ☐ c. the Irishmen's encouraging Frederick to escape.
   ☐ d. the white boys' teaching Frederick to read.

Use of Language

5. "That fatal poison of irresponsible power . . . soon commenced its <u>infernal</u> work." In this context *infernal* means
   □ a. hard.
   □ b. satisfying.
   □ c. evil.
   □ d. customary.

Interpreting the Selection

Answer each of the following questions. You may look back at the selection if necessary.

6. While he lived in Baltimore, Frederick
   □ a. did not enjoy reading.
   □ b. had some freedom of movement.
   □ c. longed to go back to the plantation.
   □ d. had no time to read.

7. From his master's words, Frederick learned
   □ a. that education was the key to the white man's power.
   □ b. that Mrs. Auld had been a weaver.
   □ c. how to deceive his master.
   □ d. the difference between city and plantation life.

8. Which of the following statements is a fact?
   ☐ a. Mrs. Auld was corrupted by slavery.
   ☐ b. Mrs. Hamilton was an example to
   Mrs. Auld.
   ☐ c. It was illegal to teach slaves to read.
   ☐ d. For Frederick Douglass, learning to
   read was more important than learning
   to write.

9. As a result of learning to read, young
   Frederick Douglass felt
   ☐ a. happy.
   ☐ b. guilty.
   ☐ c. intelligent.
   ☐ d. discontented.

10. Who was most responsible for Frederick
    Douglass's learning to read and write?
    ☐ a. Mrs. Auld
    ☐ b. Frederick himself
    ☐ c. Mr. Auld
    ☐ d. the white boys

Use of Language

Good writers choose their words carefully for several reasons. First, they want you to understand their ideas. Second, they want to present that information clearly. Third, they want to create powerful feelings in you.

A cookbook writer, for example, wants you to be able to follow the directions easily and to make the recipes successfully. But the writer also wants you to enjoy reading the cookbook and to feel eager to try the recipes. So the cookbook writer not only puts the directions in clear, simple language but also uses appealing words such as *crispy* or *tangy* to describe the food.

In writing *Narrative of the Life of Frederick Douglass, An American Slave*, Douglass had several goals. One was to convince people that he had been a slave by creating a clear, detailed picture of his life as a slave. Douglass also wanted to show how he felt about his former life and about the evils of slavery in general. To accomplish those goals, he chose his words carefully.

Informal and Formal Language

Like all writers of nonfiction, Douglass had to decide whether to use informal or formal language. <u>Informal language</u> is the language that people use in everyday conversation. It usually consists of fairly short sentences and simple vocabulary. It often includes slang words. Formal language is the language used by many writers of scholarly books. It usually has longer sentences and a greater variety of words than everyday speech does. Formal language never contains slang. In his *Narrative* Douglass chooses to use formal language. Read the following sentences:

> Very soon after I went to live with Mr. and Mrs. Auld, she very kindly commenced to teach me the A, B, C. After I had learned this, she assisted me in learning to spell words of three or four letters.

Although both sentences are short and have a simple structure, the language is formal because of the words Douglass uses. Notice that he uses the word *commenced* rather than the simpler word *began*. He also uses *assisted* rather than *helped*. Both words give the writing a more formal tone.

1. The following sentence is written in formal language. Rewrite it in informal language.

> *Few [city slaveholders] are willing to incur the odium attaching to the reputation of being a cruel master; and above all things, they would not be known as not giving a slave enough to eat.*

How does a writer decide whether to use informal or formal language? Writers usually make the choice based on who their readers will be and on what effect they want to have on their audience. For example, if you write a letter to a friend, you probably use informal language because you feel close to the reader of the letter. On the other hand, if you write a report for school, you probably use more formal language.

2. Suggest at least two reasons why Frederick Douglass chose to use formal language in his Narrative. *Think about Douglass's intended readers and what effect he wanted to have on them.*

Through his use of language, Douglass sends a powerful message about slavery. Reread the first paragraph of the selection. Douglass says of Mrs. Auld, "I was utterly astonished at her goodness," and, "The meanest slave was put fully at ease in her presence." In the second paragraph, however, he points out that "the fatal poison of irresponsible power was already in her hands, and soon commenced its infernal work."

3. What feelings about Mrs. Auld and slavery does Douglass reveal in those descriptions?

Narration and Dialogue

Douglass made other choices about how to use language. As the central character in his autobiography, he participated in the events he is describing. Yet he had to decide when to summarize the events and when to use the actual words that were spoken. When Douglass summarizes events, he is using narration—the kind of writing that gives the actions and events of the story. Dialogue is the actual conversation between the characters. Dialogue usually is more informal than narration.

In an autobiography narration allows the writer not only to summarize but also to interpret events. Dialogue, on the other hand, tells you exactly what was said in a conversation. It provides a clearer view of an event than narration because the writer has not stepped in with his or her interpretation. Like most writers of autobiographies, Douglass uses both narration and dialogue.

4. Review the third paragraph of the selection, in which Douglass describes how Mrs. Auld began to teach him to read and how Mr. Auld learned about the lessons. Compare Douglass's formal language in the narration to the informal language used by Mr. Auld. What difference between the two characters does it show? Why is Douglass's use of dialogue so effective here?

5. Find another example of dialogue and summarize what is said. What do you learn about the speaker in that dialogue? What point do you think Douglass is making by repeating the speaker's exact words?

Language and Emotion

As you have learned, Douglass wanted his autobiography to convince people of the evils of slavery. He had strong feelings about his life as a slave. Through careful choice of words, he expresses those feelings.

Sometimes, a writer wants you to notice certain words. He or she may choose to repeat similar sounds. The close repetition of the same first sounds in words is called alliteration. "A mile a minute" and "rough and ready" are examples of alliteration. Most alliteration is found at the beginnings of words. It can, however, be found within words, such as "in sunshine or shadow." Alliteration causes you to pay special attention to the words that have similar sounds.

Another way writers draw your attention to feelings or ideas is by using phrases or clauses that are similar in structure. This device is known as parallelism. There are many examples of parallelism in the Bible:

> Thou shall not kill.
> Thou shall not commit adultery.
> Thou shall not steal.

Parallelism emphasizes the writer's meaning and feelings.

6. Read the passage that follows and find examples of alliteration and parallelism. Explain what feelings or emotions each example suggests.

> *That cheerful eye, under the influence of slavery, soon became red with rage; that voice, made all of sweet accord, changed to one of harsh and horrid discord; and that angelic face gave place to that of a demon.*

Douglass, like other writers, chooses his words carefully to suggest certain emotions. Every word has a denotation, or dictionary meaning. Many words also have connotations. Connotation refers to the emotion that a word arouses or the meanings it suggests beyond its dictionary meaning. For example, Douglass uses the word *abhor*, which means to hate. That meaning is the word's denotation. The word *abhor* also suggests a deeper, more intense kind of hatred. That suggestion is the word's connotation.

7. *Read the following sentences from Douglass's* Narrative. *Give the denotation of each underlined word. Then explain the connotations of the words.*

"As I writhed *under it, I would at times feel that learning to read had been a curse rather than a blessing."*

"It was this everlasting thinking of my condition that tormented *me."*

Figurative Language

Another way writers express their feelings is by using figurative language. Figurative language refers to words and phrases used in unusual ways to create vivid images, to focus attention on certain ideas, or to compare things that are basically different. When words or phrases are used figuratively, they have meanings other than their usual, or literal, meanings. When a person says, "I was so hungry I could have eaten a horse," he or she does not actually want to eat a horse. Rather, the person is creating an image that conveys the idea of extreme hunger.

Figurative language is created through figures of speech—words or phrases that create vivid images by contrasting unlike things. A figure of speech has meanings other than its ordinary meaning. One common figure of speech is a metaphor. A metaphor is an imaginative implied comparison between two unlike things. The purpose of a metaphor is to give you an unusual way of looking at one of those things. A metaphor says, in effect, that one thing *is* another. For example, a mother might say about her children, "They are the light of my life." She does not mean that her children glow like the sun. Rather, she is suggesting that they bring joy to her, and thus brighten her life.

Frederick Douglass uses a metaphor when he says, "The silver trump of freedom had roused my soul to eternal wakefulness." The word *trump* is short for *trumpet.* Through that metaphor, Douglass suggests that the idea of freedom was like a trumpet. Once it sounded, it would not let him spend his life in slavery.

Douglass's trumpet metaphor also contains other ideas. It suggests his attitude toward the idea of freedom. Silver is a precious metal, and a trumpet is a powerful musical instrument. Thus, the metaphor shows how highly Douglass valued freedom and what a powerful influence it was in his life.

8. Find the metaphor in the following excerpt. What comparison is Douglass making here? What feelings does the metaphor express?

> *. . . I would at times feel that learning to read had been a curse rather than a blessing. It had given me a view of my wretched condition, without the remedy. It opened my eyes to the horrible pit, but to no ladder upon which to get out.*

Another figure of speech that Douglass uses in his *Narrative* is hyperbole. Hyperbole deliberately exaggerates the truth in order to emphasize an idea or feeling. "These books weigh a ton" is an example of hyperbole. The sentence is exaggerated to let people know how the speaker feels about the number or size of the books he or she is carrying.

9. Read the following passage. Then explain how Douglass uses hyperbole here. Why do you think he uses it?

> *Freedom now appeared, to disappear no more forever. . . . I saw nothing without seeing it, I heard nothing without hearing it, and felt nothing without feeling it. It looked from every star, it smiled in every calm, breathed in every wind, and moved in every storm.*

Language and Irony

Douglass uses language in many different ways. Sometimes, he turns to irony to make his point. Irony is the contrast between appearance and reality or what is expected and what actually happens. For example, if someone criticizes you, you might respond, "Thanks for the compliment." You are using irony in your reply because you really mean that you do not appreciate the criticism. You are saying the opposite of what you mean.

10. Read the following passage from the Narrative. *Pay special attention to the last line. In what way is Douglass using irony here?*

> *I am strongly tempted to give the names of two or three of those little boys [who taught him to read], as a testimonial of the gratitude and affection I bear them; but prudence forbids;—not that it would injure me, but it might embarrass them; for it is almost an unpardonable offense to teach slaves to read in this Christian country.*

As you have learned, a skillful writer such as Frederick Douglass uses language in a variety of ways to express his feelings. When you read other selections in this book, notice whether the writers use some of the same techniques. For example, are they using formal or informal language? What feelings do they express and how do they show those feelings to you? Notice examples of figurative language and try to determine the effect of the writers' use of metaphors or hyperbole.

Questions for Thought and Discussion

The questions and activities that follow will help you explore the excerpt from *Narrative of the Life of Frederick Douglass, An American Slave* in more depth and at the same time develop your critical thinking skills.

1. **Interpreting.** In the selection Frederick Douglass states that he learned an important lesson from his master. Explain what that lesson was.

2. **Analyzing Character.** List two or three reasons why you think Mrs. Auld's attitude toward Frederick's learning to read changed so dramatically. Then discuss your ideas with several classmates and listen to their ideas. Finally, choose the one reason that you think best explains the change in her and explain why you think it is the main reason.

3. **Evaluating.** Douglass wrote the *Narrative* in part to convince people that he had been a slave. Does the excerpt you read support his goal? Support your view with evidence from the selection.

4. **Drawing Conclusions.** Douglass presents two very different views of Mrs. Auld. What are those two views? What evidence does he give to support each view? What do you think he really thought of Mrs. Auld?

Writing About Literature

Several suggestions for writing projects are given below. You may be asked to complete one or more of these projects. If you have any questions about how to begin a writing assignment, review Using the Writing Process, beginning on page 341.

1. **Writing an Autobiographical Sketch.** Learning to read and write were important accomplishments for Frederick Douglass. Think about an important accomplishment in your own life. It might be learning to swim or discovering a truth about life. Write a brief sketch describing what your accomplishment involved. How did you feel about it? Use alliteration or figurative language to express your feelings about the events you are describing.

2. **Analyzing a Character.** Choose a character from the *Narrative* that is not Frederick Douglass. How would that character have viewed the events that Douglass describes? Using a scene from the excerpt, write two or three paragraphs through the eyes of the character you have chosen.

3. **Writing a Letter.** Write a letter to Frederick Douglass asking him questions about the events described in the selection. You could begin the letter by telling him what you liked about the *Narrative*. Then ask your questions. Since Douglass is not a friend, you should probably use formal language in your letter.

Chapter 2

Selection **The United States vs. Susan B. Anthony**

Excerpt from
Women of Courage

MARGARET TRUMAN

Lesson *How a Biographer Interprets Facts*

About the Selection

In Chapter 1, you read an excerpt from Frederick Douglass's autobiography. While Douglass was fighting for the abolition of slavery, other reformers were involved in different crusades to improve American society. Among those was the campaign to win suffrage for women. Suffrage means the right to vote. In the 1800s, American women were not allowed to vote. One of the leaders of the women's suffrage movement was Susan B. Anthony.

"The United States *vs.* Susan B. Anthony" is a biography—the story of a person's life told by someone else. In this selection, the biographer, or person telling the story, is Margaret Truman. Truman writes about Susan B. Anthony in only one chapter of her book *Women of Courage.* As a result, she does not include all the details of Anthony's life. She is selective about what she tells you.

The summary that follows will help you to understand what was taking place in the United States when Anthony was alive. Susan Brownell Anthony was born in 1820 into a family of Quakers. The Quakers were a religious group that allowed women equal rights, and they strongly supported the education of women. As a result of her family background, Anthony developed a strong sense of independence and a passion for social justice. The entire Anthony family was involved in movements for social reform such as women's suffrage and the abolition of slavery. In fact, soon after the family moved to Rochester, New York, they became friends with Frederick Douglass.

Anthony's first interest as a reformer was in the temperance movement. The goal of the temperance movement was to stop the sale of alcohol, which the movement's members believed destroyed family life. As you will read, Anthony's work in the temperance movement led to her involvement in the women's suffrage movement.

In the early 1800s, only white men who owned property could vote. During the 1820s and 1830s, however, there was a growing movement to give all white men the right to vote. At that time, some women asked for the same rights as men, including the right to vote.

Susan B. Anthony joined the women's suffrage movement in the 1850s, and soon became a prominent leader. During and after the Civil War (1861–1865), Anthony and others hoped that both women and blacks would win the right to vote. The Fourteenth and Fifteenth Amendments to the Constitution of the United States gave citizenship to blacks and suffrage to black men, but not to women.

In 1869, Wyoming became the first state to grant women the right to vote. Several other western states soon followed. By that time, however, supporters of suffrage for women realized that an amendment to the United States Constitution was needed to give all women the right to vote. So in 1878, the "Anthony Amendment" was introduced in Congress. It was defeated in 1887 but was reintroduced in each following Congress. Anthony died in 1906, and it was not until 1920 that the Nineteenth Amendment to the Constitution was ratified, giving all American women the right to vote.

In *Women of Courage,* Truman profiles twelve American women whose lives, she believes, illustrate the quality of courage. Margaret Truman was born in Independence, Missouri, on February 17, 1924. As a child, she had a strong interest in music and received training in piano and voice. She was planning to become a concert performer. Then President Franklin D. Roosevelt died. Margaret's father, Harry S Truman, was Roosevelt's vice president. Suddenly, he became the President of the United States.

Margaret Truman was ready to put aside her plans for a musical career. She feared that she would be criticized for taking advantage of the attention the president's daughter would automatically receive. However, her father encouraged her to continue with her career. So in 1947, after graduating from George Washington University, Margaret Truman made her debut as a concert singer. Critics praised her warmth and poise as a performer, but some suggested that she needed more vocal training.

Margaret Truman performed as a concert singer from 1947 to 1954. Since then she has worked as an actress, a broadcaster, and an author. Besides *Women of Courage,* she has written biographies of both her father and her mother. She has published a book called *White House Pets,* as well as several murder mysteries, including *Murder in the White House* and *Murder at the FBI.*

Lesson Preview

In the lesson that follows "The United States *vs.* Susan B. Anthony," you will study how Margaret Truman has chosen certain facts and has interpreted the life of Susan B. Anthony largely on the basis of a court trial. Like most biographers, Truman has chosen which facts to present about her subject's life. By selecting and emphasizing some facts and leaving out others, she gives a particular interpretation, or view, of what Susan B. Anthony was like. Truman also interprets the facts by telling us what she thinks they mean or why they are important.

In "The United States *vs.* Susan B. Anthony," Truman focuses on a trial. As you may know, the title of this selection is the name of a court case. The names of the opposing parties are separated by the abbreviation *vs.,* which stands for the Latin word *versus,* meaning against. The name of the plaintiff, or the person with a complaint, comes first. The name of the defendant, or the person who must answer the complaint, comes second. In this case, the United States had a complaint against Susan B. Anthony.

The questions that follow will help you identify Truman's interpretation of Susan B. Anthony's life. As you read, think about how you would answer these questions.

1 What are the main points Margaret Truman makes about Susan B. Anthony's life?

How a Biographer Interprets Facts

2 What facts about Susan B. Anthony's life does the author use to support her main point?

3 How does the author use language to show her attitude toward different people and events?

4 How does the trial give Truman an opportunity to interpret Susan B. Anthony's character?

Vocabulary

Here are some difficult words that appear in the selection that follows. Study the words and their definitions, as well as the sentences that show how the words are used. This will help you get the most from your reading.

advocate a person who speaks or writes in favor of something. *The council president was an advocate for strong zoning laws.*

concur agree with an opinion or decision. *At the meeting, the parents did not concur with the decision of the school board.*

demoralized weakened in spirit or discipline. *After their third defeat in a row, the soccer team felt seriously demoralized.*

disparity a lack of equality. *Despite the disparity in their ages, the children played together well.*

indefatigable tireless. *During the crisis, the negotiator was indefatigable in trying to reach a solution.*

rehabilitate bring back to a normal or good condition. *We bought an old house knowing that we could rehabilitate it ourselves.*

retrospect the act of looking back on something in the past. *In retrospect, they realized that they could have avoided their errors.*

unremitting not stopping or slowing down; continuing. *The hikers trekked through unremitting rain to reach their campsite.*

The United States
vs. *Susan B. Anthony*

Excerpt from

Women of Courage

MARGARET TRUMAN

Susan B. Anthony has never been one of my favorite characters. Stern-eyed and grim-lipped, she seemed utterly devoid of warmth and humor and much too quick to dominate the women she worked with. I always thought her personality could be summed up in one word: battle-ax. On top of that drawback, she was a fanatic. She joined the woman's suffrage movement in 1852, when she was thirty-two years old. From then until her death in 1906, she could think of little else.

The fanatics of one generation have a habit of turning into the heroes and heroines of the next, as Susan B. Anthony proved. And since I've been making a study of heroines, I decided to give Miss Anthony a second look. I have to report that my original assessment of her character was much too harsh.

Susan B. Anthony came to the woman's movement by a somewhat

circuitous route. She was a reformer by inheritance as well as by temperament. Her parents were passionate supporters of abolition, temperance,
and woman's rights. They numbered among their friends some of the
outstanding liberals of the nineteenth century, men like William Lloyd
Garrison, Frederick Douglass, and Prudence Crandall's old ally, the
Reverend Samuel J. May.[1]

Daniel Anthony had a succession of homes, a succession of jobs, and
a succession of financial ups and down. He began his career as a farmer
in Adams, Massachusetts, but gave up farming to buy a cotton mill near
Albany, New York. His business was wrecked by the panic of 1837,[2] and
he bought another farm, this one a small plot of land just outside of
Rochester, New York.

The collapse of the cotton mill left the Anthony family with a mountain of debts. Susan, by then in her late teens, became a teacher to help
pay them off. After ten years in the classroom, she resigned and took
over the management of her father's farm so Daniel Anthony could
devote his attention to still another business venture—an insurance
agency that eventually made him prosperous once more.

As I mentioned earlier, the instinct for reform had been bred into
Susan since childhood. She was particularly concerned about temperance, and her work in that movement soon brought her in contact with
Amelia Bloomer, who ran a temperance newspaper in Seneca Falls. Mrs.
Bloomer introduced her to another temperance advocate, Elizabeth Cady
Stanton, who was now pouring most of her energies into a campaign to
give women the vote. Mrs. Stanton tried to enlist Susan's support in the
suffrage movement, but Susan demurred. She was too busy with temperance activities to have time for anything else.

In 1852, Susan B. Anthony attended a rally in Albany where she

---

1. **William Lloyd Garrison** was a leader of the abolitionist movement. **Prudence Crandall**, the subject
   of an earlier chapter in *Women of Courage,* was a Quaker teacher. In 1833, she opened a school for
   black women in Canterbury, Connecticut. **The Reverend Samuel J. May** was a Unitarian minister
   who defended Crandall against critics.
2. **panic of 1837:** a severe financial depression that caused hardship for many Americans.

was refused permission to speak because of her sex. The incident made her so angry that she withdrew from the regular temperance organization and set up a separate Woman's New York State Temperance Society with Elizabeth Cady Stanton as its president.

Not long after that, Susan went to a convention of the New York State Teachers' Association. More than two-thirds of the members were women, but the men ran the entire meeting, giving the speeches, voting on resolutions, and generally ignoring the women, who sat in an isolated bloc at the back of the room.

When a panel of male speakers began a lengthy debate on the topic: "Why the profession of a teacher is not as much respected as that of a lawyer, doctor, or minister," Susan requested permission to state her opinion on the matter. After some discussion, the men agreed to let her be heard.

Susan offered a very simple answer to the question. "Do you not see," she said, "that so long as society says woman is incompetent to be a lawyer, minister, or doctor, but has ample ability to be a teacher, every man of you who chooses this profession tacitly acknowledges that he has no more brains than a woman?"

She went on to say a few words about the disparity in the salaries of men and women teachers. It would be to the men's advantage to equalize them, she maintained, because their own incomes suffered when they had to compete with the cheap labor of women.

The speech left most of Susan's audience in a state of shock. A few men rushed over to congratulate her; the women remained silent. But she made at least one convert. A woman from Rochester pushed through a resolution affirming the right of women teachers to participate in all of the association's activities, including speaking at meetings, serving on committees, and holding office.

Susan B. Anthony's success with the teachers' association convinced her that discrimination against women should—and could—be overcome. Before long she had become Elizabeth Cady Stanton's chief lieutenant in the woman's rights movement. Mrs. Stanton had young children at the time and was not free to travel extensively. She concentrated on writing letters and speeches, while Susan did most of the legwork. She proved to be a brilliant organizer and an indefatigable lecturer, a master at circulating petitions, organizing conventions, and browbeating politicians.

All of the women who had the guts to demand the right to vote were cruelly criticized in the press, but Susan was invariably singled out as a special target. The fact that she was unmarried made her particularly vulnerable. This was declared proof positive that her crusade was simply the ranting of an embittered old maid.

The insulting newspaper articles and vicious cartoons must have bothered Susan. But she never let it show. She threw herself into her work. There was always a new speech to write, a new meeting to organize, a new petition to be drawn up and presented to a state legislature.

Susan B. Anthony was a stern and single-minded woman. Like most crusaders for causes—especially unpopular causes—she had little time for fun and games. But I have a sneaky feeling that behind her severe manner and unremitting devotion to duty, she may actually have had a sense of humor. Let me tell you about my favorite episode in Susan B. Anthony's career, and perhaps you'll agree.

It began on Friday morning, November 1, 1872. Susan was reading the morning paper at her home in Rochester. There, at the top of the editorial page of the *Democrat and Chronicle,* was an exhortation to the city's residents:

> Now register! Today and tomorrow are the only remaining opportunities. If you were not permitted to vote, you would fight for the right, undergo all privations for it, face death for it. You have it now at the cost of five minutes' time to be spent in seeking your place of registration and having your name entered. And yet, on election day, less than a week hence,

hundreds of you are likely to lose your votes because you have not thought it worth while to give the five minutes. Today and tomorrow are your only opportunities. Register now!

Susan B. Anthony read the editorial again. Just as she thought, it said nothing about being addressed to men only. With a gleam in her eye, she put down the paper and summoned her sister Guelma, with whom she lived. The two women donned their hats and cloaks and went off to call on two other Anthony sisters who lived nearby. Together, the four women headed for the barber shop on West Street, where voters from the Eighth Ward were being registered.

For some time, Susan B. Anthony had been looking for an opportunity to test the Fourteenth Amendment to the Constitution as a weapon to win the vote for women. Adopted in 1870, the Amendment had been designed to protect the civil rights—especially the voting rights—of recently freed slaves. It stated that:

> All persons born or naturalized in the United States, and subject to the jurisdiction thereof, are citizens of the United States and of the State wherein they reside. No State shall make or enforce any law which shall abridge[3] the privileges or immunities of citizens of the United States, nor shall any State deprive any person of life, liberty, or property without due process of law, nor deny to any person within its jurisdiction the equal protection of the laws.

The Amendment did not say that "persons" meant only males, nor did it spell out "the privileges and immunities of citizens." Susan B. Anthony felt perfectly justified in concluding that the right to vote was among the privileges of citizenship and that it extended to women as well as men. I'm sure she must have also seen the humor of outwitting the supposedly superior males who wrote the Amendment.

3. **abridge:** lessen; decrease.

It was bad enough for a bunch of women to barge into one sacred male precinct—the barber shop—but to insist on being admitted to another holy of holies[4]—the voting booth—was absolutely outrageous. Moustaches twitched, throats were cleared, a whispered conference was held in the corner.

Susan had brought along a copy of the Fourteenth Amendment. She read it aloud, carefully pointing out to the men in charge of registration that the document failed to state that the privilege of voting extended only to males.

Only one man in the barber shop had the nerve to refuse the Anthony sisters the right to register. The rest buckled under Susan's determined oratory and allowed them to sign the huge, leather-bound voter registration book. If the men in the barber shop thought they were getting rid of a little band of crackpots the easy way, they were wrong. Susan urged all her followers in Rochester to register. The next day, a dozen women invaded the Eighth Ward barber shop, and another thirty-five appeared at registration sites elsewhere in the city. The *Democrat and Chronicle,* which had inadvertently prompted the registrations, expressed no editorial opinion on the phenomenon, but its rival, the *Union and Advertiser,* denounced the women. If they were allowed to vote, the paper declared, the poll inspectors "should be prosecuted to the full extent of the law."

The following Tuesday, November 5, was Election Day. Most of the poll inspectors in Rochester had read the editorial in the *Union and Advertiser* and were too intimidated to allow any of the women who had registered to vote. Only in the Eighth Ward did the males weaken. Maybe the inspectors were *Democrat and Chronicle* readers, or perhaps they were more afraid of Susan B. Anthony than they were of the law. Whatever the reason, when Susan and her sisters showed up at the polls shortly after 7 A.M., there was only a minimum of fuss. A couple of inspectors were hesitant about letting the women vote, but when Susan

4. **holy of holies:** a very sacred place.

assured them that she would pay all their legal expenses if they were prosecuted, the men relented, and one by one, the women took their ballots and stepped into the voting booth. There were no insults or sneers, no rude remarks. They marked their ballots, dropped them into the ballot box, and returned to their homes.

Susan B. Anthony's feat quickly became the talk of the country. She was applauded in some circles, vilified in others. But the day of reckoning was not long in arriving. On November 28, Deputy U.S. Marshal E. J. Keeney appeared at her door with a warrant for her arrest. She had violated Section 19 of the Enforcement Act of the Fourteenth Amendment, which held that anyone who voted illegally was to be arrested and tried on criminal charges.

Susan B. Anthony was a great believer in planning ahead. The day after she registered, she decided to get a legal opinion on whether or not she should attempt to vote. A number of lawyers turned her away, but she finally found one who agreed to consider the case. He was Henry R. Selden, a former judge of the Court of Appeals, now a partner in one of Rochester's most prestigious law firms.

On the Monday before Election Day, Henry Selden informed his new client that he agreed with her interpretation of the Fourteenth Amendment and that in his opinion, she had every right to cast her ballot. The U.S. Commissioner of Elections in Rochester, William C. Storrs, did not concur.

E. J. Keeney, the marshal dispatched to arrest Susan B. Anthony, was not at all happy with his assignment. He nervously twirled his tall felt hat while waiting for her to come to the front door. When she finally appeared, he blushed and stammered, shifted uncomfortably from one foot to the other, and finally blurted out, "The Commissioner wishes to arrest you."

Susan couldn't help being amused at Keeney's embarrassment. "Is this your usual method of serving a warrant?" she asked calmly. With that, the marshal recovered his official dignity, presented her with the warrant, and told her that he had come to escort her to the office of the Commissioner of Elections.

When Susan asked if she could change into a more suitable dress, the marshal saw his opportunity to escape. "Of course," he said, turning to leave. "Just come down to the Commissioner's office whenever you're ready."

"I'll do no such thing," Susan informed him curtly. "You were sent here to arrest me and take me to court. It's your duty to do so."

Keeney had no choice but to wait while his prisoner went upstairs and put on a more appropriate outfit. When she returned, she thrust out her wrists and said, "Don't you want to handcuff me, too?"

"I assure you, madam," Marshal Keeney stuttered, "it isn't at all necessary."

With the U.S. Marshal at her side, Susan was brought before the Federal Commissioner of Elections, William C. Storrs. Her arrest was recorded, and she was ordered to appear the next day for a hearing. It was conducted by U.S. District Attorney Richard Crowley and his assistant, John E. Pound.

Susan answered Dictrict Attorney Crowley's questions politely. She said that she thought the Fourteenth Amendment gave her the right to vote. She admitted that she had consulted an attorney on the question but said that she would have voted even if he had not advised her to do so. When Crowley asked if she had voted deliberately to test the law, she said, "Yes, sir. I have been determined for three years to vote the first time I happened to be at home for the required thirty days before an election."

The District Attorney's next step was to convene a grand jury to draw up a bill of indictment.[5] He and his assistant fell to wrangling over a suitable trial date. Susan interrupted them. "I have lecture dates that will take me to central Ohio," she said. "I won't be available until December 10."

5. **bill of indictment:** charge of a crime.

"But you're supposed to be in custody until the hearing," Crowley informed her.

"Is that so?" said Susan coolly. "I didn't know that."

The District Attorney backed down without an argument and scheduled the grand jury session for December 23.

Sixteen women had voted in Rochester. All sixteen were arrested and taken before the grand jury, but Susan alone was brought to trial. The District Attorney had decided to single her out as a test case. The three poll inspectors who had allowed the women to vote were also arrested. The grand jury indicted them too, set bail at five hundred dollars each, and ordered their trial set for the summer term of the U.S. District Court.

Susan Anthony's case now involved nineteen other men and women. All of them—including Susan—were liable to go to prison if they were found guilty and the judge was in a sentencing mood. Prison in the 1870s was a very unpleasant place. There were no minimum security setups where a benevolent government allowed corrupt politicians, crooked labor leaders, and political agitators to rest and rehabilitate, as we do today. Prison meant a cold cell, wretched food, the company of thieves and murderers.

For a while it looked as if Susan might be behind bars even before her trial. She refused to post a bond[6] for her five-hundred-dollar bail. Henry Selden paid the money for her. "I could not see a lady I respected put in jail," he said.

It must be agonizing to sweat out the weeks before a trial. There is time to look ahead and brood about the possibility of an unfavorable verdict and time to look back, perhaps with regret, at the decision that placed you in the hands of the law. But Susan B. Anthony had no regrets. Nor did she appear to have any anxieties about her trial. She had already proved her fortitude by devoting twenty years of her life to fighting for the right to vote. If she won her case, the struggle would be over. But

6. **post a bond:** put up money to guarantee that one will appear for a court appearance.

even if she lost, Susan was not ready to give up the fight.

Some prospective defendants are too demoralized to do anything but sit around and worry. Not Susan B. Anthony. In the course of the next few months, she attended woman's rights conventions in Ohio, Illinois, and Indiana. She appeared before a session that was meeting in Albany to revise the New York State Constitution and tried to persuade them to include equal suffrage among its provisions. Then she went back to Rochester to cast her ballot again in the city elections on March 4, 1873.

Deputy Marshal Keeney appeared at the railroad every time she left Rochester. He reminded her that she was not supposed to leave the city while she was out on bail. Susan would smile, nod, and get on the train. Keeney never tried to stop her.

The summer term of the District Court opened in May. In mid-March, Susan launched a new lecture tour. Her topic: Is it a crime for a citizen of the United States to vote? The lecture centered on the U.S. Constitution, particularly the Fourteenth Amendment.

She spoke in every town in New York's Monroe County and drew surprisingly large audiences. When she polled the crowd at the end of each lecture, the majority invariably supported her. Even those who had been skeptics when they entered the hall usually changed their minds when they heard her arguments.

District Attorney Crowley soon decided that Susan was making it difficult for him to find an unprejudiced jury anywhere in the vicinity of Rochester. When he voiced his concern to Susan, she replied by asking him if he honestly believed that a jury could be prejudiced by having the Constitution of the United States read and explained to them.

Crowley became so exasperated that when the District Court opened on May 13, he requested a change of venue[7] from Rochester to Canandaigua in adjacent Ontario County. The change forced a postponement of the trial until June 17. Susan promptly launched a whirlwind lecture tour of the villages around Canandaigua. She managed to cover twenty-one

7. **change of venue:** change of location.

postal districts on her own, while her good friend and supporter, Matilda Joslyn Gage, covered the remaining sixteen.

The trial of *The United States* vs. *Susan B. Anthony* opened on the afternoon of June 17, 1873, with the tolling of the Canandaigua Courthouse bell. The presiding justice was Ward Hunt, a prim, pale man, who owed his judgeship to the good offices of Senator Roscoe Conkling, the Republican boss of New York State. Conkling was a fierce foe of woman suffrage, and Hunt, who had no wish to offend his powerful patron, had written his decision before the trial started.

District Attorney Crowley opened the arguments for the prosecution. They didn't make much sense at the time, and in retrospect, they sound nothing short of ridiculous. The District Attorney mentioned that Susan B. Anthony was a woman and therefore she had no right to vote. His principal witness was an inspector of elections for the Eighth Ward, who swore that on November 5 he had seen Miss Anthony put her ballot in the ballot box. To back up his testimony, the inspector produced the voter registration book with Susan B. Anthony's signature in it.

Henry Selden's reply for the defense was equally simple. He contended that Susan Anthony had registered and voted in good faith, believing that it was her constitutional right to do so. When he attempted to call his client to the stand, however, District Attorney Crowley announced that she was not competent to testify in her own behalf. Judge Hunt agreed, and the only thing Henry Selden could do was read excerpts from the testimony Susan had given at her previous hearings when presumably she was no less incompetent than she was right now.

Henry Selden tried to make up for this gross injustice by making his closing argument a dramatic, three-hour speech on behalf of woman suffrage. District Attorney Crowley replied with a two-hour rehash of the original charge.

By the afternoon of June 18, the case of *The United States* vs. *Susan B. Anthony* was ready to go to the jury. It was impossible to predict what their verdict might be, so Judge Hunt, determined to make it the verdict he and

Roscoe Conkling wanted, took matters into his own hands. "Gentlemen of the jury," he said, "I direct that you find the defendant guilty."

Henry Selden leaped to his feet. "I object, your honor," he thundered. "The court has no power to direct the jury in a criminal case."

Judge Hunt ignored him. "Take the verdict, Mr. Clerk," he said.

The clerk of the court must have been another Conkling man. "Gentlemen of the jury," he intoned as if the whole proceeding was perfectly normal, "hearken to the verdict as the court hath recorded it. You say you find the defendant guilty of the offense charged. So say you all."

The twelve jurymen looked stunned. They had not even met to discuss the case, much less agree on a verdict. When Henry Selden asked if the clerk could at least poll the jury, Judge Hunt rapped his gavel sharply and declared, "That cannot be allowed. Gentlemen of the jury, you are discharged."

An enraged Henry Selden lost no time in introducing a motion for a new trial on the grounds that his client had been denied the right to a jury verdict. Judge Hunt denied the motion. He turned to Susan B. Anthony and said, "The prisoner will stand up. Has the prisoner anything to say why sentence shall not be pronounced?"

Thus far in the trial, Susan B. Anthony had remained silent. Now she rose to her feet and said slowly, "Yes, your honor, I have many things to say."

Without further preliminaries, she launched into a scathing denunciation of Judge Hunt's conduct of her trial. ". . . In your ordered verdict of guilty," she said, "you have trampled underfoot every vital principle of our government. My natural rights, my civil rights, my political rights, are all alike ignored. Robbed of the fundamental privilege of citizenship, I am degraded from the status of a citizen to that of a subject; and not only myself individually, but all of my sex, are, by your honor's verdict, doomed to political subjection under this so-called Republican government."

Judge Hunt reached for his gavel, but Susan B. Anthony refused to be silenced.

"May it please your honor," she continued. "Your denial of my citizen's right to vote is the denial of my right to a trial by a jury of my peers as an offender against law, therefore, the denial of my sacred rights to life, liberty, property, and—"

"The court cannot allow the prisoner to go on," Judge Hunt cried out.

Susan ignored him and continued her impassioned tirade against the court. Hunt frantically rapped his gavel and ordered her to sit down and be quiet. But Susan, who must have been taking delight in his consternation, kept on talking. She deplored the fact that she had been denied the right to a fair trial. Even if she had been given such a trial, she insisted, it would not have been by her peers. Jury, judges, and lawyers were not her equals, but her superiors, because they could vote and she could not. Susan was adamant about the fact that she had been denied the justice guaranteed in the Constitution to every citizen of the United States.

Judge Hunt was sufficiently cowed by now to try to defend himself. "The prisoner has been tried according to the established forms of law," he sputtered.

"Yes, your honor," retorted Susan, overlooking his blatant lie, "but by forms of law all made by men, interpreted by men, administered by men, in favor of men, and against women; and hence your honor's ordered verdict of guilty, against a United States citizen for the exercise of that citizen's right to vote, simply because that citizen was a woman and not a man. But yesterday, the same manmade forms of law declared it a crime punishable with a one-thousand-dollar fine and six months imprisonment, for you, or me, or any of us, to give a cup of cold water, a crust of bread, or a night's shelter to a panting fugitive[8] while he was tracking his way to Canada. And every man or woman in whose veins coursed a drop of human sympathy violated that wicked law, reckless of consequences, and was justified in so doing. As, then, the slaves who got their freedom must take it over, or under, or through the unjust

8. **fugitive:** runaway slave.

How a Biographer Interprets Facts

forms of law, precisely so now must women, to get their right to a voice in this government, take it, and I have taken mine, and mean to take it at every opportunity."

Judge Hunt flailed his gavel and gave the by now futile order for the prisoner to sit down and be quiet. Susan kept right on talking.

"When I was brought before your honor for trial," she said, "I hoped for a broad and liberal interpretation of the Constitution and its recent Amendments. One that would declare all United States citizens under its protection. But failing to get this justice—failing, even, to get a trial by a jury *not* of my peers—I ask no leniency at your hands—but to take the full rigors of the law."

With that Susan finally obeyed Judge Hunt's orders and sat down. Now he had to reverse himself and order her to stand up so he could impose sentence. As soon as he pronounced the sentence—a fine of one hundred dollars plus the costs of prosecuting the trial—Susan spoke up again. "May it please your honor," she said, "I shall never pay a dollar of your unjust penalty. All the stock in trade I possess is a ten-thousand-dollar debt, incurred by publishing my paper—*The Revolution*—four years ago, the sole object of which was to educate all women to do pre-cisely as I have done, rebel against your manmade, unjust, unconstitu-tional forms of law, that tax, fine, imprison, and hang women, while they deny them the right of representation in the government; and I shall work on with might and main to pay every dollar of that honest debt, but not a penny shall go to this unjust claim. And I shall earnestly and persistently continue to urge all women to the practical recognition of the old Revolutionary maxim, that 'Resistance to tyranny is obedience to God.' "

Judge Hunt must have had strict orders not only to see that the defendant was convicted, but to do everything he could to prevent the case from going on to a higher court. He allowed Susan to walk out of the courtroom without imposing a prison sentence in lieu of her unpaid fine. If he had sent her to prison, she could have been released on a writ of habeas corpus[9] and would have the right to appeal. As it was, the case was closed.

Although she was disappointed that her case would not go to the Supreme Court as she had originally hoped, Susan knew that she had struck an important blow for woman's suffrage. Henry Selden's arguments and her own speech at the end of the trial were widely publicized, and Judge Hunt's conduct of the trial stood as proof that women were treated unjustly before the law.

Susan did not forget the election inspectors who had allowed her to cast her ballot. The men were fined twenty-five dollars each and sent to jail when they refused to pay. In all, they spent about a week behind bars before Susan, through the influence of friends in Washington, obtained presidential pardons for each of them. In the meantime, her followers, who included some of the best cooks in Rochester, saw to it that the men were supplied with delicious hot meals and home-baked pies.

True to her promise, Susan paid the legal expenses for the three inspectors. With the help of contributions from sympathetic admirers, she paid the costs of her own trial. But she never paid that one-hundred-dollar fine. Susan B. Anthony was a woman of her word as well as a woman of courage.

9. **writ of habeas corpus:** an order to bring an imprisoned person before a court.

Reviewing the Selection

Answer each of the following questions without looking back at the selection.

Recalling Facts

1. Susan B. Anthony was tried on charges of
   - ☐ a. disturbing the peace.
   - ☐ b. resisting arrest.
   - ☐ c. voting illegally.
   - ☐ d. speaking in public.

Understanding Main Ideas

2. Susan B. Anthony was a "woman of courage" because she
   - ☐ a. traveled alone to make speeches.
   - ☐ b. was willing to go to jail for her beliefs.
   - ☐ c. paid off all her debts.
   - ☐ d. enjoyed breaking the law.

Placing Events in Order

3. Which of the following events happened first?
   - ☐ a. Susan B. Anthony registered to vote.
   - ☐ b. Susan B. Anthony met Henry Selden.
   - ☐ c. Susan B. Anthony became a teacher.
   - ☐ d. Susan B. Anthony became a leader of the woman's suffrage movement.

Finding Supporting Details

4. Susan B. Anthony showed that she was a "woman of her word" when she
   - ☐ a. paid the legal expenses of the three inspectors.
   - ☐ b. left the temperance movement to protest discrimination against women.
   - ☐ c. stayed in Rochester while waiting for her trial.
   - ☐ d. registered to vote.

5. "She was applauded in some circles, <u>vilified</u> in others." In this context *vilified* means
☐ a. welcomed.
☐ b. attacked.
☐ c. relieved.
☐ d. rewarded.

Interpreting the Selection

Answer each of the following questions. You may look back at the selection if necessary.

6. As a crusader for woman's rights, Susan B. Anthony
☐ a. was disliked by all the men she knew.
☐ b. was not very effective as a speaker.
☐ c. was too busy to consider marriage.
☐ d. traveled widely.

7. Abolition, temperance, and woman's suffrage
☐ a. were all reform movements of the 1800s.
☐ b. were all movements run by women.
☐ c. used methods of nonviolent resistance.
☐ d. accomplished all their goals by 1900.

8. In the opinion of the author, Susan B. Anthony
   - ☐ a. was an embittered woman.
   - ☐ b. became a teacher to help pay off her father's debts.
   - ☐ c. may have had a sense of humor.
   - ☐ d. consulted with a lawyer before she voted.

9. According to Susan B. Anthony, teachers received less respect than other professionals because
   - ☐ a. they worked with young people.
   - ☐ b. they were paid less than others.
   - ☐ c. many of them had little education.
   - ☐ d. many of them were women.

10. Before her trial, Susan B. Anthony lectured on the Fourteenth Amendment in order to
    - ☐ a. fulfill a promise.
    - ☐ b. win support for her case.
    - ☐ c. earn money for her court expenses.
    - ☐ d. change the place where the trial was held.

How a Biographer Interprets Facts

Nonfiction is about real people and real events. It is based on facts. By reading "The United States *vs.* Susan B. Anthony," you have learned some facts about Susan B. Anthony's life. You have also learned Margaret Truman's interpretation of those facts. An <u>interpretation</u> is one person's view of the meaning of certain words, events, or actions. As a biographer, Margaret Truman tries to explain the meaning of her subject's goals and actions by answering questions such as these:

- Which facts about Susan B. Anthony's life are most important?
- What do those facts mean when they are all put together? Are there patterns in Anthony's life?
- Why did Susan B. Anthony behave in certain ways or say certain things?
- How did Anthony feel about the events in which she was involved?

Interpretation and Theme

A biographer's first task is to organize important details about the subject's life. Think of the task in this way: Imagine that you kept a diary in which you wrote down everything that happened to you every day.

But you did not record your feelings about those events. Later, if your diary were found, people might conclude that going to the store to buy milk mattered just as much to you as doing well on a math test. Unless you had interpreted, or explained, the meanings of the events in your diary, your future reader would not understand their relative importance.

Since people want to understand the lives of those they read about, they usually appreciate an author's interpretation of the facts. How does an author, such as Margaret Truman, interpret facts? First, she establishes a theme. The <u>theme</u> is the underlying message or the central idea of a piece of writing. Sometimes, the author introduces several related themes.

The main theme of Margaret Truman's book *Women of Courage* is that throughout the history of the United States, many women have shown courage in a variety of ways. Truman's theme is evident from the title of her book. By choosing to include Susan B. Anthony in the book, Truman has already begun to interpret Anthony's life. Although she does not directly state that Susan B. Anthony was courageous, she interprets Anthony's life as a series of courageous acts.

1. Find three examples of Susan B. Anthony's courage. Summarize each example and indicate whether Truman states directly that each example is an act of courage.

In the introduction to *Women of Courage*, Margaret Truman defines three separate types of courage. Bravery, she says, "is daring and defiant." Heroism is "noble and self-sacrificing." Fortitude is "patient and persevering [steady and hardworking]." Truman discusses Susan B. Anthony in the section of the book that she calls "Three Faces of Fortitude." By including Anthony's biography under that title, she introduces the theme that Susan B. Anthony was patient and persevering.

2. Reread the three examples of Susan B. Anthony's courage that you summarized in question 1. Explain whether any or all of them are examples of fortitude, as Margaret Truman defines it.

By creating those two themes, Truman gives you some clues to understanding Susan B. Anthony. First, you can view Anthony as a woman of courage. Second, you can see her behavior as an example of a particular kind of courage, called fortitude.

The Biographer's Opinion

A biographer naturally has an opinion, or judgment, about his or her subject. Often, an author organizes the facts and events of a subject's life to support that opinion.

Reread the first two paragraphs of the selection. Truman bluntly says that she originally thought of Susan B. Anthony as a "battle-ax" and a "fanatic." But she admits, "The fanatics of one generation have a habit of turning into the heroes and heroines of the next, as Susan B. Anthony proved." Truman examined Anthony again and decided her first judgment had been "much too harsh."

In this biography Truman shows her opinion of Susan B. Anthony in many ways. Notice, for example, some of the adjectives she uses to describe Anthony: "a *brilliant* organizer and an *indefatigable* lecturer." Then think of the stories she chooses to illustrate Anthony's life.

Truman spends most of the chapter describing her "favorite episode in Susan B. Anthony's career." Her opinion of that episode is stated outright. She likes the particular episode because she believes it clearly shows Anthony's character.

3. Read the paragraph on page 38 that begins "Susan B. Anthony was a stern and single-minded woman." What adjectives does Truman use in that paragraph to describe Anthony?

Selecting the Facts

In "The United States *vs.* Susan B. Anthony," Margaret Truman carefully selects facts to support her interpretation of Anthony's character. For example, she says of Anthony: "She was a reformer by inheritance as well as by temperament." Truman then explains how Anthony's parents were supporters of abolition, temperance, and woman's rights. She adds that they were friends of liberals such as William Lloyd Garrison and Frederick Douglass. By selecting that information, she clarifies the main idea of the paragraph and shows the environment in which Anthony grew up.

Later in the chapter, she describes Anthony's decision to vote and the consequences of that action. Here, Truman shows her subject's character even more clearly. Reread the paragraph on page 43 that begins, "It must be agonizing to sweat out the weeks before a trial."

4. What facts does Truman select to support her view that Anthony did not "appear to have any anxieties about her trial"? How do those facts support Truman's interpretation of her subject's character?

Inference and Interpretation

Margaret Truman does more than explain what kind of person Susan B. Anthony was. She also presents her own view of how Anthony and others felt at certain times and why they behaved as they did. Sometimes, this type of interpretation is based on recorded facts. For example, Anthony may have told people how she felt or why she did certain things. Often, however, this type of interpretation is based on inferences.

An inference is an educated guess based on limited facts. To draw a conclusion from an inference, you must decide what those limited facts imply, or suggest. For example, if your dog is alone all day in the house and you come home to find a sweater chewed up, it is reasonable to infer that the dog chewed up the sweater. That inference is not a fact because no one witnessed it, but it is based on the facts that the dog was alone and the sweater was chewed.

When you are reading, you must examine an author's inferences carefully. Decide for yourself if an author's conclusion is a reasonable interpretation of the facts.

Study this inference that Truman makes about Anthony: "The insulting newspaper articles and vicious cartoons must have bothered Susan. But she never let it show." You might ask yourself, If Susan never let her pain show, how does Margaret Truman know that she felt pain? In fact, Truman does *not* know. That is why she used the phrase "must have bothered" rather than just the word *bothered*. Truman is basing her inference on the way most people feel if they are attacked in newspapers.

Some inferences in the selection are probably based on evidence from the time. For example, read this description:

> E. J. Keeney, the marshal dispatched to arrest Susan B. Anthony, was not at all happy with his assignment. He nervously twirled his tall felt hat while waiting for her to come to the front door. When she finally appeared, he blushed and stammered, shifted uncomfortably from one foot to the other, and finally blurted out, "The Commissioner wishes to arrest you."

How does the author know that Keeney was unhappy with his assignment? Perhaps Keeney told someone who later recalled the information. Perhaps someone who witnessed the scene later wrote down that Keeney blushed, stammered, and twirled his hat nervously. In doing her research, Margaret Truman may have read that record and made the inference that Keeney was not happy with his job.

   5. Each of the following passages contains an inference about feelings or motives. Read each passage. First, identify the inference in each. Then describe what evidence Truman might have found that led her to make each inference.

   a. *She joined the woman's suffrage movement in 1852, when she was thirty-two years old. From then until her death in 1906, she could think of little else.*

   b. *Judge Hunt must have had strict orders not only to see that the defendant was convicted, but to do everything he could to prevent the case from going on to a higher court.*

Language and Interpretation

Margaret Truman's use of language also supports her interpretation of Susan B. Anthony. If you study Truman's language, you will notice that she generally uses an informal style. Although she begins the chapter by talking about *Susan B. Anthony*, Truman soon relaxes her language to *Susan*. Truman even includes herself in the story. "As I mentioned earlier, this instinct for reform had been bred into Susan since childhood." As a biographer, therefore, Truman is placing herself close to her subject and telling you about Susan B. Anthony as though they were friends.

Truman's informal language contrasts with the "stern and single-minded" woman she is describing. Truman uses the language of today to describe the situations in which Anthony found herself. Read the description of the Anthony sisters going to the barber shop to register to vote:

> It was bad enough for a bunch of women to barge into one sacred male precinct—the barber shop—but to insist on being admitted to another holy of holies—the voting booth—was absolutely outrageous. . . . If the men in the barber shop thought they were getting rid of a little band of crackpots the easy way, they were wrong.

Think about what is suggested by the phrase "little band of crackpots." Truman herself does not believe that Anthony and her followers were "crackpots." Instead, she is suggesting that the men in the barber shop were making that judgment.

6. *List three other examples of informal language in the description of the barber shop. How does Truman's use of informal language affect your view of Susan B. Anthony?*

7. *Examine the underlined words in the passages that follow. Explain how each underlined word offers an interpretation of the people or events in the selection. Then find another word that simply reports rather than interprets.*

   a. *All of the women who had the <u>guts</u> to demand the right to vote were cruelly criticized in the press. . . .*

   b. *Henry Selden tried to make up for this gross injustice by making his closing argument a dramatic, three-hour speech on behalf of woman suffrage. District Attorney Crowley replied with a two-hour* <u>*rehash*</u> *of the original charge.*

c. *Judge Hunt was sufficiently cowed by now to try to defend himself. "The prisoner has been tried according to the established forms of law," he* <u>*sputtered.*</u>

Margaret Truman is a twentieth-century woman looking back at a woman who was born more than a hundred years ago. Truman thinks of her subject, Susan B. Anthony, as a courageous, patient, and persevering leader of the woman's suffrage movement. Another biographer might have interpreted the facts about Anthony differently by choosing a different theme and using other incidents from her life. When you read other nonfiction writing, especially biographies, take time to find the author's interpretation.

Questions for Thought and Discussion

The questions and activities that follow will help you explore "The United States *vs.* Susan B. Anthony" in more depth and at the same time develop your critical thinking skills.

1. **Comparing and Contrasting.** Margaret Truman's opinion of Susan B. Anthony changed after she started to write about her. What did Truman think of Anthony at the end of the chapter? Why do you think her opinion changed? Did you share Truman's final opinion of Anthony? Explain your answer.

2. **Performing a Scene.** As a class project, prepare a reenactment of Susan B. Anthony's trial. You will need to have people take the parts of Anthony, her lawyer, the judge, the clerk, the jurors, and the courtroom audience. Plan and prepare the dialogue based on the selection you read. After the trial, hold a discussion in which each of the major actors discusses how he or she felt about the events of the trial. Finally, take a vote on who actually "won" the case of "The United States *vs.* Susan B. Anthony."

3. **Analyzing.** In this selection Margaret Truman uses both narration and dialogue. When does she use dialogue? How does the use of dialogue make the selection more interesting?

4. **Evaluating.** Before describing the central episode of this biography, Truman states, "But I have a sneaky feeling that behind her severe manner and unremitting devotion to duty, she may actually have had a sense of humor." Study the voting incident and the trial that followed. Do those events support Truman's statement? Find evidence to support your evaluation.

Writing About Literature

Several suggestions for writing projects are given below. You may be asked to complete one or more of these projects. If you have any questions about how to begin a writing assignment, review Using the Writing Process, beginning on page 341.

1. **Writing a Review.** Imagine that you have been asked to review "The United States *vs.* Susan B. Anthony" for a school newspaper. In two or three paragraphs, explain what you liked about the biography and what you think could have been improved. Conclude your review by making a recommendation as to who might enjoy reading the biography.

2. **Reporting on Research.** Find out more about the life of Susan B. Anthony in a full-length biography, reference book, or history of woman's suffrage. Find additional information to support Truman's interpretation of Anthony's character. Summarize the information in a brief report.

3. **Write a Character Sketch.** Write a character sketch of someone whom you think is a person of courage. You might choose a famous person from the past or present, or you might write about someone you know personally. Before you begin to write, think about your interpretation of the person's character. Then use episodes from the person's life and other details to support your interpretation.

Chapter 3

Selection

Homecoming for a Jazz Musician
Excerpt from
Willie and Dwike: An American Profile

WILLIAM ZINSSER

Lesson

Character Development

About the Selection

In this chapter you will meet jazz musician Willie Ruff. When writer William Zinsser met Ruff and his partner Dwike Mitchell, he found them so interesting that he decided to write a book about them. Biographies traditionally are about people who are famous. But more and more writers are realizing that readers enjoy learning about contemporary people who lead interesting lives, even if such people are not very famous.

Zinsser has called his book *Willie and Dwike: An American Profile*. A profile is a short, concise biography. Often, the subject of a profile is still living. The advantage of writing about a person who is still alive is that the author can meet the person and get a firsthand impression of him or her. Profiles often appear as magazine articles. In fact, three chapters of *Willie and Dwike* first appeared as magazine articles.

Many profiles differ from traditional biographies because they are not told in chronological order. They do not start with the birth of the subject and follow him or her year by year. A profile may start with the present and then flash back to the subject's childhood. Very often a profile is more concerned with analyzing the character of the subject than with recounting all the details of that person's life. The last selection you read, Margaret Truman's portrait of Susan B. Anthony, is also a biographical profile. It focuses on a few incidents in Anthony's life that show you her strength and persistence.

The subject of this excerpt is Willie Henry Ruff, Jr. He was born in Sheffield, Alabama, in 1931. He grew up surrounded by music and by people who encouraged his interest in music. As a boy, Ruff's greatest desire was to be a drummer. He spent hours with a young neighbor, Mutt McCord, learning everything Mutt could teach him about the drums. Another strong influence on Ruff was the rich music that he heard in the local Baptist church.

Ruff's musical education continued when he enlisted in the United States Army. He was assigned to a base where there was a band. The band, however, needed French horn players, not drummers. Preferring the band to driving a truck, Ruff soon learned to play the French horn. He won a place in the highly regarded band at Lockbourne Air Force Base, near Columbus, Ohio. There, in 1947, young Willie Ruff met a pianist named Dwike Mitchell. Ruff started playing the bass in a jazz band with Mitchell, but when both left the army, they lost track of each other.

Several years later, the two musicians met again in New York, where both played with the Lionel Hampton Orchestra. In 1955 they formed the Mitchell-Ruff Duo, and they have been performing together ever since. Ruff calls the duo "the oldest continuous group in jazz without personnel changes."

Ruff and Mitchell have performed all over the United States and have traveled as far as the Soviet Union and China. Their mission is two-fold: to bring jazz music to a wide audience and to educate people about the nature and history of jazz. When they travel, they not only give concerts, but they also give "lecture/performances" in schools and in other community facilities. In these "lecture/performances" Willie Ruff is the spokesman for the duo.

It was Ruff's idea to take the duo to the Soviet Union, and he arranged the trip with Soviet officials. During their five-week visit, Ruff and Mitchell taught and performed at various music conservatories. When it was time for them to leave Moscow, nine hundred people gathered at the train station to see them off and to throw flowers into their compartment.

In 1981 Ruff again decided to travel. This time he planned a trip to China. In preparation he taught himself Chinese so that he could lecture to the people in their own language. By this time, writer William Zinsser had come to know and admire these two jazz musicians. He invited himself along on the China trip. After that trip, he wrote the first of several magazine articles about the Mitchell-Ruff Duo. Zinsser also went on other trips with them. As a result of those travels, he wrote *Willie and Dwike: An American Profile.*

The excerpt from *Willie and Dwike* that you will read is part of a chapter called "Muscle Shoals." Muscle Shoals is the area around Sheffield, Alabama, where Willie Ruff grew up and to which he still returns on regular visits. Until the week of February 15, 1982, however, he and Mitchell had never performed there.

Ruff felt that the young people in his home area had lost touch with the musical tradition that had nourished him. Many did not know that Muscle Shoals was the birthplace of the great W. C. Handy, known as "the father of the blues." So Ruff persuaded a group of local citizens to organize a W. C. Handy Music Festival. He and Mitchell agreed to help raise money for the festival by giving a benefit performance. Author William Zinsser went with them. He used the opportunity to find out more about Ruff's boyhood.

William Zinsser was born in New York City in 1922. After graduating from Princeton University in 1944, he became a writer for a newspaper, the *New York Herald Tribune.* Since 1959, he has been a free-lance writer, contributing articles and columns to magazines, including *Life, Look,* and *The New Yorker.* From 1971 to 1979, he taught writing at Yale University.

Zinsser has written eleven books, including *Seen Any Good Movies Lately?, The Lunacy Boom,* and *On Writing Well.* Most recently, he has edited a book called *Extraordinary Lives: The Art and Craft of American Biography,* in which several writers talk about their experiences writing biographies.

Lesson Preview

The lesson that follows "Homecoming for a Jazz Musician" focuses on character development. When writing a profile, a biographer tries to paint a vivid portrait of the subject's character. Biographers use several methods to reveal character.

In the excerpt you are about to read, you will learn about Willie Ruff from his own words, from what others say about him, from what he does, and from what William Zinsser says about him. The questions that follow will help you see how Zinsser reveals Ruff's character. As you read, think about how you would answer these questions.

1 What do you learn about Willie Ruff from his own words?

2 What do you learn about Ruff from his actions?

3 What do other people think of Ruff?

4 What does William Zinsser think of Ruff?

Vocabulary

Here are some difficult words that appear in the selection that follows. Study the words and their definitions, as well as the sentences that show how the words are used. This will help you get the most from your reading.

vaudeville a stage entertainment composed of various acts such as songs, dances, and comic skits. *The theater director suggested that we stage a vaudeville show.*

cornet a valved brass instrument resembling a trumpet. *Whenever George practices his cornet he makes a lot of noise.*

idioms phrases or expressions characteristic of a particular region, people, or class. *Although she has not lived in Maine for several years, her speech still contains many Maine idioms.*

Homecoming for a Jazz Musician

Excerpt from
Willie and Dwike: An American Profile

WILLIAM ZINSSER

In this excerpt, Zinsser has come to Willie Ruff's hometown of Sheffield, Alabama. Ruff is participating in a week of celebrations honoring the region's musical traditions. At the end of the week, Ruff's partner, Dwike Mitchell, will join him for a benefit concert to raise money for the W. C. Handy Music Festival.

Music was literally in the air during [Willie] Ruff's boyhood, brought by boat and by train. Stern-wheelers going up and down the Tennessee River would put in at Sheffield to unload passengers and cargo, and many of them had calliopes[1] out on the deck. "You'd hear them coming a couple of miles away because the sound carried across the water," Ruff recalled. "I'd hear that calliope and I'd run down to the river. The boats would leave off some freight and take on wood for fuel and maybe pick up some cotton, and while they were there at dockside the calliope player would give a free concert. Those men were great players. They wore red-and-white-striped shirts and sleeve garters, and when they played the calliope these big clouds

1. **calliope:** a keyboard instrument like an organ that has a series of steam whistles.

of steam would billow up over their heads and evaporate. People standing on the dock would marvel at that. They'd say, 'Watch that booger play till it rains on him.' "

Minstrel shows also came to Sheffield regularly. They would set up their tent in a field several blocks from Ruff's house, and he and Mutt McCord would hurry over to hear the drummers, whom they greatly admired. I was surprised to learn that minstrel shows traveled through the South; I had always thought they were offensive to blacks because they consisted of white actors doing black acts in blackface. Ruff explained their somewhat circular history. They started in the time of slavery, he said, as an entertainment on plantations: blacks making fun of whites. "What you'd see was slaves strutting around in tails and high hats, imitating how the white folks acted in the big house, and that was genuinely funny. Later these acts were seen as such a vibrant theatrical form that they were adapted to the commercial stage, and at that point it became whites imitating blacks who were imitating whites. Some of the white entertainers were very funny, and they also were good actors and dancers and mimics. Those were the minstrel shows that eventually made their way up North and that made people like Jolson[2] famous with his Mammy songs.

"Meanwhile, in the South, minstrel shows branched off into still another form. The performers were blacks, but they no longer imitated whites. They did comedy routines on black subjects—the kind that Pigmeat Markham became famous for—and they played a circuit of black vaudeville houses that sprang up throughout the South. The acts were booked by an organization called the Theater Owners Booking Association, or TOBA. . . . Many great musicians like Fats Waller were part of those traveling minstrel shows, and forty years later when I had them up to Yale they still remembered coming through our town. Pigmeat Markham said, 'Man, are you from *Muscle* Shoals?' He remembered being there in 1928. Some black minstrel shows also made their way North because the North was so heavily populated by Southerners.

2. **Al Jolson:** a famous jazz singer.

Theaters like the Apollo in Harlem would book them, especially if they featured gospel quartets or rhythm-and-blues singers that the Southern blacks missed. But down here they always played in tents. And the town where they put up their tents was always Sheffield, because that's where the action was."

One other external influence was records. When Ruff was about ten he began plowing, near the neighboring town of Killen, for a family that one of his sisters had married into. "My brother-in-law's mother, Mrs. Hardin, owned all these records," Ruff said. "She'd buy every new blues record that came out—and as soon as I got home from the fields she and I would put those records on an old wind-up Victrola. The needle had to be changed about every four records—I remember they came in dime packets—and I'd keep up with the needles and just play the records over and over while she cooked. I didn't know who I was listening to; later I realized that I'd been listening to men like Lester Young and Jo Jones. There was one record with a saxophone sound that was one of my favorite records of all time. I grew up with it. It was called 'Evening,' and it had Lester Young on the sax and a vocal by Jimmy Rushing. Some other songs in that period were 'Cow-Cow Boogie' and 'One O'Clock Jump' and 'The Honey Dripper' and 'Tuxedo Junction,' and all of Count Basie. But radio wasn't an influence on me at all. I never listened to the radio because we never had electricity."

Ruff himself hadn't yet learned any instrument except the drums, and opportunities to play were sparse. The black school in Sheffield, which ran from kindergarten through twelfth grade, didn't have a band because no equipment was provided by the board of education, as it was in white schools. Instead, the state sent a black teacher from town to town to try to get black children interested in music. Every three weeks he came to Sheffield, where he tried to start a band. "I was the only kid in the school who had his own instrument and knew how to read music," Ruff said. "It was a pitiful beginning—this man played the piccolo, and I played the drum, and there was a dentist's son who had a cornet."

It was common in the South at that time for black schools to be given hand-me-down equipment that the white schools no longer wanted—old footballs, for instance, and old books—but not old instruments. Ruff took a certain strength from the inequities. "There were marvelous ways that people invented to overcome in style," he said. "In fact, I know a lot of people who credit that disadvantage for their being able to make themselves better than they otherwise would have been. We had a brilliant black doctor in Sheffield named Dr. Long. He was one of the most inspirational men I've ever known and also one of the most tragic. He was frustrated because he wasn't given hospital privileges and many other rights that he had earned. But he had no patience with kids in Sheffield who complained about having to study out of books that had the backs torn off. He said, 'If there's not a page missing out of it, it's not a secondhand book. It's got as much learning with the back off as it has with the back on. Of *course* it's an injustice. But you can waste your time complaining about it, or you can get what's in it.' "

What finally made a difference in Sheffield was World War II. "The war touched our lives in ways that are hard to understand even now," Ruff says. "Suddenly there was great prosperity—everybody's parents had a good job, or a better job than they'd had before. Musical instruments finally began to materialize. But before our little school band could get to be anything, my mother died and I had to move away." Ruff was sent to Evansville, Indiana, to stay with his father, whom he hardly knew. Less than a year later he happened to meet a cousin who had gone into the army and who told him about such appealing aspects of army life as regular meals and the possibility of playing in the band. Ruff faked his age and his father's signature on a parental consent form and became a fourteen-year-old soldier. In another year he would meet a soldier named Dwike Mitchell who would teach him to play the bass. But if he was beginning to think about any instrument besides the drums, it was one of the horns.

I asked Ruff where that idea came from. I assumed that it was the memory of those powerful trombonists who came from Memphis to play in the Sanctified church. Or the memory of those evenings out in

Killen listening to Lester Young's saxophone on Mrs. Hardin's Victrola.

"The thing that gave me the notion of playing the horn," Ruff said, "was the sound of a great contralto[3] in our Baptist church named Miss Celia Appleton. She had that rich, horn-like quality in her voice. When people used to ask me how I decided to play the French horn I said that it was the closest I could get to Miss Celia. Or to Mr. Buddy Jenkins, who sang bass in the church choir. They both sang a lot of solos, and people in the church were just overwhelmed by the extraordinary quality of those two voices. It wasn't only the beauty of the voice; it was the poetic expressiveness. It was what they could bring to a melody. I can't ever remember a funeral in Sheffield when people didn't have it in their will that they wanted Miss Celia or Mr. Buddy to sing. That's a sound that I'll never forget. It's more distinctive in my ear than Louis Armstrong."

After Ruff and I had walked around his old neighborhood we got back in his car. He had tickets to the Mitchell-Ruff concert that he wanted to give to various friends and relatives. (Ruff was once married, incidentally, and has a twenty-five-year-old daughter, Michele.) As it turned out, some of the friends and relatives seemed to have no interest in the tickets and almost no grasp of the event he was inviting them to attend. He was just Willie Ruff. If he had a career somewhere else, that was his business. For now he appeared to be someone who had never left small-town Alabama. I was delighted by the down-home cadences that had crept into his speech, by idioms and regionalisms that were as old as the black South. It wasn't the first time I had been struck by Ruff's gifts of adaptation. I had heard him charm foundation[4] executives in Manhattan and conservatory students in Shanghai—both in their native language. His remarkable ear was one of the agencies of his survival and his success.

We stopped at one house to drop off three tickets with Ruff's stepbrother, an old man named Buddy-Boy Pruitt, who had been a truckdriver

---

3. **contralto:** the lowest range of woman's singing voice.
4. **foundation:** a charitable organization that gives funds to various causes, such as the arts, education, or medical research.

Character Development

for the TVA[5] but was now retired—seemingly to a chair out in the yard, in which he sat as motionless as a cat. Ruff told Buddy-Boy that the tickets were for him and his daughter, Ann, and her husband, Bubba, who also lived there. "When that piano picker starts to play," Ruff said, "they're going to have to strap 'em to the seats." I had never heard Mitchell (or anyone else) called a piano picker, but the term had a vitality that conveyed Ruff's admiration for Mitchell. Buddy-Boy didn't trouble himself over exactly what was going to happen on Sunday night; all that really mattered was the transaction of giving and receiving the tickets. As we got back into the car Buddy-Boy said he'd wait and see what Ann and Bubba were planning to do. If they came, he would probably come too. That, Ruff explained to me, was a certainty: Buddy-Boy can't stand to be alone after dark.

Next we dropped off a pair of tickets with a white man of about seventy-five named James Kirsch, who owns an auto body shop and, by virtue of that fact, is Ruff's most unusual music student. Ruff's car is a 1948 Packard that he coveted for four years as it sat rusting in a weed field outside the Muscle Shoals Recording Studio. After Nashville the studio is the most popular one with the brightest stars of rock, gospel and country-and-western music, and many of them come there to make records; thus Muscle Shoals is again a magnet for musicians. The sound engineer who owned the Packard was too busy to fix it, and he finally sold it to Ruff in 1979 for three hundred dollars—by far the smallest of the sums that would go into its revival. Ruff had the engine rebuilt and then faced the task of restoring the dilapidated body and interior. He took his problem to Mr. Kirsch, who said he was too old to do the work himself but that he would teach Ruff how and would let him keep the car in his shop. Ruff would pay in money for the parts and the paint; but for the instruction and the space Mr. Kirsch wanted a different kind of payment.

"I knew that Mr. Kirsch was a great admirer of a honky-tonk sax

5. TVA: Tennessee Valley Authority, a federal agency created in 1933. It employed thousands of people to bring electricity and other conveniences to the Tennessee River Valley.

player named Boots Randolph, out of Nashville," Ruff told me. "But one night—just before I went to see him about the car—he was watching a religious television program and he heard a saxophonist playing 'The Lord's Prayer.' Mr. Kirsch said it was so beautiful that the preacher congratulated the sax player and told him that old Gabriel was going to have to move over. Mr. Kirsch said to me, 'If I could play that song like that feller played it on TV, just one time in church before I died, I'd *have* to be let into heaven.' Hearing that song reminded him that he had a saxophone down in his basement—he had bought it thirty years before for his son, who didn't take to it. It was a wreck. But I knew I had to teach Mr. Kirsch that song if I wanted to get my car restored."

Ruff can teach anybody anything, but this was one of his knottiest challenges, for, as he soon found out, Mr. Kirsch had little aptitude for music. "And 'The Lord's Prayer' happens to be an unusually difficult piece—it rambles all over the place," Ruff said. His only hope would be to devise a special system of notation. He made a chart consisting of X's and O's to correspond to the words and to Mr. Kirsch's fingers—an X meant that he should keep the finger down, an O that he should lift it up—and the odd-looking document was tacked to Mr. Kirsch's wall. Luckily for Ruff, the tricky climactic measures of "The Lord's Prayer" continued to give Mr. Kirsch trouble. "He got the first part O.K., " Ruff said, "and told me he hoped to have the whole thing memorized soon. That had me worried. I thought, 'He's almost up to Amen and we haven't even started spray painting.' "

Mr. Kirsch came out of his house and greeted Ruff warmly. He was a short, bald man with a fringe of white hair. Around his neck he was wearing the leather strap that saxophonists wear to hold their instrument and that some of the great ones wear habitually as a badge of their art.

"How are you coming on 'The Lord's Prayer,' Mr. Kirsch?" Ruff asked him.

"Pretty good, Willie," he said. "I'm up to 'Forgive us our trespasses,' but I still can't get 'For thine is the kingdom.' " Ruff reassured him that all those high notes would be hard for anybody, but Mr. Kirsch was obviously disappointed. He said he thought he had the whole piece memorized and only last week had persuaded his wife to let him play it for her Wednesday afternoon ladies' group. Evidently this was no small act of persuasion—his wife, an organist, had exiled him to the basement for his practice sessions. Ruff had told me that Mr. Kirsch was both very nervous as a student and very proud of his new skill. "Anybody who comes into the body shop with a torn fender, Mr. Kirsch gets his sax and plays as much of 'The Lord's Prayer' as he can remember."

I asked Mr. Kirsch how it had gone on Wednesday afternoon. "I started off fine," he said, "right up through 'Hallowed be Thy name.' But then I froze. I think it was at 'Thy will be done.' Or maybe I got up to 'Give us this day.' Anyway it wasn't very far. I couldn't go on. Finally I just had to turn around and walk out of the room."

Ruff told him he had made charts for two more songs that use similar fingering—"My Country 'Tis of Thee" and "You Are My Sunshine"—and Mr. Kirsch brightened at this news of fresh territory to conquer. Mrs. Kirsch came out of the house and Ruff asked if they needed more than two tickets to Sunday night's concert. They said that two was just right and that they were looking forward to it. Mrs. Kirsch gave Ruff a curious look.

"Jimmy," she said to her husband, "I don't know how that feller can get you to put the right finger on those keys."

On Saturday morning Mitchell arrived, and he and Ruff put in two days of giving informal jazz demonstrations for children and for the citizens who had organized the week's events. Sunday night brought the long-awaited concert. It was held in the large and handsome auditorium of the University of North Alabama, whose campus is in Florence. Some of the patrons were worried that the turnout would be small, despite all the publicity, and that this would jeopardize the W. C. Handy Music Festival. But one look at the people flocking into the auditorium put those fears to rest. It was a big crowd and a happy one.

I saw many faces that were familiar: students from the high school in Florence where Ruff had talked, friends from his old neighborhood in Sheffield. I saw Buddy-Boy and Ann and Bubba. I saw Mr. Kirsch—nicely dressed and wearing his saxophone strap—and Mrs. Kirsch. In the front row I saw a sandy-haired man of about sixty who was conspicuous for his pleasure at being there. I asked someone who it was and learned that it was Mutt McCord. It hadn't occurred to me that Ruff's first teacher might still be around. I introduced myself to him.

"This is a thrill of a lifetime for me," Mutt said. He had brought his two granddaughters, Christy and Melanie, and he introduced them to me. I asked him for his early memories of Ruff. "You know, I just can't imagine a more wonderful friendship than that boy and I had," he said. "Bill Henry[6] was a skinny little kid with red hair, and he always had manners. That's how his mother brought him up. During the war when I went into the service he was very good to my mama and daddy. He'd come over every day and ask if they needed any wood cut, or anything else done, and he wouldn't ever take any money for it.

"That boy loved music. After I took up drumming I got a big bass drum that I played in the high school band, and Bill Henry thought that was the prettiest thing in the world—it was like a Christmas tree to him. When I walked to school for band practice he'd walk beside me beating that drum, and his eyes would just sparkle and shine. Blacks weren't allowed on the football field of the white high school, so while we practiced he'd sit at the edge of the cotton patch next to the field and wait till band practice was over, and then he'd walk back home with me, beating that big drum."

I asked Mutt whether he had kept up with his own drumming. He said that when he came home after World War II he became a builder and a construction superintendent, but that he continued to be a part-time drummer, sitting in with bands that accompanied many Grand Ole Opry singers and other soloists who gave community concerts at the National Guard armory in Sheffield. In 1968, however, a head-on car crash almost killed him and broke so many bones, including his wrists

6. **Bill Henry:** a nickname for Willie Henry Ruff.

and his right foot, that doctors told him he wouldn't walk again. He did walk again, but his drumming days were over. To take the place that drumming had filled in his life, he became a professional dog trainer and is now the contented proprietor of Mutt's School of Canine Control. He has kept in touch with Ruff not only as a friend but as a builder. When Ruff built his house out in Killen, on the land he had once plowed, it was Mutt who taught him how and helped him to build it.

The concert began. Ruff made a brief homecoming speech that thanked the people for their attendance, which had raised the money necessary to proceed with the W. C. Handy festival in August. (It was duly held, with Dizzy Gillespie as its principal star.) Ruff was unabashedly proud to be on that particular stage on that particular night. Mitchell struck the first few chords of "The More I See You"—chords of unusual elegance—and was off in high gear. Usually it takes him a while to achieve the emotional breakthrough that at some point in every Mitchell-Ruff concert lifts it to a high plane of excitement. This time excitement was in the air from the beginning.

Afterward, people from all of Ruff's old and new constituencies came backstage to see him. One of them was Buddy-Boy.

"Willie Henry," he said when he got to Ruff, "I never did know what you does for a living. But you sure does it."

Reviewing the Selection

Answer each of the following questions without looking back at the selection.

Recalling Facts

1. Willie Ruff was giving Mr. Kirsch saxophone lessons in exchange for
   - [ ] a. room and board.
   - [ ] b. advice on repairing a car.
   - [ ] c. advice on building a house.
   - [ ] d. concert tickets.

Understanding Main Ideas

2. When visiting his hometown, Willie Ruff
   - [ ] a. becomes angry about discrimination.
   - [ ] b. feels like an outsider.
   - [ ] c. is sad when he thinks about his past.
   - [ ] d. is at ease with friends and relatives.

Placing Events in Order

3. The first instrument that Ruff learned to play was the
   - [ ] a. trombone.
   - [ ] b. piano.
   - [ ] c. drums.
   - [ ] d. French horn.

Finding Supporting Details

4. Ruff shows his pleasure in teaching when he
   - [ ] a. explains the history of minstrel shows.
   - [ ] b. gives away tickets to the concert.
   - [ ] c. restores a 1948 Packard.
   - [ ] d. joins the army.

Character Development

5. "Ruff had the engine rebuilt and then faced the task of restoring the <u>dilapidated</u> body and interior." In this context *dilapidated* means
   ☐ a. colorful.
   ☐ b. run-down.
   ☐ c. unpainted.
   ☐ d. fancy.

Interpreting the Selection

Answer each of the following questions. You may look back at the selection if necessary.

6. As a young boy, Willie Ruff
   ☐ a. started a school band.
   ☐ b. disliked practicing the drums.
   ☐ c. was shy and withdrawn.
   ☐ d. was fascinated by music.

7. Willie Ruff can best be described as
   ☐ a. enthusiastic and energetic.
   ☐ b. nervous and musical.
   ☐ c. proud and unfriendly.
   ☐ d. quiet and shy.

8. Which of the following statements is
   not a fact?
   ☐ a. World War II brought prosperity
      to Sheffield.
   ☐ b. Ruff joined the army at the age
      of fourteen.
   ☐ c. Willie Ruff can teach anybody to
      do anything.
   ☐ d. Mr. Kirsch wanted to learn to play
      the saxophone.

Identifying Cause and Effect

9. As a result of his mother's death, Willie Ruff
   ☐ a. stopped playing music.
   ☐ b. joined the army.
   ☐ c. had to get a job.
   ☐ d. left Sheffield, Alabama.

Drawing Conclusions

10. When Willie Ruff was growing up, his
    parents
    ☐ a. were willing to buy him new books.
    ☐ b. were separated.
    ☐ c. discouraged his interest in music.
    ☐ d. moved around a lot.

Character Development

In "Homecoming for a Jazz Musician," William Zinsser has tried to show what Willie Ruff is like. A successful writer *shows* you a person's character, rather than *tells* you about the person. What is the difference between showing and telling?

Suppose a classmate is trying to give away a puppy. Before you consider taking the puppy, you might ask, "What is it like?" Your classmate might say, "Well, it's cute and playful and loves people." That is telling you what the puppy is like. On the other hand, your classmate might say, "Come over to our house and I'll show it to you." You are much more likely to want the puppy if you see it than if you just hear about it.

Since biographers cannot introduce you to their subjects in person, they try to show you what their subjects are like. They want you to be able to see and hear the people. Character development refers to the methods that writers use to show you what a person is like. In this lesson you will learn about several methods of character development.

Character Development Through Monologue

As you learned in Chapter 1, dialogue is the actual conversation between the characters in a story. What people say and how they say it can reveal a lot about them. In this selection William Zinsser uses some dialogue, but he also lets Willie Ruff tell his own story. Ruff sometimes gives a monologue, or a long uninterrupted speech given by one person. Like dialogue, a monologue gives you information about a person's character. Notice what Willie Ruff's words reveal about him in the monologue in the following excerpt.

It was common in the South at that time for black schools to be given hand-me-down equipment that the white schools no longer wanted—old footballs, for instance, and old books—but not old instruments. Ruff took a certain strength from the inequities. "There were marvelous ways that people invented to overcome in style," he said. "In fact, I know a lot of people who credit that disadvantage for their being able to make themselves better than they otherwise would have been. We had a brilliant black doctor in Sheffield named Dr. Long. He was one of the most inspirational men I've ever known and also one of the most tragic. He was frustrated because he wasn't given hospital privileges and many other rights that he had earned. But he had no patience with kids in Sheffield who complained about having to study out of books that had the backs torn off. He said, 'If there's not a page missing out of it, it's not a secondhand book. It's got as much learning with the back off as it has with the back on. Of *course* it's an injustice. But you can waste your time complaining about it, or you can get what's in it.' "

Zinsser describes a situation and then summarizes Ruff's attitude toward it in the short sentence, "Ruff took a certain strength from the inequities." Then he lets Ruff explain what that means in Ruff's own words. The author could simply have told you that Willie Ruff was not bitter about his experiences in a segregated school system. Instead, he shows you Ruff's positive attitude. Notice the words Ruff uses—*marvelous, brilliant,* and *inspirational.*

Through Ruff's description, you also understand his admiration for Dr. Long. By letting Ruff speak for himself, Zinsser provides concrete, or specific, evidence to support the statement that "Ruff took a certain

Character Development

strength from the inequities." Because you have read Ruff's own words, you know that Zinsser's interpretation of Ruff's character is correct.

1. Find another place in the selection where Willie Ruff talks about his past. Summarize what Ruff says. Then explain what you learn about Ruff's character from reading his own words.

Character Development Through Description

Another way that a writer reveals a person's character is through description. Description is the kind of writing that helps you to picture a person, a place, or an event. It is a common method of character development, but it gives you only the writer's view of what is important about the person. Although description is not as effective as dialogue or monologue, it is still an important aspect of character development. Read the following passage in which Zinsser describes Willie Ruff's use of the spoken language.

> I was delighted by the down-home cadences that had crept into his speech, by idioms and regionalisms that were as old as the black South. It wasn't the first time I had been struck by Ruff's gifts of adaptation. I had heard him charm foundation executives in Manhattan and conservatory students in Shanghai—both in their native language. His remarkable ear was one of the agencies of his survival and his success.

2. In your own words summarize what William Zinsser is saying about Willie Ruff's speech. What generalization can you make about Ruff's character from that description?

Character Development and Action

Actions speak louder than words is an old saying that applies to character development. A writer tries to capture a person's character by showing that person in action. A writer can easily tell you that a person is kind and considerate of others. However, the writer creates a much more effective picture by relating an incident in which a person takes time from a busy schedule to visit a sick friend or to help a neighbor hunt for a lost pet.

How does William Zinsser show Willie Ruff in action? In the excerpt you read, you see Willie Ruff walking around his hometown and telling Zinsser about growing up in Sheffield. Those actions suggest two characteristics of Ruff. First, they show that he is an energetic man. Instead of sitting in a hotel room and reminiscing, he talks to Zinsser while showing him around the town. Second, Ruff's actions show that he has positive feelings about his youth. If he did not have those positive feelings, he would probably not be interested in seeing his old neighborhood.

As Ruff and Zinsser walk around Sheffield, Ruff explains the history of minstrel shows. That incident not only reveals Ruff's knowledge of his field, but also shows how naturally he falls into the role of teacher. What is more, he clearly enjoys teaching. Although later Zinsser tells you about Ruff's teaching, in this episode he actually shows Willie Ruff as a teacher.

3. *Several scenes in the selection show Willie Ruff visiting friends and relatives and giving them concert tickets. What do those actions reveal about Ruff?*

4. *When Ruff and the author visit Mr. Kirsch, you learn about two activities of Ruff's. What are those activities? What do they show you about him?*

Character Development and the Opinions of Others

In addition to letting Ruff tell his own story and showing him in action, Zinsser also records other people's opinions of Ruff. In that way, you get more than one view of Ruff's character. It is revealing to learn what other people remember about a person they have known. Ruff's boyhood friend and drum teacher, Mutt McCord, remembers the young Willie Ruff in this way:

"You know, I just can't imagine a more wonderful friendship than that boy and I had," he said. "Bill Henry was a skinny little kid with red hair, and he always had manners. That's how

Character Development

his mother brought him up. During the war when I went into the service he was very good to my mama and daddy. He'd come over every day and ask if they needed any wood cut, or anything else done, and he wouldn't ever take any money for it."

5. What does that passage reveal about Willie Ruff as a boy? List at least two things that you learn about Ruff's character from Mutt McCord's words.

In the selection Zinsser not only reveals what Mutt McCord thought of Willie Ruff but also shows the relationship that existed between the two musicians. Think about this piece of information: "When Ruff built his house out in Killen, on the land he had once plowed, it was Mutt who taught him how and helped him to build it."

6. What does that scene reveal about both Willie Ruff and Mutt?

Character Development and Interpretation

Even though Zinsser lets Willie Ruff tell much of his own story, the author does interpret Ruff's character. As you learned in Chapter 2, a biographer's interpretation helps you notice patterns and themes in a subject's life.

One advantage that Zinsser has is that he can see Ruff in action. He can also see other people's reactions to Ruff. Thus, instead of relying on written records, Zinsser gets his information firsthand. Still, he must organize those details to show you the patterns in Willie Ruff's life.

One pattern that Zinsser finds is repeated evidence of Ruff's teaching ability. "Ruff can teach anybody anything," he states. By the time you read that interpretation, Zinsser has already shown one example of Ruff's teaching—the lecture about minstrel shows. But that example alone is not enough to support Zinsser's opinion that Ruff could "teach anybody anything."

7. Find another example of Willie Ruff's ability to "teach anybody anything." Summarize the example. Then decide whether it supports the author's interpretation.

While William Zinsser focuses on Willie Ruff's character, he also interprets the actions of people around Ruff. By showing you the people with whom Ruff associates, the author adds to your picture of Ruff's character. Notice, for example, the author's interpretation of how Ruff's friends and relatives responded to receiving the concert tickets.

> As it turned out, some of the friends and relatives seemed to have no interest in the tickets and almost no grasp of the event he was inviting them to attend. He was just Willie Ruff. If he had a career somewhere else, that was his business. For now he appeared to be someone who had never left small-town Alabama.

Although that comment gives you information about the friends and relatives, it also shows you something about Willie Ruff. It suggests that Ruff is not someone who insists on impressing people with his own importance. When he goes home, he is interested in the people there. He does not insist on making others recognize his accomplishments.

8. Read the last two paragraphs of the selection. Why do you think William Zinsser chose to end the episode with the quotation from Willie Ruff's stepbrother?

Questions for Thought and Discussion

The questions and activities that follow will help you explore "Homecoming for a Jazz Musician" in more depth and at the same time develop your critical thinking skills.

1. **Analyzing.** What were some of the musical influences on Willie Ruff during his early years in Sheffield, Alabama? List at least four influences and explain how each of them affected Ruff.

2. **Finding Examples.** Zinsser shows that Willie Ruff was both a teacher and a student. Find at least two examples of each.

3. **Interpreting.** In your opinion what is the author's attitude toward Willie Ruff? Give specific evidence to support your interpretation.

4. **Organizing a Debate.** Reread the paragraph in which Willie Ruff talks about Dr. Long's impatience "with kids . . . who complained about having to study out of books that had the backs torn off." Organize a debate in which one side supports Dr. Long's position and the other supports the position of the students. Each side should develop strong reasons for its stand.

Writing About Literature

Several suggestions for writing projects are given below. You may be asked to complete one or more of these projects. If you have any questions about how to begin a writing assignment, review Using the Writing Process, beginning on page 341.

1. **Writing a Profile.** Write a two-page profile of someone you know and admire. Use one or more of the methods that you studied in this chapter to develop your subject's character. For example, try to use dialogue, description, and the opinions of others to show the different sides of your subject's character.

2. **Preparing an Interview.** Imagine that you are a radio or television talk-show host. Choose to interview one of the three people you have read about in this unit—Frederick Douglass, Susan B. Anthony, or Willie Ruff. In a paragraph or two, explain why you would like to interview that person for your show. Then draw up a list of questions you would ask the person.

3. **Writing Dialogue.** Imagine that there was some way for Frederick Douglass and Willie Ruff to meet. Think about what they might say to each other. Then write a dialogue of their conversation. (Remember that Frederick Douglass died in 1895. Remember also that Willie Ruff is a teacher as well as a musician.)

Essays
and Articles

*T*he selections in Unit Two represent two forms of nonfiction writing—essays and articles. An <u>essay</u> is a brief composition that expresses a person's opinions or views about a particular subject. The essayist does not say everything there is to say about a subject. Instead, he or she usually tries to persuade you to accept his or her views about that subject. In fact, the word *essay* comes from a French word meaning "to try."

An essay may be either informal or formal. An <u>informal essay,</u> which is sometimes called a personal essay, uses informal language and often reveals the writer's personality. A <u>formal essay</u> uses formal language and often sounds impersonal. Serious subjects such as philosophy and history are usually discussed formally in essays.

Unlike an essay, in which the author's opinions or views are very important, an <u>article</u> is a written work that tries to give you an unbiased, or balanced, view of a topic. Writers of articles do not try to influence you by including their opinions in their articles. Instead, they present the information and let you develop your own opinions about it. Articles often appear in newspapers and magazines.

All nonfiction writers, including essayists and writers of articles, rely on four basic kinds of writing to develop their ideas—description, narration, exposition, and argumentation. Description, as you have learned, is the kind of writing that helps you picture a person, a place, or an event. Narration, which you studied in Chapter 1, is the kind of writing that gives the events and actions of the story.

<u>Exposition</u>, sometimes called expository writing, is the kind of writing that presents information. An article about how to care for an animal is an example of exposition. <u>Argumentation</u> is the kind of writing that tries to persuade you to accept the author's opinions. Essayists, for example, use argumentation to convince you that their opinions are correct.

In the selections in Unit Two, you will read examples of all four kinds of writing. In the lessons you will examine how writers use those kinds of writing to create effective essays and articles.

Chapter 4

Selection   *Keeping Up with the Joneses, Jr.*
PHYLLIS MCGINLEY

Lesson   *Evaluating Opinions in an Essay*

About the Selection

"Keeping Up with the Joneses, Jr." is an essay in which Phyllis McGinley expresses some strong opinions about children in the United States in the 1960s. Although McGinley is serious about her subject, "Keeping Up with the Joneses, Jr." is an informal essay. In it McGinley recalls many personal experiences. She speaks casually to you rather than lectures about her ideas or opinions.

The title of the essay is revealing. "Keeping up with the Joneses" was a common phrase in the 1950s and 1960s and it is still used today. The phrase grew out of the new prosperity that the United States enjoyed in the 1950s.

During the 1930s and 1940s, people in the United States suffered first the hardships of the Great Depression and then the shortages of World War II. By the 1950s factories were again producing consumer goods, such as cars, appliances, and television sets. People had jobs and the money to buy those goods. To some observers, it seemed as though the whole country was on a gigantic spending spree.

Sometimes, people bought goods whether or not they needed them. They simply bought an item because their friends and neighbors had it. If one person in the neighborhood bought a pool for the backyard, then others bought similar pools for their backyards. Some even bought pools when they did not enjoy swimming. "Keeping up with the Joneses" was the phrase used to describe that behavior. "The Joneses" were the typical family next door with whom everyone else was trying to compete.

Who are the "Joneses, Jr." in McGinley's title? According to McGinley, they are the children of the Joneses. The Joneses, Jr., were growing up in the 1960s and they faced the same kind of competition their parents did. Even though this essay was written in the 1960s, McGinley's opinions still apply to today's society.

"Keeping Up with the Joneses, Jr." first appeared as a magazine article. Later, it was published with other essays by Phyllis McGinley in a book called *Sixpence in Her Shoe*. The title of the book refers to an old English legend. According to the legend, if a housewife was thrifty, clean, kind, and hardworking, she might occasionally find a sixpence coin in her shoe. It would have been put there by an elf as a reward. McGinley chose that title because the essays in her book are about the rewards, challenges, and difficulties of being a homemaker and raising a family.

Phyllis McGinley is best known as a writer of light verse. In that kind of poetry, the writer exhibits a humorous attitude toward the problems of everyday life. McGinley's poetry deals with such commonplace topics as television, department stores, and homework. Her poems, however, are thought-provoking as well as entertaining. In 1961 her book *Times Three: Selected Verse from Three Decades* won the Pulitzer Prize for poetry. It was the first collection of light verse to receive that honor.

Phyllis McGinley was born in Oregon in 1905. When she was three, her parents took her to live on a ranch in eastern Colorado. She said in her own words that she was raised in "the real Wild West." Phyllis and her brother rode ponies to the country school where they were the only pupils.

After her father died, the family moved to Ogden, Utah, where Phyllis attended high school. She graduated from the University of Utah and in 1928 went east to teach English in a suburb of New York City. She taught for four and a half years and wrote poetry in her free time. When she began to have some success as a writer, she left teaching, moved into the city, and became a full-time writer.

In 1937 Phyllis McGinley married and moved back to the suburbs. There, she raised two daughters and continued to write poetry, essays, and children's books. McGinley was a keen observer of suburban life. She once confessed that she enjoyed cooking, gardening, and "sticking pins into the smugger aspects of the social scene."

In her later years Phyllis McGinley devoted most of her time to writing prose rather than poetry. The last of her eighteen books, called *Saint Watching*, was published in 1969. On her seventieth birthday, however, she composed these lines, showing that she had not lost her touch for light verse:

> Seventy is wormwood,
> Seventy is gall.
> But it's better to be 70
> Than not alive at all.

In 1978 Phyllis McGinley died at the age of seventy-two.

Lesson Preview

The lesson that follows "Keeping Up with the Joneses, Jr." focuses on evaluating opinions. The selection is an essay. As you read in the introduction to Unit Two, an essay is a brief composition that expresses a writer's opinions or views about a particular subject. You may or may not agree with the writer. Before you can make your judgment, however, you need to identify the writer's opinions and decide whether they are reasonably supported by facts.

The questions that follow will help you identify Phyllis McGinley's opinions and decide how well she supports them. As you read, think about how you would answer these questions.

1 What are the main opinions that McGinley expresses in her essay?

2 What kinds of information does the author give to support her opinions? Does she support her opinions effectively?

3 What attitude does the writer take toward her subject? For example, is she angry, bitter, playful, or concerned?

Vocabulary

Here are some difficult words that appear in the selection that follows. Study the words and their definitions, as well as the sentences that show how the words are used. This will help you get the most from your reading.

benefactions gifts. *The kind woman's generous benefactions were greatly appreciated by the church.*

dervishes members of a Muslim religious group, some of whom practice whirling, howling dances as religious acts. *The dead leaves spun like dervishes in the strong wind.*

dilettante dabbler; amateur. *That dilettante George can never stay with one hobby long enough to get good at it.*

predilection preference; partiality. *I have a predilection for popcorn, so I make it frequently.*

emulate imitate; copy. *A good way to learn to dance is to emulate someone who dances well.*

misogyny hatred or distrust of women. *An employer's misogyny does not mean he can discriminate against women.*

ennui boredom; weariness. *During vacations, some children suffer from ennui, not knowing what to do with so much free time.*

coterie close circle of friends; clique. *Only the actress's small coterie was ever invited to her home.*

Keeping Up with the Joneses, Jr.

PHYLLIS MCGINLEY

*E*very now and then when I am in a benign mood, I stop to count my blessings. I give thanks for friends and for drip-dry underwear; for the sun in the morning and my new electric blanket at night; for my dentist, my husband, my automatic pencil sharpener. But chiefly I am grateful that I don't have to be a child in this era.

Youth is a perfectly wonderful commodity and far too valuable, as Shaw[1] has pointed out, to be wasted on the young. Yet like all human benefactions, it has its penalties, which in today's urgent society have frighteningly increased. I don't think I am merely nostalgic when I contend that being a child nowadays is a tougher proposition than it was when my generation and I compared arithmetic answers between classes or devoured bread-and-pickle sandwiches on the front porch after school. For one thing, it isn't as much fun.

On the surface this assertion may sound like gibbering nonsense.

1. Shaw: George Bernard Shaw, an Irish dramatist, known for his witty sayings.

Never before in history has childhood had so much attention paid to its welfare and its amusement. It is cosseted, pampered, immunized against unhappiness as against polio or whooping cough.

Also on the surface, its pattern of traditional play seems not to have changed very much since my time—or since Tom Sawyer's or Alexander's.[2] Little boys still scuffle on pavements with friends as truculently as if they were enemies. Little girls, curls or pigtails bobbing, still swing ropes to identical chants I remember, leaping like dervishes at the climactic command of "Salt, Vinegar, Mustard—PEPPER!" Baseballs thud into gloves too large for hands they encase. Kites fly, forts get built out of snow, summer waters divide where frolicking bodies flash through them like dolphins. But there is a difference in the way the games are played.

That nimble child with the skip rope may not be bounding merely for the pleasure of physical activity. Perhaps she practices leaps so that at ballet class on Saturday morning she can improve her *tour jeté*[3] and be able to star in the spring show. There is a contest arranged for kite flyers, with cash awards donated for the winners by the chamber of commerce—so reeling a paper toy in and out of the sky is serious business. The champion builder of snowmen has his picture in the paper. That ballplayer exercises his arm apprehensively. Will he or will he not be included in a Little League, where he and the rest of his team can own uniforms and a coach and listen to parents cheering from genuine grandstands? The swimmer vies for medals. Those vague dreams and rewards of "When I grow up" have suddenly become concrete goals, scaled to child's size. The play has turned professional. And the ordinary competitive instinct of the young is being channeled into a frenzy of keeping up with, or learning to surpass, all the little Joneses in the neighborhood.

There is nothing wrong with healthy competition. But there is, it seems to me, something both wrong and unwholesome about harassing those below their teens into too early insistence on success. A success,

---

2. **Tom Sawyer:** the hero of a novel by Mark Twain. **Alexander:** the young leader who conquered ancient Greece and Persia in the fourth century B.C.
3. *tour jeté*: a French term used in ballet to mean a high turning leap.

that is, imposed from above. In the same society which has made so much recent outcry about the perils of conformity in the adult world, a kind of terrible conformity of effort is being forced upon youth.

Not all boys are natural material for Little League, and thank God for it. Not all little girls are born to be prima ballerinas. Olympic standards in swimming or hurling a ball or brandishing a tennis racket are not for everyone. Left to themselves, the duffers might find some field in which they could excel—making up stories for younger brothers and sisters, maybe, or naming wild flowers, or just rejoicing in their own thoughts. But they are *not* left to themselves. No quarter is given to the dilettante.

A bookish nine-year-old girl I know was discovered lying face down on her bed one spring afternoon not long ago, alternately crying her heart out and exclaiming, as if she were the heroine of a Victorian novel,[4] "In vain! In vain! All in vain!"

Her matter-of-fact mother told me about it with amusement, but I was appalled by the reason for the tears. The child's heart had been broken, not for any realistic tragedy (like being left out of a party list or receiving few Valentines in the school Valentine box). She had simply, after hours of practice, trailed the field in the fourth-grade square-dancing competition. She had chasséd left when she was supposed to promenade right or made some such other public faux pas.[5] The shame was more than she could bear.

Had so much stress not been laid on conforming to a pattern, she wouldn't have cared a fig about her *dos-à-dos*.[6] It wasn't her talent, and she ought not to have minded. I can recall, for instance, being the worst map drawer for my age and weight in the whole school when I was a fourth grader. I was also the clumsiest volleyball player on our side when we chose up teams at recess. But no iron entered my soul. If my maps

---

4. **Victorian novel:** a fictional work written during the reign of Queen Victoria, in the last half of the 1800s. Victorian novels were often very melodramatic.

5. **faux pas:** false steps; mistake.

6. *dos-à-dos:* a French phrase meaning back to back. It describes a square dancing step and is often written in English as dosido or dosy-do.

were lopsided, at least I got A's on my compositions. And if I couldn't knock the ball back across the net two-thirds of the time, I was valued by my contemporaries in spite of it because I made up such involved signals for Saturday games of Run, Sheep, Run. No parent, no teacher, was breathing down my neck, expecting me to beat a community record in some field. The most irksome admonition I received was an exasperated, "Do take your nose out of that book and get into the fresh air." And while such tolerance kept me from perfecting my swimming stroke, made me the eternal amateur at sports, it left my self-confidence intact. I went on, however ineptly, building my snow forts and turning my ankles skating on winter ice and floundering in warm ponds as happily as if I were champion of every art. I was following Chesterton's[7] sound advice that "whatever is worth doing is worth doing badly."

That is what today's generation is not permitted. Fear of failure is indoctrinated in them early—nor is it only fear of failure at games. Socially, also, children are expected to star, are required to follow a pattern exact as a diet list. Are bananas good for twelve-week-old babies? Is strained liver prescribed a little later, whole milk at eight months? Well and good. There is a chart for gregarious behavior just as rigid. At seven, little girls ought to start casting warm looks on their favorite cub scout. At nine, they should be inviting "mixed groups" to their birthday galas. They must master the day's approximation of the waltz or the Twist at, say, eleven, and no later than twelve months afterwards wangle from some masculine contemporary in junior high school an invitation to the movies. At thirteen or fourteen, they should have turned into accomplished sirens.

If the pattern does not become them, if they are more interested in books or tropical fish than in experimenting with lipstick, mothers wring their hands over their predilection for spinsterhood. When I was a tomboy in middy blouse and pleated skirt, no such precocious behavior was demanded of us. Boys might carry home our book bags or help us with geography lessons; they might even be invited in for a casual piece of chocolate cake by hospitable mothers. But little girls too given to giggles

7. **Chesterton:** Gilbert K. Chesterton, a British writer.

and melting glances were earmarked "boy-struck" and their conduct frowned on. Today, though, if there is a Thelma Jones in the neighborhood who has known from her cradle how to toss an alluring tress over her shoulder and assure the class hero that he is Tarzan and Hector and Socrates[8] all rolled into one, she is called "socially adjusted." And it is Thelma whom her peers are urged to emulate. Even the boys, sturdy bachelors of ten or eleven, are prodded into following paths their elders think suitable. To be a boy scout now, it is not enough to stay reverent, courteous, and clean; to camp ecstatically if uncomfortably in sleeping bags; and to track the fierce woodchuck down spring trails. A loyal scout must also attend the troop's two dances a year, complete with date.

(Their opposite numbers, with true feminine excess, have gone farther. The Girl Scouts of America have just announced the formation of a new group, the Cadettes, who will study not marching and good deeds, but how to get along with young men and the most efficient ways of applying cosmetics.)

That children might want to wait a while before they cast off childhood is scarcely taken into consideration by schools, parents, community leaders, busy keeping little Joneses on their mettle. It is now possible to be a social failure earlier than twelve. Girls learn to be wallflowers before their petals open and boys to retreat into premature misogyny with voices still unbroken.

They can also be academic failures as early as kindergarten. For prosperous middle-class America has suddenly discovered the prestige of education and is bowing down before it as before a golden calf.[9] I am not, naturally, against education. To enlarge and elevate the mind, particularly the child mind, is the noblest of all human activities. Moreover, the hungry intelligence of youth has always been able to assimilate more learning than our schools were prepared to feed it. What I deplore is the new race toward measured achievement, the frantic struggle of all parents to set their children competing for grades, marks, triumphs in

8. Hector: a great hero in ancient Greek literature. **Socrates:** a brilliant philosopher of ancient Greece.
9. golden calf: something that is worshiped as an idol.

aptitude tests, not for the love of knowledge, but because only triumph will get them into future colleges.

That the struggle has innocent motives, that the snobbery of a high IQ proceeds from a good cause does not reduce tensions for the children involved. There used to be room in childhood's world for every kind of mentality. If schools offered less challenge in my day than in this, at least they gave to us, who sat in unassorted classrooms, a kind of anonymous safety. We were not branded by the Test. Now the specter of the intelligence test, the examination for aptitude, achievement, special skills, hangs over our schools like a nightmare, haunting our young from the time they enter first grade until they walk onstage for a diploma. Tests sort them, classify them, winnow them out as if they were gradable peas from a commercial garden. Into one compartment go the jumbo-sized IQ's; into another the medium, into a third the inferior. And the fact that such tests measure neither leadership nor talent nor emotional adjustment, nor even promise, stops no educator from doing the classifying— nor the sortie from feeling its impact. Again, success or failure comes too soon.

"Jane isn't a student," Jane's mother used to say with a lenient smile. She knew perfectly well Jane could straggle on somehow toward graduation, no doubt marry young, and let fall her lines in pleasant places. Jane was able to wear her academic inability gaily, as if it were a corsage.

Or, "Howard's impossible at math," Howard's father was inclined to boast. "Just like his old man. But you ought to see the way he'll hit that scrimmage line when he gets to Princeton."

Now Howard, Sr., is having his eight-year-old son tutored in arithmetic, burdening him with summer-school lessons, making him feel guilty of some juvenile sin for not achieving the same marks as the Jones lad. He is aware, and makes the boy aware, that there will be no Princeton in his future—perhaps not even a Siwash University—unless things improve. Jane's mother, eager for the prestige a good college bestows now on a girl (socially, important as a debut), is nagging her daughter into hysterics or moving her from school to school, hoping somehow to redesign her charming if unscholarly mind. No wonder the neuroses of childhood increase and unsuccessful victims of the System turn delinquent at twelve. One needs an adult shell to withstand the knowledge that the path one walks will lead into no enchanted land. And even for the successful, some of the fun of undetermined aims has vanished.

I know a young woman with four children all still under six. She lives in a delightful suburb but is deserting it for Larkspur Manor. In Larkspur Manor she has no friends, her house will not be so attractive as the one she owns.

"But Larkspur has this awfully good school," she admits candidly. "The principal gets practically the entire senior class into college. I have to think ahead."

Already, you see, she is waging that battle for status. Higher education is not a dim vision on a faraway horizon but a prize for which the battle begins in the perambulator. And the prize is a pragmatic one—a social rather than an intellectual reward. Her brood will be trained for winning scholastic merit as they will be groomed for appearance and poise. First-rate schooling has to her the identical value of orthodontics, summer camps, riding lessons, and a talking doll for the baby. It is a Thing which she competitively tries to buy for them, like a rocking horse.

She is not unique. The operative word in juvenile upbringing today is Things. American children are afflicted with a glut of possessions. Peer into any ordinary middle-class nursery. Its material accumulations overwhelm the grown-up who remembers from her own youth how exciting it was to receive, say, a new set of paper dolls, or how the neighborhood Midas[10] swaggered when he finally came into his inheritance of a real catcher's mask and glove.

My childhood was not deprived, except by current standards. But it was certainly not animated by all the fire engines, dolls, educational puzzles, pogo sticks, electric pianos, giant pandas, personal radios and television sets with which parents of even moderate means now smother

10. **Midas:** in Greek mythology, a king who was granted the power of turning everything he touched into gold. Here the term means the golden boy of the neighborhood.

infants. And this in spite of the fact that any experienced mother knows babies are democratic about toys. Hand them an empty oatmeal box and a spoon and they will contentedly beat time on that improvised drum. Give them pie plates to pound, a chain of buttons to finger, and no jungle gym amuses them more validly. But there is status involved. What the little Joneses have, all must have. A bicycle used to be an approximation, for a boy, of the exurbanite's Jaguar—a glittering dream acquired only after months of coaxing, saving up, delivering papers on a local route, or dropping hints to generous grandparents. When it arrived at last, some delirious Christmas or glorious birthday morning, the child marched like a monarch into his kingdom. Now bicycles come in so many sizes, appear so early on the juvenile scene, that a jaded owner has often possessed (or wrecked or lost) several by the time he learns long division. For him it has never been an achievement, merely an expected convenience, like his book bag or his winter snowsuit.

By the same token he has probably found his interest waning early in the complicated system of electric railroads his father bought him before he was old enough to know a culvert from a coupling. Familiarity breeds not only contempt but ennui.

The other day I saw three little boys ambling down a rural road. Young as they were, they knew the gambit of the thumb, and I obligingly stopped the car to pick them up. As they shambled into the back seat, each of them flicked off the transistor radio he had been carrying along on his nature walk. I was less amused than horrified. What was the excitement of exploring woods and rocks to these world-weary Croesuses[11] whose imaginative resources had grown so limited by riches that only an adult gadget could entertain them? It is little wonder that by adolescence such possession-drowned children have no dreams left to wait for and take to crashing parties or doing a bit of shoplifting in supermarkets by way of diversion.

When I think of riches I am reminded of dollhouses. Of all symbols

---

11. **Croesus:** a very wealthy king of ancient times.

of childhood (at least to me, who have only daughters) the dollhouse seems the most enduring. The little girl lucky enough to be given one used to be empress of her coterie. And eight years old used to be judged the proper age to become a chatelaine,[12] as, indeed, it still is. Eight is house-proud. Eight arranges furniture, dusts the living room, sets Lilliputian[13] tables, is as careful with her things as a Dutch housewife. She is not a destroyer but a guardian of her hearth. Yet in half the nurseries I enter nowadays, babies of three and four are already tearing to pieces the little dwellings they cannot yet appreciate. What will they have left to yearn for?

Our younger daughter, patly on her eighth birthday, received a dollhouse. Her clever father had constructed it himself in our basement over five hardworking months. We knew at the time that the project was partly for ourselves, a labor of personal gratification. And it turned out to be the most rewarding busywork we ever embarked on. We were architects, contractors, interior decorators. All the windows opened and closed. There was a real staircase with a newel-post, fireplaces, book-shelves, a bathroom with its own tiny scales and towels. Lights turned on in every room by individual switches made from radio appliances. Everything was built to scale. The walls we papered with material designed for bookbinders, since ordinary wallpaper of even the smallest pattern loomed immoderately large. We covered the floors with uphol-stery fabrics, stretched and tacked by hand. There was a telephone. There was a grandfather clock. The doll's refrigerator bulged with food. I, who do not willingly sew on a button or put up a hem, spent weeks stitching tiny tablecloths and curtains. And of course the secret (for we managed somehow to keep it secret) was the greatest imaginable success. The birthday child eclipsed the grandest of the Joneses. She began to be courted even by little boys, who would not admit to being interested in

---

12. **chatelaine:** the mistress of a castle or any large household.
13. **Lilliputian:** tiny. The Lilliputians were imaginary people, six inches tall, who appeared in Jonathan Swift's novel, *Gulliver's Travels*.

anything concerning dolls but who professed, nevertheless, to admire the ingenious way you could press a button at the front door and hear a bell ring in that splendid house.

She loved it, naturally. She loves it still, and we store it now in the attic against the day her own daughter turns eight. Yet I think we gave her, again, too much too early. If we had let her paint her own walls, invent her own furniture, design her own curtains, however ill-made, the gift might have held a greater magic. Wealth can be stifling. The houses I made out of shoe boxes when *I* was eight, with their cardboard beds and pasted-up draperies and chairs concocted from acorn caps, afforded me more actual pleasure, I believe, than any child gets now from a prefabricated mansion. They made me a creator.

It is the fun of creation which today's overindulged children are in danger of missing.

I would tell all these things to novice parents if they would listen. I would beg them to hold off their well-meant efforts to provide the young with all joys and accomplishments before their hands (or their hearts) were large enough to hold them. I would remind them that the copybook maxim still holds: Happiness is not manufactured from goods but from good. At the same time I would ask tolerance from them; tolerance of mediocrity, casual acceptance of their children's limitations as of their talents.

"Let them walk forward at their own speed," I would say. "Give love rather than possessions, moral standards rather than a sense of competition, an education fitted not to any arbitrary test or the ambitions of the Joneses, but to their individual and fledgling minds. Then, when success or failure comes, they will be better able to cope with it."

Surely on a planet increasingly chilly to the touch, uncomplicated childhood ought to remain the last warm and lighted house in which the human animal can shelter for a time while he grows strong enough to face the gathering winds of the world.

Reviewing the Selection

Answer each of the following questions without looking back at the selection.

Recalling Facts

1. As a child, Phyllis McGinley
    - ☐ a. excelled at everything she tried.
    - ☐ b. was allowed to pursue her own interests.
    - ☐ c. envied children who could draw maps.
    - ☐ d. was a wallflower.

Understanding Main Ideas

2. According to McGinley, modern parents
    - ☐ a. do not show much interest in their children.
    - ☐ b. do not discipline their children enough.
    - ☐ c. put too much pressure on their children to succeed.
    - ☐ d. understand their children better than her parents understood her.

Placing Events in Order

3. Which of the following events took place last?
    - ☐ a. Even little boys enjoyed playing with the dollhouse.
    - ☐ b. McGinley decided it might have been best for her daughter to decorate her own dollhouse.
    - ☐ c. McGinley's husband built a dollhouse.
    - ☐ d. McGinley decided that eight was the perfect age for a girl to have a dollhouse.

Finding Supporting Details

4. As an example of giving children too much too early, McGinley describes the
    - ☐ a. bicycles parents buy for their boys.
    - ☐ b. fourth-grader who did not win the square dancing competition.
    - ☐ c. tests that students must constantly take.
    - ☐ d. competition to get into college.

Evaluating Opinions in an Essay

5. "Every now and then when I am in a <u>benign</u> mood, I stop to count my blessings." In this context *benign* means
   - ☐ a. silly.
   - ☐ b. angry.
   - ☐ c. nervous.
   - ☐ d. kindly.

Interpreting the Selection

Answer each of the following questions. You may look back at the selection if necessary.

6. From this essay, you can infer that Phyllis McGinley believes that
   - ☐ a. all children enjoy ballet lessons.
   - ☐ b. not everyone should go to college.
   - ☐ c. parents should not help their children with homework.
   - ☐ d. girls should not be given dollhouses until they are at least ten years old.

7. The opinions in this essay are mostly based on
   - ☐ a. personal experience.
   - ☐ b. opinion polls.
   - ☐ c. research.
   - ☐ d. interviews.

8. Based on the essay, which of the following statements is a fact?
   □ a. Children today still play many of the same games that McGinley played as a child.
   □ b. Being a child today is not as much fun as it used to be.
   □ c. Children today are under pressure to succeed at everything.
   □ d. Children today are given too many toys.

9. Because McGinley was allowed to follow her own interests as a child, she
   □ a. felt inadequate as an adult.
   □ b. hated sports.
   □ c. developed self-confidence.
   □ d. was ignored by her classmates.

10. From the essay, you could conclude that
    □ a. children do not enjoy competition.
    □ b. parents do not spend enough time with their children.
    □ c. parents are forcing their children to be overly competitive.
    □ d. children have too much free time.

Evaluating Opinions in an Essay

In "Keeping Up with the Joneses, Jr." Phyllis McGinley describes what she thinks it is like "to be a child in this era." Her essay presents a very personal view and is filled with her opinions, or her feelings, thoughts, or ideas about a subject.

Writers express their opinions in different ways. They may be part of general statements or predictions. Other opinions depend on personal values. A general statement of opinion is "Competition is healthy." The prediction "Sue is going to win the tennis match" is an opinion based on a particular situation. "Joe shouldn't be so competitive" is an opinion that depends on personal values.

Writers cannot prove that their opinions are true. But they can show their opinions to be reasonable by using facts to support them. A fact is a thing that has actually happened or that is really true.

An essayist, such as Phyllis McGinley, presents several opinions on a particular subject. Sometimes the essayist lists a series of facts and then presents an opinion based on those facts. At other times the essayist may express an opinion and then give the supporting facts. In either case, you need to identify which statements are opinions and which are facts. You should also decide how well the writer uses facts to support opinions.

Identifying Opinions

Why do opinions have to be identified? Aren't they obvious? The answer is that opinions are often not easy to identify. Of course, if a writer says, "I think" or "I believe" or "it seems to me" or "in my opinion," then you know that he or she is expressing an opinion. But writers do not always use such phrases. More often, they state an opinion as though it were a fact. They are not trying to fool you. They assume that you are able to distinguish between a fact and an opinion.

In "Keeping Up with the Joneses, Jr.", Phyllis McGinley gives a whole series of opinions. Most of them concern the challenges of childhood and youth and the differences between growing up when McGinley did and growing up today.

Read the following passage taken from the second paragraph of McGinley's essay. Here, she expresses two opinions, but only one is labeled as an opinion.

> I don't think I am merely nostalgic when I contend that being a child nowadays is a tougher proposition than it was when my generation and I compared arithmetic answers between classes or devoured bread-and-pickle sandwiches on the front porch after school. For one thing, it isn't as much fun.

In the first sentence McGinley uses two phrases—"I don't think" and "when I contend"—that clearly label her statement an opinion. In the second sentence she gives no such clue. Yet the second statement is an opinion, too, because it reflects her feelings. Perhaps to many children childhood still *is* a lot of fun.

Those two statements contain two main points that McGinley makes in her essay. First, she argues that being a child today is much harder than it was when she was growing up. Second, she insists that "it isn't as much fun." In the rest of her essay, McGinley supports those opinions. She also tries to convince you that her opinions are valid.

1. Read the sixth paragraph of the essay, which begins "There is nothing wrong with healthy competition." Find two statements of opinion in that paragraph—one that is labeled an opinion and one that is not.

Throughout the essay, McGinley supports her main opinions. She feels that children are being forced to conform to unrealistic standards set by the adult world. She complains that children "are *not* left to themselves" to explore their own world. "No quarter [mercy] is given to the dilettante," she says. In other words, the child who wants to be a dilettante, a dabbler who tries different things, receives no consideration from the adult world.

2. Skim the essay. Find at least three other opinions and summarize them.

Identifying Facts

As you have learned, McGinley has strong opinions about the pressures that are put on children. What facts does she give to support those opinions?

Writers use different kinds of facts to support their opinions. Statistics are one kind of fact. Statistics are numerical data on a given subject, arranged in an orderly fashion. Phyllis McGinley could have used statistics to support her opinions. She could have cited statistical surveys that showed how many children felt great pressure to achieve and how many did not. She could have listed data such as how much money parents spent on special tutoring for their children. McGinley, however, took another approach to support her statements. She relied on experiences from her own life and the lives of people she knew.

Personal experience is generally judged to be as true as other kinds of facts. When a writer recounts personal experiences, you tend to accept them as true, especially if the writer is well known, respected, and reliable. For example, when Phyllis McGinley says that she and her husband built a dollhouse for their daughter, there is no reason to doubt that fact. Similarly, when she tells you about a young mother who decides to move to Larkspur Manor because of its school, you are willing to accept that as fact.

3. Skim the essay to find two other personal experiences that McGinley uses to support her opinions. Summarize each example. Then explain what opinion each supports.

Identifying Anecdotes

Many of the personal experiences McGinley relates are told in the form of anecdotes. An <u>anecdote</u> is a brief story about an interesting incident. Like a short story, an anecdote has characters, a setting, and a plot. McGinley's anecdotes not only support her opinions but also add interest to her essay.

Think about the story of the fourth-grade girl who cried because she had lost the square-dancing competition. McGinley uses that anecdote to support at least two opinions—that children are forced to conform to what others are doing and that too much emphasis is placed on competition.

McGinley also uses that story to add humor to her essay. She quotes the words the girl uses to express her despair: "In vain! In vain! All in vain!" When McGinley compares that cry to the cry of a Victorian heroine, she gently mocks the child's overly dramatic distress.

Notice how McGinley describes the girl's mistake: "She had chasséd left when she was supposed to promenade right or made some such other public faux pas." The writer is laughing at the whole scene. You may want to laugh, too, even though you know that the girl took her mistake very seriously. And despite her humorous anecdote, McGinley is serious in her judgment about the episode.

4. Find the anecdote about the three boys who were hitchhiking. What opinion is McGinley supporting with that anecdote? Does she show a sense of humor in telling the story? Explain your answer.

Anecdotes are entertaining, but they also must support the author's opinions. Ask yourself if one anecdote alone can support an opinion or if the incident described is likely to happen again in a similar way. You must rely on your own experiences and common sense to analyze the effectiveness of an anecdote.

Identifying Generalizations

Another way in which Phyllis McGinley supports her opinions is by making generalizations. A <u>generalization</u> is a broad, unspecific statement that is based on a number of facts. Imagine that you looked around the classroom and noticed that more than half the students in the class were wearing red shirts or red blouses. You might then make the generalization that people in your class liked red.

McGinley makes a number of generalizations in the following passage.

> Socially, also, children . . . are required to follow a pattern exact as a diet list. . . . At seven, little girls ought to start casting warm looks on their favorite cub scout. At nine, they should be inviting "mixed groups" to their birthday galas. They must master the day's approximation of the waltz or the Twist at, say, eleven, and no later than twelve months afterward wangle from some masculine contemporary in junior high school an invitation to the movies. At thirteen or fourteen, they should have turned into accomplished sirens.

McGinley has based those generalizations on facts that she observed. But she does not reveal her sources. How can you evaluate such generalizations? How do you know if they are true? You evaluate them the same way you evaluate anecdotes. You must rely on your own experiences and common sense to judge the author's generalizations.

5. Reread the excerpt just cited. Are the generalizations made in it reasonable? Which of McGinley's opinions do they support?

Identifying the Author's Attitude

An essayist establishes a <u>tone</u>, or attitude toward his or her subject or toward the audience. The content and language of the essay contribute to the overall tone. Some essayists are very serious about their opinions. Others are lighter and more humorous. They may simply enjoy writing about their thoughts without worrying too much if anyone agrees or disagrees with those thoughts.

Phyllis McGinley's attitude is a mixture of lightness and seriousness. You have already studied the combination of humor and seriousness in her story about the fourth-grader who lost the square-dancing contest.

6. Consider McGinley's opinion that "American children are afflicted with a glut of possessions" (page 103). Then read the paragraphs following that general statement. How does McGinley show both humor and concern about possessions?

The subject of possessions leads McGinley to talk about dollhouses. Age eight "used to be judged the proper age to become a chatelaine, as indeed, it still is. Eight is house-proud. Eight arranges furniture, dusts the living room, sets Lilliputian tables, is as careful with her things as a Dutch housewife." Notice the humorous language in that description.

McGinley later tells how she and her husband built a dollhouse as a gift for their daughter. She describes the elaborate details of the house and the success of the gift. "The birthday child eclipsed the grandest of the Joneses. She began to be courted even by little boys. . . ." Again, McGinley is treating the subject lightly although she concludes on a serious note. She now believes that she and her husband gave their daughter too many possessions too early.

7. Find examples of the author's tone in the first paragraph of the essay. Is it humorous, serious, or both? Explain your answer. Then compare the first paragraph of the essay to the last one. Which is more serious? What makes it more serious?

In her essay Phyllis McGinley writes about a serious subject in an entertaining way. She uses a number of techniques to convince readers that her views are true. As you read other selections in this book, notice the authors' opinions and how they support them.

Questions for Thought and Discussion

The questions and activities that follow will help you explore "Keeping Up with the Joneses, Jr." in more depth and at the same time develop your critical thinking skills.

1. **Comparing and Contrasting.** Compare Phyllis McGinley's childhood with the kind of childhood she criticizes in her essay. What are the

similarities? What are the differences? Was your childhood more like McGinley's or that of the children for whom McGinley is expressing sympathy? Explain.

2. **Organizing a Debate.** Organize a class debate around this statement: Phyllis McGinley's views about childhood are no longer true today. First, as a class, make a list of her views on childhood. Then divide the class into two groups. One group should find information to support the debate statement, and the other group should provide reasons to oppose it.

3. **Predicting Outcomes.** In the future how do you think childhood will be different from today? What are the chances that it may become more like Phyllis McGinley's childhood? Give reasons for your answer.

4. **Identifying Main Ideas.** What opinion does Phyllis McGinley express about education? List the supporting evidence that she offers for this opinion. Label each piece of supporting evidence as personal experience, anecdote, or generalization.

Writing About Literature

Several suggestions for writing projects follow. You may be asked to complete one or more of these projects. If you have any questions about how to begin a writing assignment, review Using the Writing Process, beginning on page 341.

1. **Offering New Evidence.** Choose one of Phyllis McGinley's main opinions. Support or oppose her position with evidence of your own. Try to use personal experience, anecdotes, and generalizations, as McGinley does in her essay.

2. **Reporting on Interviews.** The people who were nine and ten years old when McGinley wrote this essay are now in their thirties. Interview two or three people in that age bracket whom you know. Summarize McGinley's opinions for them. Then ask if they remember a "too early

insistence on success" and a "glut of possessions." If they do, find out what effect they think those things had on them. Finally, write a report about their responses.

3. **Expressing Your Opinions in an Essay.** Think of some aspect of the relationship between adults and children about which you feel strongly. Write an informal essay on the topic you select, using a style similar to Phyllis McGinley's. Be sure to focus your essay on one or more opinions.

4. **Telling an Anecdote.** In a paragraph or two tell an anecdote that illustrates your attitude toward possessions. The anecdote can be from your own life or from the experience of someone you know.

Chapter 5

Selection   *The Dog That Bit People*

JAMES THURBER

Lesson   *The Humorous Essay*

About the Selection

James Thurber has been called one of America's greatest humorists. The essay "The Dog That Bit People" is a classic example of Thurber humor. The essay first appeared in a book called *My Life and Hard Times*. Although Thurber called this book his autobiography, not everything in the book is factual. *My Life and Hard Times* was published just before Thurber's fortieth birthday. It consists of nine essays that tell about his youth in Columbus, Ohio.

The essays have titles such as "The Car We Had to Push," "The Day the Dam Broke" (it didn't, but everyone in Columbus was convinced that it had), "The Night the Ghost Got In," and "The Night the Bed Fell." As you can imagine from those titles, Thurber's stories are not typical of an autobiography. In them, however, he introduces some of the most entertaining characters you will ever meet. One of these characters is Muggs, the dog that bit people.

Muggs was an Airedale, a breed of terrier with a wiry tan coat and black markings. Muggs bit anyone who had the misfortune to cross his path, including almost everyone in the Thurber household. Only Thurber's mother escaped Muggs's attacks. In the essay Thurber describes Muggs's battles with family members, a visiting congressman, and various tradespeople.

As you read "The Dog That Bit People," you may wonder just how much of it is really true. Even though the essay is nonfiction, can you believe all the facts? According to Burton Bernstein, who wrote a biography of Thurber, that is a question worth asking. Bernstein claims that what Thurber did in *My Life and Hard Times* was to "take a seed of truth from his real past" and let it take root in his imagination. The result was his collection of fanciful essays.

Still, the "seed of truth" is there. According to Thurber, his mother was upset when "The Dog That Bit People" was published. She objected to his *truthful* story about her putting out food for the mice. After reading it, she told him, "People will think we're trash." Yet Thurber himself believed that "the disinterested reader is not impressed by facts as such." He wrote about the mice incident in a letter to his family, "Now nobody in the world believes that I didn't make it up."

Thurber did not expect his readers to believe every word of his autobiography. Like many writers of humorous pieces, he often crossed the dividing line between nonfiction and fiction. Thurber was just as funny in fiction as he was in nonfiction.

Probably his best-known fiction work is a short story called "The Secret Life of Walter Mitty." The story's main character is a mild-mannered, henpecked man who daydreams himself into different heroic situations. Walter Mitty has become a symbol for the daydreamer in everyone.

James Thurber was born in Columbus, Ohio, in 1894. His family was as unusual as they appear to be in *My Life and Hard Times.* Thurber's mother, who was known to the family as Mame, was a practical joker. She once "borrowed" a wheelchair at a faith-healing meeting, rolled herself down the aisle, then stood up and announced that she had been cured.

His father was never very financially successful. At one point, the Thurbers had to live with Mame's parents. Young James was then sent to live with a family friend because there were too many people in his grandfather's house.

After graduating from Ohio State University, Thurber worked as a newspaper reporter. On his own time, he wrote humorous sketches, which he sold to newspapers and magazines. In 1925 he moved to

New York City. He soon went to work for *The New Yorker*, a new magazine that was attracting talented writers and artists to its staff. Although Thurber eventually left that job, he continued to write for the magazine all his life.

At *The New Yorker*, Thurber shared an office with E. B. White. White noticed that Thurber constantly doodled on any blank space. One day, White suggested that Thurber submit some drawings for publication in the magazine. That suggestion led to Thurber's second career, as a cartoonist. The "Thurber dog" is his most famous cartoon.

As a child, Thurber lost the sight in his left eye after his brother accidentally shot him with an arrow. As a result of the accident, the other eye also became inflamed. It gave Thurber trouble throughout his life. Despite several operations, his eyesight grew worse. For the last twenty years of his life, he was almost completely blind. His drawing days were over, but he continued to write.

Besides short stories, fables, and nonfiction works, Thurber wrote two books for children and several plays. He was a perfectionist, and was known to revise a piece as many as twenty-five times to get it right!

Lesson Preview

The lesson that follows "The Dog That Bit People" focuses on the methods James Thurber uses to make his essay humorous. The author's main purpose is to entertain you with his version of autobiographical events. The questions that follow will help you to learn how Thurber uses humor. As you read, think about how you would answer these questions.

1 What parts of the essay make you smile or laugh? Why do you think those parts are humorous?

2 Which character or characters do you find most humorous? Why?

3 Can you picture some of the scenes that Thurber is describing? How do those images add to the humor of the essay?

The Humorous Essay

Vocabulary

Here are some difficult words that appear in the selection that follows. Study the words and their definitions, as well as the sentences that show how the words are used. This will help you get the most from your reading.

incredulity disbelief. *We stared with incredulity at the damage the storm had done to the house.*

choleric easily angered. *Tom's choleric temper often turned discussions into arguments.*

oblivious inattentive; not noticing. *George was so engrossed in his book that he was oblivious to Sue's question.*

irascible quick-tempered. *Tom's irascible temper was provoked by George's annoying questions.*

ingenious clever; skillful. *The inventor has patented several of his ingenious devices.*

indelible permanent. *That ink will leave an indelible mark on your shirt.*

The Dog That Bit People

JAMES THURBER

*P*robably no one man should have as many dogs in his life as I have had, but there was more pleasure than distress in them for me except in the case of an Airedale named Muggs. He gave me more trouble than all the other fifty-four or five put together, although my moment of keenest embarrassment was the time a Scotch terrier named Jeannie, who had just had six puppies in the clothes closet of a fourth floor apartment in New York, had the unexpected seventh and last at the corner of Eleventh Street and Fifth Avenue during a walk she had insisted on taking. Then, too, there was the prize winning French poodle, a great big black poodle—none of your little, troublesome white miniatures—who got sick riding in the rumble seat[1] of a car with me on her way to the Greenwich Dog Show. She had a red rubber bib tucked around her throat and, since a rain storm came up when we were

---

1. **rumble seat:** an open seat in the rear of some early automobiles, which could be folded shut when not in use.

half way through the Bronx, I had to hold over her a small green umbrella, really more of a parasol. The rain beat down fearfully and suddenly the driver of the car drove into a big garage, filled with mechanics. It happened so quickly that I forgot to put the umbrella down and I will always remember, with sickening distress, the look of incredulity mixed with hatred that came over the face of the particular hardened garage man that came over to see what we wanted, when he took a look at me and the poodle. All garage men, and people of that intolerant stripe, hate poodles with their curious hair cut, especially the pom-poms that you got to leave on their hips if you expect the dogs to win a prize.

But the Airedale, as I have said, was the worst of all my dogs. He really wasn't my dog, as a matter of fact: I came home from a vacation one summer to find that my brother Roy had bought him while I was away. A big, burly, choleric dog, he always acted as if he thought I wasn't one of the family. There was a slight advantage in being one of the family, for he didn't bite the family as often as he bit strangers. Still, in the years that we had him he bit everybody but mother, and he made a pass at her once but missed. That was during the month when we suddenly had mice, and Muggs refused to do anything about them. Nobody ever had mice exactly like the mice we had that month. They acted like pet mice, almost like mice somebody had trained. They were so friendly that one night when mother entertained at dinner the Friraliras, a club she and my father had belonged to for twenty years, she put down a lot of little dishes with food in them on the pantry floor so that the mice wouldn't come into the dining room. Muggs stayed out in the pantry with the mice, lying on the floor, growling to himself—not at the mice, but about all the people in the next room that he would have liked to get at. Mother slipped out into the pantry once to see how everything was going. Everything was going fine. It made her so mad to see Muggs lying there, oblivious of the mice—they came running up to her—that she slapped him and he slashed at her, but didn't make it. He was sorry immediately, mother said. He was always sorry, she said, after he bit someone, but we could not understand how she figured this out. He didn't act sorry.

Mother used to send a box of candy every Christmas to the people the Airedale bit. The list finally contained forty or more names. Nobody could understand why we didn't get rid of the dog. I didn't understand it very well myself, but we didn't get rid of him. I think that one or two people tried to poison Muggs—he acted poisoned once in a while—and old Major Moberly fired at him once with his service revolver near the Seneca Hotel in East Broad Street—but Muggs lived to be almost eleven years old and even when he could hardly get around he bit a Congressman who had called to see my father on business. My mother had never liked the Congressman—she said the signs of his horoscope showed he couldn't be trusted (he was Saturn with the moon in Virgo)—but she sent him a box of candy that Christmas. He sent it right back, probably because he suspected it was trick candy. Mother persuaded herself it was all for the best that the dog had bitten him, even though father lost an important business association because of it. "I wouldn't be associated with such a man," mother said, "Muggs could read him like a book."

We used to take turns feeding Muggs to be on his good side, but that didn't always work. He was never in a very good humor, even after a meal. Nobody knew exactly what was the matter with him, but whatever it was it made him irascible, especially in the morning. Roy never felt very well in the morning, either, especially before breakfast, and once when he came downstairs and found that Muggs had moodily chewed up the morning paper he hit him in the face with a grapefruit and then jumped up on the dining room table, scattering dishes and silverware and spilling the coffee. Muggs' first free leap carried him all the way across the table and into a brass fire screen in front of the gas grate but he was back on his feet in a moment and in the end he got Roy and gave him a pretty vicious bite in the leg. Then he was all over it; he never bit anyone more than once at a time. Mother always mentioned that as an argument in his favor; she said he had a quick temper but that he didn't hold a grudge. She was forever defending him. I think she liked him because he wasn't well. "He's not strong," she would say, pityingly, but that was inaccurate; he may not have been well but he was terribly strong.

The Humorous Essay

One time my mother went to the Chittenden Hotel to call on a woman mental healer who was lecturing in Columbus on the subject of "Harmonious Vibrations." She wanted to find out if it was possible to get harmonious vibrations into a dog. "He's a large tan-colored Airedale," mother explained. The woman said that she had never treated a dog but she advised my mother to hold the thought that he did not bite and would not bite. Mother was holding the thought the very next morning when Muggs got the iceman but she blamed that slip-up on the iceman. "If you didn't think he would bite you, he wouldn't," mother told him. He stomped out of the house in a terrible jangle of vibrations.

One morning when Muggs bit me slightly, more or less in passing, I reached down and grabbed his short stumpy tail and hoisted him into the air. It was a foolhardy thing to do and the last time I saw my mother, about six months ago, she said she didn't know what possessed me. I don't either, except that I was pretty mad. As long as I held the dog off the floor by his tail he couldn't get me, but he twisted and jerked so, snarling all the time, that I realized I couldn't hold him that way very long. I carried him to the kitchen and flung him onto the floor and shut the door on him just as he crashed against it. But I forgot about the backstairs. Muggs went up the backstairs and down the frontstairs and had me cornered in the living room. I managed to get up onto the mantelpiece above the fireplace, but it gave way and came down with a tremendous crash throwing a large marble clock, several vases, and myself heavily to the floor. Muggs was so alarmed by the racket that when I picked myself up he had disappeared. We couldn't find him anywhere, although we whistled and shouted, until old Mrs. Detweiler called after dinner that night. Muggs had bitten her once, in the leg, and she came into the living room only after we assured her that Muggs had run away. She had just seated herself when, with a great growling and scratching of claws, Muggs emerged from under a davenport where he had been quietly hiding all the time, and bit her again. Mother examined the bite and put arnica[2] on it and told Mrs. Detweiler that it was only

2. **arnica:** a preparation of herbs used on bruises and sprains.

a bruise. "He just bumped you," she said. But Mrs. Detweiler left the house in a nasty state of mind.

Lots of people reported our Airedale to the police but my father held a municipal office at the time and was on friendly terms with the police. Even so, the cops had been out a couple of times—once when Muggs bit Mrs. Rufus Sturtevant and again when he bit Lieutenant-Governor Malloy—but mother told them that it hadn't been Muggs' fault but the fault of the people who were bitten. "When he starts for them, they scream," she explained, "and that excites him." The cops suggested that it might be a good idea to tie the dog up, but mother said that it mortified him to be tied up and that he wouldn't eat when he was tied up.

Muggs at his meals was an unusual sight. Because of the fact that if you reached toward the floor he would bite you, we usually put his food plate on top of an old kitchen table with a bench alongside the table. Muggs would stand on the bench and eat. I remember that my mother's Uncle Horatio, who boasted that he was the third man up Missionary Ridge,[3] was splutteringly indignant when he found out that we fed the dog on a table because we were afraid to put his plate on the floor. He said he wasn't afraid of any dog that ever lived and that he would put the dog's plate on the floor if we would give it to him. Roy said that if Uncle Horatio had fed Muggs on the ground just before the battle he would have been the first man up Missionary Ridge. Uncle Horatio was furious. "Bring him in! Bring him in now!" he shouted. "I'll feed the—— on the floor!" Roy was all for giving him a chance, but my father wouldn't hear of it. He said that Muggs had already been fed. "I'll feed him again!" bawled Uncle Horatio. We had quite a time quieting him.

In his last year Muggs used to spend practically all of his time out-doors. He didn't like to stay in the house for some reason or other— perhaps it held too many unpleasant memories for him. Anyway, it was hard to get him to come in and as a result the garbage man, the iceman, and the laundryman wouldn't come near the house. We had to haul the garbage down to the corner, take the laundry out and bring it back, and

3. **Missionary Ridge:** site of a major Civil War battle, near Chattanooga, Tennessee.

meet the iceman a block from home. After this had gone on for some time we hit on an ingenious arrangement for getting the dog in the house so that we could lock him up while the gas meter was read, and so on. Muggs was afraid of only one thing, an electrical storm. Thunder and lightning frightened him out of his senses (I think he thought a storm had broken the day the mantelpiece fell). He would rush into the house and hide under a bed or in a clothes closet. So we fixed up a thunder machine out of a long narrow piece of sheet iron with a wooden handle on one end. Mother would shake this vigorously when she wanted to get Muggs into the house. It made an excellent imitation of thunder, but I suppose it was the most roundabout system for running a household that was ever devised. It took a lot out of mother.

A few months before Muggs died, he got to "seeing things." He would rise slowly from the floor, growling low, and stalk stiff-legged and menacing toward nothing at all. Sometimes the Thing would be just a little to the right or left of a visitor. Once a Fuller Brush salesman got hysterics. Muggs came wandering into the room like Hamlet [4] following his father's ghost. His eyes were fixed on a spot just to the left of the Fuller Brush man, who stood it until Muggs was about three slow, creeping paces from him. Then he shouted. Muggs wavered on past him into the hallway grumbling to himself but the Fuller man went on shouting. I think mother had to throw a pan of cold water on him before he stopped. That was the way she used to stop us boys when we got into fights.

Muggs died quite suddenly one night. Mother wanted to bury him in the family lot under a marble stone with some such inscription as "Flights of angels sing thee to thy rest" but we persuaded her it was against the law. In the end we just put up a smooth board above his grave along a lonely road. On the board I wrote with an indelible pencil "Cave Canem." [5] Mother was quite pleased with the simple classic dignity of the old Latin epitaph.

4. **Hamlet:** the main character in a play by Shakespeare. In the play, Hamlet sees his father's ghost.
5. **Cave Canem:** Latin phrase meaning "Beware of the Dog."

Reviewing the Selection

Answer each of the following questions without looking back at the selection.

Recalling Facts

1. The only thing that Muggs feared was
   - ☐ a. mice.
   - ☐ b. noise.
   - ☐ c. revolvers.
   - ☐ d. electrical storms.

Understanding Main Ideas

2. The main idea of the essay is that
   - ☐ a. the Thurbers' dog, Muggs, disrupted their lives.
   - ☐ b. James Thurber loved dogs.
   - ☐ c. Muggs should have been tied up.
   - ☐ d. Thurber's mother loved Muggs better than she loved her children.

Placing Events in Order

3. When did Muggs start "seeing things" that did not exist?
   - ☐ a. a few months before he died
   - ☐ b. as a young puppy
   - ☐ c. after James Thurber shut him in the kitchen
   - ☐ d. whenever the police came to the house

Finding Supporting Details

4. Thurber's mother sent candy every Christmas to
   - ☐ a. people who were kind to Muggs.
   - ☐ b. the Friraliras club.
   - ☐ c. Uncle Horatio.
   - ☐ d. everyone Muggs had bitten.

The Humorous Essay

5. "... I reached down and grabbed his short stumpy tail and <u>hoisted</u> him into the air." In this context *hoisted* means
   ☐ a. helped.
   ☐ b. lifted.
   ☐ c. kicked.
   ☐ d. ran.

Interpreting the Selection

Answer each of the following questions. You may look back at the selection if necessary.

6. After Muggs died, the family probably felt
   ☐ a. bitter.
   ☐ b. relieved.
   ☐ c. angry.
   ☐ d. guilty.

7. Which generalization is true based on this story?
   ☐ a. All garage men hate poodles.
   ☐ b. Only Thurber's mother had any sympathy for Muggs.
   ☐ c. Muggs only bit family members.
   ☐ d. Muggs hated to be indoors.

8. Which of the following statements is a fact?
   - ☐ a. Muggs was probably mistreated as a puppy.
   - ☐ b. The police should have put Muggs in the dog pound.
   - ☐ c. Muggs liked Thurber's mother because she fed him.
   - ☐ d. Muggs was a large Airedale.

9. The only time Muggs ever tried to bite Thurber's mother was after she slapped him. She slapped him because he
   - ☐ a. had bitten her son James.
   - ☐ b. had bitten an important congressman.
   - ☐ c. was paying no attention to the mice in the kitchen.
   - ☐ d. refused to come in when she shook the thunder machine.

10. The Thurbers probably kept Muggs for eleven years because
    - ☐ a. they needed his protection.
    - ☐ b. they expected he would learn to behave.
    - ☐ c. Roy had paid a lot of money for him.
    - ☐ d. James Thurber's mother felt sorry for him.

The Humorous Essay

Have you ever heard someone tell a story that was so funny you laughed until you hurt? Have you tried telling the same story and found that it did not sound nearly as funny? If you have had this experience, then you know that an event itself may not be very humorous. The storyteller makes the incident funny. For example, think about the events in "The Dog That Bit People." Taken by themselves they are not funny. Here is a simple summary of the events.

> The Thurber family acquired a dog that bit people for no
> good reason. During the dog's eleven years with the family, he
> bit at least forty people, including a congressman and every
> family member except the mother. The police called on the
> family a few times, but nothing was ever done about the dog.
> It finally died of natural causes.

That summary does not sound like the story you read in Thurber's essay. What makes Thurber's story funny is the way he tells it. Humor is often the result of the writer's <u>style</u>—the way in which a piece of literature is written. How an author writes is part of his or her style. Because of differing styles, one writer may make a story sound tragic while another may make the same story sound comic.

In this lesson you will study some of the ways in which humorists such as James Thurber tell stories that make you laugh. You may think that analyzing humor can spoil the fun of it. But an analysis can make you appreciate a writer's skill. It can make the humor in a story more enjoyable. You can also learn new ways to tell funny stories yourself.

Two Techniques of Humor

If you were a witness at a trial, the judge would caution you to tell "just the facts." To a writer of humor, however, the facts are probably the least important part of the story. Many techniques used by the writer of humor involve changing or adjusting the facts. A common technique that James Thurber uses is exaggeration, an intentional overstatement of facts or events so that their meanings are intensified. Exaggeration is not meant to trick you but to create humorous results.

Reread the story of the mice in the second paragraph of the essay. At one point, Thurber says that they "acted like pet mice, almost like mice somebody had trained." He is clearly exaggerating the situation.

1. How does that exaggeration make the story more humorous? What would the effect be if Thurber had not exaggerated the friendliness of the mice?

A second technique of humor that Thurber uses is digression. Digression is a wandering from the main point of a story. In "The Dog That Bit People," Thurber states his main point in the first sentence. He says that he has had "more pleasure than distress" from all his dogs. The only exception was an Airedale named Muggs. You are probably curious to find out what was so troublesome about Muggs. But having caught your interest, Thurber is not going to satisfy your curiosity right away.

He digresses into telling two stories about other dogs that caused problems. Those two dogs have nothing to do with Muggs and the main point of the story. Yet the two incidents are amusing in themselves. Thurber wanders from his main point in the second sentence of the essay. That digression tells you that his goal is not just to get from

The Humorous Essay

the beginning of the story to the end. He is more concerned with entertaining you than with telling a story in the most efficient way.

2. Do you think Thurber's digression adds anything to the story? Give reasons for your answer. Would it have been more effective if the digression had come at the end of the story instead of at the beginning? Explain your answer.

Consider the incident of the congressman whom Muggs bit. Thurber gives details that are unrelated to the main idea of the story.

> My mother had never liked the Congressman—she said the signs of his horoscope showed he couldn't be trusted (he was Saturn with the moon in Virgo)—but she sent him a box of candy that Christmas.

The fact that the congressman was born under the sign of Saturn with the moon in Virgo certainly has no bearing on the story. Yet it makes the story more entertaining. You cannot help smiling at the mother's strange logic, and perhaps you are even interested to know whether there is any truth in her reasoning.

3. The information about the congressman's horoscope actually tells you more about Thurber's mother than about the congressman. What does it tell you about her? How does that information add to the humor of the essay?

Character Development and Humor

The main character in "The Dog That Bit People" is the dog. If James Thurber had not made Muggs a humorous character, the story would not have been funny. Read the following passages from the essay. See if you can find what is humorous about Thurber's description of Muggs.

a. "I wouldn't be associated with such a man," mother said, "Muggs could read him like a book."

b. Mother always mentioned that as an argument in his favor; she said he had a quick temper but that he didn't hold a grudge.

c. The cops suggested that it might be a good idea to tie the dog up, but mother said that it mortified him to be tied up and that he wouldn't eat when he was tied up.

What those descriptions have in common is that they give human qualities and feelings to the dog. In literature that is called personification. Personification is a figure of speech in which an animal, an object, or an idea is given human qualities. You know that a dog does not have the same thoughts and feelings as a person. Yet Thurber makes you willing to accept that Muggs takes certain deliberate actions just as a human does. The personification serves another purpose. At the same time that Thurber is showing Muggs as a thinking creature, he is also revealing Muggs to be a particularly unpleasant dog.

4. Skim the essay and make a list of Muggs's "human" qualities. Then write a paragraph describing what kind of person Muggs might have been.

Although Muggs is the central character in "The Dog That Bit People," he is not the only character. Part of the humor in the essay comes from the human characters and their reactions to Muggs. You learned about character development in Chapter 3. Writers of humor also develop characters. They use dialogue, description, action, and the opinions of others to make their humorous characters seem real.

Recall the story of Thurber's mother visiting the mental healer. She wanted to find out if it was possible "to get harmonious vibrations into a dog."

"He's a large, tan-colored Airedale," mother explained. The woman said that she had never treated a dog but she advised my mother to hold the thought that he did not bite and would not bite. Mother was holding the thought the very next morning when Muggs got the iceman but she blamed that slip-up on the iceman. "If you didn't think he would bite you, he wouldn't," mother told him.

Mother's actions and words show you that she would go to unusual lengths to help Muggs overcome his bad habit. The picture of a woman asking a mental healer to treat her dog is so unexpected that it is humorous. Instead of saying, "My mother was an eccentric woman," Thurber shows you her unusual behavior.

5. Find two other examples in which Thurber shows his mother's actions. What does each incident tell you about his mother? How do those incidents make her a humorous character?

Visual Images and Humor

In "The Dog That Bit People" James Thurber creates vivid pictures with words. You can almost see the scenes of Muggs and his victims. Such word pictures contribute greatly to the humor of the essay. Read the following passage:

> Roy never felt very well in the morning, either, especially before breakfast, and once when he came downstairs and found that Muggs had moodily chewed up the morning paper he hit him in the face with a grapefruit and then jumped up on the dining room table, scattering dishes and silverware and spilling the coffee. Muggs's first free leap carried him all the way across the table and into a brass fire screen in front of the gas grate but he was back on his feet in a moment and in the end he got Roy and gave him a pretty vicious bite in the leg.

6. Make a diagram or sketch of the scene. Why does the grapefruit incident make the scene especially funny?

7. Skim the essay to find another humorous scene that Thurber creates with words. Explain what makes the scene humorous.

Language and Humor

In Chapter 1 you learned, by examining the writing of Frederick Douglass, how writers use language to express strong feelings. Language can also be used to create a humorous effect. In his essay James Thurber chooses words that create humorous images.

Think about the scene with the iceman after Thurber's mother has tried "to get harmonious vibrations" into Muggs. She informed the iceman that Muggs would not have bitten him if he did not think Muggs would bite him. The iceman then "stomped out of the house in a terrible jangle of vibrations."

Humor often develops from the contrast between what is expected and what actually happens. In the scene with the iceman, Thurber has chosen words and created images that set up a humorous contrast between the intended "harmonious vibrations" and the actual "jangle of vibrations." One meaning of the word *vibration* is one's emotional response to a person or thing. Thurber's mother wanted Muggs to feel friendly toward people, and she expected people to feel the same toward Muggs. Instead of creating that atmosphere of harmony, the encounter between the dog and the iceman results in just the opposite. The dog bites the iceman and sends the iceman off in a furious state.

The phrase "in a terrible jangle of vibrations" creates humor in another way because it suggests sounds that echo the iceman's feelings. You can almost hear the clashing, crashing sounds that surround the departing iceman.

The humor of the scene also comes from the unexpected reasoning of Thurber's mother. She blames the iceman for Muggs's attack instead of blaming the dog.

8. Read the following passages from Thurber's essay. In each passage find an example of how Thurber uses language to create a humorous image. Explain why each image is funny.

    a. *I remember that my mother's Uncle Horatio, who boasted that he was the third man up Missionary Ridge, was sputteringly indignant when he found out that we fed the dog on a table because we were afraid to put his plate on the floor.*

    b. *A few months before Muggs died, he got to "seeing things." He would rise slowly from the floor, growling low, and stalk stiff-legged and menacing toward nothing at all. Sometimes the Thing would be just a little to the right or left of a visitor.*

James Thurber had the rare gift of being able to write humorously. As you have learned, he used a number of methods to turn a simple story into a very funny one. His style of humor depended to some extent on creating humorous characters and using exaggeration and digression. It also relied on creating vivid pictures of his characters and their behavior.

Questions for Thought and Discussion

The questions and activities that follow will help you explore "The Dog That Bit People" in more depth and at the same time develop your critical thinking skills.

1. **Expressing an Opinion.** Which scene in "The Dog That Bit People" did you find most amusing? Why? Compare your choice and your reasons for choosing the scene with those of your classmates.

2. **Analyzing and Solving a Problem.** Imagine that you are Muggs's owner and want to train him to behave better. First, make a list of the possible reasons for his bad behavior. Then explain what you would do to try to improve Muggs's behavior, based on what you think its causes might be. What would you do if none of your ideas worked and Muggs continued to bite people?

3. **Drawing a Conclusion.** Compare "The Dog That Bit People" with Phyllis McGinley's essay "Keeping Up with the Joneses, Jr." and with the excerpt from Frederick Douglass's autobiography. Then decide whether "The Dog That Bit People" is more like an essay or more like an autobiography. Give reasons for your answer.

4. **Inferring.** Thurber's mother has an important role in the essay, and you learn a lot about her from her actions and words. What do you think Thurber thought of his mother? Give reasons for your answer.

Writing About Literature

Several suggestions for writing projects follow. You may be asked to complete one or more of these projects. If you have any questions about

how to begin a writing assignment, review Using the Writing Process, beginning on page 341.

1. **Taking Another Point of View.** The only character in "The Dog That Bit People" who seems to appreciate Muggs is Thurber's mother. Rewrite two incidents in the essay, telling them from her point of view. Remember that her opinions of the people in the essay may be different from those of the author.

2. **Telling a Humorous Incident.** Choose a humorous incident from your life or from the experience of someone you know. Write a description of the incident using at least one of the techniques discussed in this chapter. You can use exaggeration, digression, character development, or visual imagery.

3. **Writing an Essay.** In a one- or two-page essay, explain why people have pets. You can write from personal experience or from your observation of pet owners. In your essay use at least one of the techniques of humor that you studied in this chapter.

Selection	*That Astounding Creator—Nature*
	JEAN GEORGE
Lesson	*Main Ideas and Supporting Details*

❖

About the Selection

"That Astounding Creator—Nature" is a magazine article about the unusual ways in which animals adapt to their surroundings. As an article, its main purpose is to inform. An article is different from an essay, although both are short nonfiction works. Unlike an essay, which often centers on the author's feelings and opinions, an article usually focuses on factual information.

Jean George's article is based on the theory of evolution. According to that theory, a species of plant or animal may evolve, or change gradually, to adapt itself to a particular environment. What do scientists mean when they say that a species evolves? They do *not* mean that animals suddenly change their appearance or behavior. Evolution is a very slow process, taking thousands of years. No one is sure exactly how long it takes or how it happens.

Many scientists, however, suggest that it follows a pattern similar to this: In any given species, a few individuals may be born that are different from the rest. They may look different or behave differently. If the difference makes the individual better able to survive, that individual will probably live longer than other members of its species.

During its longer life, it may produce more offspring than the others. Some of the offspring may have the different look or behavior of the parent. Over hundreds, thousands, or tens of thousands of years, the number of individuals with this special survival adaptation will increase.

Eventually, most members of the species will have that adaptation.

Read this imaginary example. Suppose that there is a species of bird called the rockwalker living in Antarctica. It feeds on just one kind of seaweed that grows only in the narrow cracks between the rocks at the water's edge.

Now suppose that a rockwalker is born with a longer, narrower bill than most rockwalkers have. As a result, this individual can reach the seaweed more easily. It can, therefore, get more to eat, especially when seaweed is scarce. So the rockwalker with the longer, narrower bill will probably live longer. It may produce many offspring that have longer, narrower bills. The offspring, too, may all live longer and produce more baby rockwalkers with the longer, narrower bill. As the centuries go by, rockwalkers with the longer, narrower bill come to outnumber those with the shorter bill. Eventually, the short-billed rockwalker will be an oddity.

In "That Astounding Creator—Nature" Jean George describes many unusual creatures. As you read the article, notice the large number of facts that the author includes in a short space. Yet she does that without confusing you. Like any good writer, Jean George presents her information clearly. Writers of articles must also have other important skills. They need to be curious and to look for answers. They need to talk to experts and to ask the right questions. They must also be able to report their findings objectively—that is, without showing their own opinions. When you read this article, you will discover that Jean George has those important skills.

Jean George was born in 1919 into a family that was interested in plants and animals. Her father was an entomologist, a scientist who studies insects. Her two brothers became ecologists—scientists concerned with the conditions in which living things exist. When Jean and her brothers were growing up, their house was full of animals such as owls, raccoons, crickets, turtles, and dogs. Every weekend, Jean's father took the family canoeing, fishing, and swimming on the Potomac River. There, he taught them about plants and animals.

When Jean George was eight years old, she decided to become a writer. As she later wrote, "My third grade teacher sent our class to the blackboard to solve arithmetic problems. I had no idea how to do my assignment, but the blackboard was before me, the chalk in my hands, and I thought I should do something. I wrote a poem and sat down. Fortunately, Mrs. Clark was an extraordinary teacher. She did not reprimand me but quietly announced that I had written a lovely poem. I have been writing ever since."

After graduating from college, Jean George worked as a newspaper reporter in Washington, D.C., and in New York City. In Washington one night, as she watched the city lights go on from her window, she began to think about the Potomac River and the beauty of the nearby woods where the foxes ran. That night, she began her first book, *Vulpes, the Red Fox.* Since then, she has written more than fifty books of fiction and nonfiction, as well as many articles on nature.

One of Jean George's best-known books is *My Side of the Mountain,* the story of a teenager who runs away from his family in New York City and spends a year living in the Catskill Mountains. Another popular Jean George book is *Julie of the Wolves.* It tells about an Eskimo girl and the pack of wolves that helps her survive in the Arctic.

Jean George lives in a suburb of New York City with plenty of woods around her house. She has raised three children, each now involved in science. One of her sons once counted all of the animals that had lived with them over the years. The total came to one hundred seventy-three, not counting cats and dogs. Jean George says that most wild animals that live with her depart in autumn when they feel the urge to migrate or go off alone. But while they are with her, they become the basis for characters in her books, stories, and articles.

Lesson Preview

The lesson that follows "That Astounding Creator—Nature" focuses on main ideas and supporting details in an article. An article is an informative piece of writing that appears in a newspaper or magazine. For an article to be useful, it must be well organized. The most common way a writer organizes an article is by establishing one or more main ideas and supporting them with details.

Often, an article has an overall main idea and several secondary ideas that are related to the main idea. The questions that follow will help you notice the main ideas and supporting details in Jean George's article. As you read, think about how you would answer these questions.

1 What is the main idea of Jean George's article? How can you tell it is the main idea?

2 Does the article contain any secondary ideas? If so, what are they?

3 How does the author support her main idea? Does she give enough details or too many? What kinds of details does she give?

Vocabulary

Here are some difficult words that appear in the selection that follows. Study the words and their definitions, as well as the sentences that show how the words are used. This will help you get the most from your reading.

niche an activity for which a person or a thing is best fitted. *Because George enjoys reading, he feels that a job in the library might be his niche.*

longevity length of life. *My elderly aunt's longevity is the result of a healthy diet and an active life.*

forages wanders in search of food. *The deer forages for berries in the underbrush.*

submerges goes under water. *After rising to the water's surface, the whale again submerges.*

endowed gave or provided. *The bride's mother endowed her daughter with several antique bracelets.*

That Astounding Creator—Nature

JEAN GEORGE

A bird that eats feathers, a mammal that never drinks, a fish that grows a fishing line and worm on its head to catch other fish. Creatures in a nightmare? No, they are very much with us as co-inhabitants of this earth.

Nature has fashioned most animals to fit the many faces of the land—moose to marshes, squirrels to trees, camels to deserts, frogs to lily pads. Give nature an environment or situation and she will evolve a creature, adapting a toe here, an eye there, until the being fits the niche. As a result of this hammering and fitting, however, some really unbelievable creatures circle the sun with us.

One summer in Maine I saw a sleek mother horned grebe herding her three bobbing young to supper among the green pickerelweed. Suddenly I noticed through my binoculars that she was feeding her babies quantities of feathers from a deserted duck's nest. As she stuffed the dry

Main Ideas and Supporting Details

feathers into the gaping mouths, she made two or three pokes to get each one down. Finally she worked a dozen or so down her own throat; then, sailing low on the water, she vanished contentedly among the plants.

I later learned that 60 percent of the grebe's diet is feathers. When I asked why, a biologist from the U.S. Fish and Wildlife Service answered, "Because nature finds a use for everything. Feathers seem to act as a strainer to prevent fishbones from entering and damaging the intestines."

Australia has many strange beasts, one of the oddest of which is the koala. Perfectly adapted to one specific tree, the eucalyptus, this living teddy bear does not need anything else, not even a drink! The moisture in the leaves is just right for the koala, making it the only land animal that doesn't need water to supplement its food.

The creature with the fishing line on its head was created for the dark canyons of the sea. Here food is so scarce that the deep-sea angler fish, which preys on smaller fish, grew a line, and an appendage on the end that wiggles like a worm. This catches the attention of the occasional passerby. A fish approaches the bait, and the toothy angler swirls up and swallows him.

The gigantic ocean bottom creates other problems. A male angler fish could swim for years without meeting a female of his own species. Nature's solution to this problem is for the female to carry a dwarfed husband tightly fused to her body. Marine biologists believe that this nuptial begins when the eggs first hatch and there are many fry of both sexes. A male then grabs hold of a female with his mouth and hangs on until he has literally become a part of her. His mouth becomes fused to her stomach, and for the rest of his life the male remains attached to his mate, marking the most amazing union on earth.

Sound has shaped the bodies of many beasts. Noise tapped away at the bullfrog until his ears became bigger than his eyes. Now he hears so well that at the slightest sound of danger he quickly plops to safety under a sunken leaf. The rabbit has long ears to hear the quiet "whoosh" of the owl's wings, while the grasshopper's ears are on the base of his abdomen, the lowest point of his body, where he can detect the tread of a crow's foot or the stealthy approach of a shrew.

Sometimes food will determine an animal's appearance. Earthworms have shaped the woodcock, a snipelike bird of the forest floor. This creature has a long narrow bill that looks like a pencil and fits neatly into the burrows of the worms. But the bill has its disadvantages; with it buried deep in a worm hole the woodcock is vulnerable to attack from above. To counteract this danger the woodcock has eyes near the top of his head. This singular device permits him to scan the trees for danger even when his beak is buried. A successful arrangement for longevity—but it certainly creates an odd-looking creature.

The need to catch elusive prey has evolved some staggering biological tricks. The sea anemone, a flower-like animal of the tidemark, is usually riveted to one spot, yet it feeds on darting fish. A diabolically clever trap was necessary to catch them, so the anemone developed tentacles with bombs in the end of each. When a fish forages into these tentacles the ends shoot a thin thread into the fish's body. The thread in turn explodes a paralyzing poison. The stunned fish is hauled in by the tentacles and shoved into the anemone's gullet.

Nature seems to have gone all out in creating preposterous gadgets for self-defense. The jacana, a bird of the American tropics, for instance, is endowed with spurs which unfold like a switchblade at the bend of the bird's wings and with which he can slash his enemies to shreds.

Lizards are professionals in the art of warding off attack. The two-headed skink, whose tail is shaped like his head, confuses his enemy. A hawk, upon attacking this fellow, anticipates that he will run in the direction of the lifted head and makes allowance for the movement. However, the bird usually strikes nothing, for he is aiming at the tail. The real head took off the other way.

In order to travel in a hostile world, the Portuguese man-of-war first mastered the art of floating. To do this it evolved a purple bag and inflated it with gas from a special gland. As a crowning idea it also grew a sail! Launched, the man-of-war can blow away from enemies or approach food by putting its sail up and down. When severely threatened, it forces the gas out of the float and submerges.

There is hardly any environment, however hostile, that some creature has not mastered. Land is, of course, the nemesis of the fish. If they flop out on it they die. If their ponds dry up, they are helpless. Given this situation, it was almost certain that some fish would evolve a way to beat it; and so there is a lungfish. It is an air breather and must come to the surface every 20 minutes or so; otherwise it drowns. When the ponds of Africa dry up in the arid season, the lungfish wrap themselves in mud and wait it out, sometimes for years. When the rains finally return, they resume their water life.

Just as nature adds things on creatures that need them, so she occasionally takes things away from those that don't. The adult Mayfly, for example, has no mouth or stomach. Last year, by a northern New York lake, I found myself amid hundreds of thousands of these insects. I told the conservation officer whom I was with that I was glad they didn't bite. He replied that they have no mouths to bite with. "An adult Mayfly lives but one day," he explained, "and that day is devoted entirely to pleasure. They do nothing but dance and mate all their short life, and so they do not need a mouth."

With all this elaborate evolution, it is not surprising that some of nature's inventions got out of hand. Into this category falls the speedometer of reindeer. A tendon snaps back and forth over a bone in the reindeer's foot, noisily tapping out the speed of his gait. Useless. And so is the nose on the stomach of the scorpion and the feather-like tongue of the toucan, a bird of Africa.

But probably the most dumbfounding of nature's extraordinary creations is the horned toad of our Southwest. A herpetologist once invited me to observe one of these lizards right after it had molted. In a sand-filled glass cage I saw a large male. Beside him lay his old skin. The herpetologist began to annoy the beast with mock attacks, and the old man of the desert with his vulnerable new suit became frightened. Suddenly his eyeballs reddened. A final fast lunge from my friend at the beast and I froze in astonishment—a fine spray of blood shot from the lizard's eye, like fire from a dragon! The beast had struck back with a weapon so shocking that it terrifies even the fiercest enemy.

Later I walked home, pondering the bizarre methods for survival with which evolution has endowed earth's creatures, sometimes comical, sometimes pathetic. I knew the biologists were right: If any adaptation is possible, nature has tried it.

Reviewing the Selection

Answer each of the following questions without looking back at the selection.

Recalling Facts
1. The feathers that the horned grebe swallows and feeds to her young
   - ☐ a. come from newly hatched grebes.
   - ☐ b. act as a strainer for fishbones.
   - ☐ c. help the grebe fight its enemies.
   - ☐ d. provide protein for the grebe.

Understanding Main Ideas
2. Most of the adaptations described in the article
   - ☐ a. help animals escape from human hunters.
   - ☐ b. are useless.
   - ☐ c. help animals survive.
   - ☐ d. work against the animals.

Placing Events in Order
3. The herpetologist annoyed the horned toad
   - ☐ a. after the author left the laboratory.
   - ☐ b. while the horned toad was sleeping.
   - ☐ c. while the horned toad was eating.
   - ☐ d. after the horned toad had shed its old skin.

Finding Supporting Details
4. An example of how "sound has shaped the bodies of many beasts" can be found in
   - ☐ a. the long ears of rabbits.
   - ☐ b. creatures with a fishing line on their heads.
   - ☐ c. the floating ability of the Portuguese man-of-war.
   - ☐ d. the presence of feathers in the grebe's diet.

5. "The sea anemone, a flowerlike animal of the
   tidemark, is usually <u>riveted</u> to one spot." In
   this context *riveted* means
   ☐ a. fastened.
   ☐ b. trapped.
   ☐ c. helped.
   ☐ d. attracted.

Interpreting the Selection

Answer each of the following questions. You may look back at the
selection if necessary.

*Making
Inferences*

6. Although Jean George does not say so
   directly, you can infer that a major part of the
   woodcock's diet is
   ☐ a. earthworms.
   ☐ b. snipes.
   ☐ c. hawks.
   ☐ d. grasses.

Generalizing

7. Which of the following generalizations can
   you make based on the article?
   ☐ a. Nature is destructive.
   ☐ b. Only bizarre creatures will survive in
       nature.
   ☐ c. Nature has designed creatures for
       almost every environment.
   ☐ d. The purpose of evolution is to create
       new and strange creatures.

8. Which of the following statements is an
   opinion?
   ☐ a. The koala is found in Australia.
   ☐ b. The koala is an odd beast.
   ☐ c. The koala does not need to drink water.
   ☐ d. The leaves of the eucalyptus tree contain
      all the moisture the koala needs.

9. The Mayfly does not need a mouth or a
   stomach because it
   ☐ a. absorbs food through its skin.
   ☐ b. makes food in its own body.
   ☐ c. lives for only one day.
   ☐ d. gets its energy from the air.

10. From the information that Jean George gives
    in the article, you can conclude that
    ☐ a. adaptation goes on all the time in
       nature.
    ☐ b. most bizarre creatures do not live
       very long.
    ☐ c. only land animals can adapt to harsh
       environments.
    ☐ d. the sea is a less hostile environment
       than the land.

Main Ideas and
Supporting Details

"That Astounding Creator—Nature" contains many fascinating facts about animals. But if the author had just presented those facts in a random way, you might have found the article confusing. It might also have been hard to remember most of the facts.

To avoid confusing her audience, Jean George organized her facts into a clear framework. She used the most common kind of framework for articles—presenting main ideas and supporting details. In this lesson you will identify the main ideas and supporting details in her article. In addition to studying her organization, you will explore other techniques that Jean George used to help you understand and remember the information she chose to present.

The Thesis Statement

In an article there is usually an overall main idea. It is the central point that the author is trying to make. A <u>thesis statement</u> is the way in which the main idea of an article is expressed. A thesis is an idea or viewpoint that someone intends to support with evidence. A thesis statement can consist of one or more complete sentences.

A thesis statement is usually worded as a generalization and it is often not very interesting by itself. It becomes interesting only when it is supported by concrete, or specific, evidence.

A writer must decide on the main idea, or thesis statement, before beginning an article. The main idea holds the article together, just as a central beam holds up a house. The main idea provides the focus. The writer then builds onto the main idea to create a fully developed work.

1. Imagine that you are asked to write an article about your school, town, or city. Think of an idea that you have about one of those topics. Write a thesis statement that expresses your idea and that could be the basis of your article. The thesis statement should be a general statement that you can support with concrete evidence.

How do you find the thesis statement in an article? Sometimes, the title of the article suggests it. In Jean George's article you find clues to the thesis statement in the title. "That Astounding Creator—Nature" gives you a hint that the main idea will be about the unusual creations of nature.

The thesis statement is often found in the <u>lead paragraph</u>, or opening paragraph of an article. But many writers of magazine or newspaper articles prefer to use the lead paragraph to catch your attention. In that case, the thesis statement may not appear until the second or third paragraph. Or it may not even appear until the conclusion of the article.

Read the beginning of Jean George's article. She uses the lead paragraph to catch your interest, offering tidbits about some strange animals. In the middle of the second paragraph, however, she clearly states her main idea:

> Give nature an environment or situation and she will evolve a creature, adapting a toe here, an eye there, until the being fits the niche. As a result of this hammering and fitting, however, some really unbelievable creatures circle the sun with us.

Sometimes a writer will repeat the thesis statement two or three times. It may be suggested in the title, stated at the beginning of the article, and reworded in the conclusion. The repetition helps to connect the ideas in the article.

2. Read the conclusion of the article. Does Jean George repeat her thesis statement? If so, what words does she use?

A thesis is not always stated directly. Even though a writer does not use a thesis statement, a thesis can still be implied, or suggested. In such a case, you must identify the author's central point.

Secondary Ideas

Some articles have only one main idea. Most articles, however, include one or more secondary ideas that are related to the thesis statement. The secondary ideas support the thesis statement. In "That Astounding Creator—Nature," the secondary ideas often appear as topic sentences. A topic sentence is a sentence that states the main idea of a paragraph. Read paragraph 8, which begins, "Sound has shaped the bodies of many beasts." As you learned earlier, the thesis statement says that animals adapt their appearance or behavior to their environment. Now this secondary idea presents sound as one part of the environment to which animals have adapted.

3. The article includes six other secondary ideas. List at least two of them. Explain how each is connected to the thesis statement.

Supporting Details

A thesis statement is not very meaningful unless it is supported with concrete evidence, or supporting details. In an article such as this one, supporting details fall into a number of categories. One kind of supporting detail is facts, statements that can be proved or disproved by research or experimentation. When talking about the grebe that fed feathers to its young, Jean George gives you this fact: "I later learned that 60 percent of the grebe's diet is feathers."

A fact can also be a statement by an expert in a field. Since writers are not always experts in the subjects of their articles, they often quote people who are. You are likely to accept such information because it comes from a knowledgeable source.

4. Reread paragraph 4 of "That Astounding Creator—Nature." What expert does George consult? What does the expert say? How does the expert's information support George's thesis statement?

A second type of supporting detail is the anecdote. As you learned in Chapter 4, an anecdote is a brief story about an interesting incident. In an article it can be used to illustrate the main idea. The story Jean George tells of watching the mother grebe feed feathers to her young is an anecdote. She uses that anecdote to support the idea that "some really unbelievable creatures circle the sun with us."

5. Skim the article and find another anecdote that supports the main idea or a secondary idea. Briefly summarize the anecdote. Then tell what idea it supports.

A third type of supporting detail is the example. An example is chosen to explain or specifically illustrate a general statement. In an article an example often illustrates a main idea.

Review the paragraph that begins, "Nature seems to have gone all out in creating preposterous gadgets for self-defense." In that topic sentence Jean George presents an idea that she supports with the example of the jacana. With spurs like switchblades, a jacana "can slash his enemies to shreds." In the next paragraph George gives another example of unusual self-defense—the example of the two-headed skink.

6. Find an example that the author uses to support one of her ideas. What is the example? What idea does it illustrate?

Transitions Between Ideas

An article can be organized into main ideas and supporting details and still be confusing unless the writer connects the ideas. In a piece of writing the connection between two or more ideas is called a <u>transition</u>. A transition may connect one sentence to the next or one paragraph to another. It may also connect a paragraph to the thesis statement.

Read the paragraph that begins, "Australia has many strange beasts, one of the oddest of which is the koala." That paragraph comes right after the story about the feather-eating grebe. The only connection between the two stories is that both the koala and the grebe have unusual behaviors, and Jean George makes this point clear. The strange behavior of those animals also connects them to the thesis statement.

Repeating Words. Transitions between paragraphs can be made in several ways. Sometimes the writer repeats a word to connect two ideas. Below are the first sentences of two consecutive paragraphs in "That Astounding Creator—Nature."

a. In order to travel in a hostile world, the Portuguese man-of-war first mastered the art of floating.
b. There is hardly any environment, however hostile, that some creature has not mastered.

Notice that the words *hostile* and *mastered* appear in both sentences. *Hostile* is used to describe a particular kind of environment. *Mastered* suggests that nature's creatures have succeeded in overcoming the difficulties of certain environments. By repeating those words, Jean George connects the two paragraphs and lets you know that she has an orderly plan for her article.

Synonyms. Another type of transition is one made through the use of a synonym—a word or phrase having practically the same meaning as another word or phrase. Jean George often uses phrases that are synonyms. Read the following topic sentences from two consecutive paragraphs. Find the synonyms in each sentence.

a. The creature with the fishing line on its head was created for the dark canyons of the sea.
b. The gigantic ocean bottom creates other problems.

The phrases *canyons of the sea* and *ocean bottom* refer to the same place. Therefore, they can be considered synonyms. Those two phrases connect the paragraphs by telling you that both paragraphs are about life at the bottom of the sea.

Transitional Words. A third way that authors connect ideas is by using transitional words and phrases. Transitional words help connect ideas in the same way that longer transitions between paragraphs do. Common words and phrases used in transitions include *however, nevertheless, on the other hand, also, in addition, as a result, in comparison,* and so on.

Notice the transitional words in this sentence: "Just as nature adds things on creatures that need them, so she occasionally takes things away from those that don't." Jean George uses the phrase *just as . . . so* to connect a new idea to the earlier parts of the article. In the first half of the article, she has described the various body parts animals have grown to better adjust to their environments. In a later part of the article, she wants to tell about body parts that they do not have. She then gives the example of the Mayfly that has no mouth or stomach.

7. Near the end of the article, Jean George writes: "But probably the most dumbfounding of nature's extraordinary creations is the horned toad of our Southwest." How does that sentence create a connection between the story of the horned toad and George's thesis statement?

All good nonfiction writers build a framework of main ideas and supporting details into whatever they write. Like Jean George, the other writers you have read in this book have built their works around a framework. As you read the remaining selections, notice how the authors have presented their ideas and then supplied evidence to support them.

Questions for Thought and Discussion

The questions and activities that follow will help you explore "That Astounding Creator—Nature" in more depth and at the same time develop your critical thinking skills.

1. **Questioning.** Besides giving information, a good article will often raise questions in your mind. Skim "That Astounding Creator—Nature" and write down any questions you may have. Next to each question, note how you might find the answer.

2. **Categorizing.** Jean George could have organized her article in various other ways. She could, for example, have discussed the odd adaptations in nature by types of animals, such as insects, fish, reptiles,

and mammals. Divide the class into small groups. With your group, think of at least one other way that Jean George could have categorized, or divided, the unusual adaptations of animals. Then share your group's ideas with the class.

3. **Analyzing Language.** Jean George's article is entertaining as well as informative. It is interesting in part because of her lively language. Find three examples of how her language adds interest to the article. Explain your choice.

4. **Analyzing Differences.** "That Astounding Creator—Nature" and "The Dog That Bit People" are both about animals. Yet the two selections are very different. Describe the main differences between Jean George's article and James Thurber's essay.

Writing About Literature

Several suggestions for writing projects are given below. You may be asked to complete one or more of these projects. If you have any questions about how to begin a writing assignment, review Using the Writing Process, beginning on page 341.

1. **Summarizing.** Write a letter to a friend explaining what you found most interesting in "That Astounding Creator—Nature." Your letter should have at least four paragraphs. Be sure to organize the information in your letter into main ideas and supporting details.

2. **Writing from Research.** Research an animal or some aspect of animal behavior that interests you. Remember that research can involve interviewing people, reading books and magazines, or watching educational films. Take notes on your topic and develop a thesis statement. Then write an article about your findings.

3. **Turning Facts into Fiction.** Jean George often writes fiction, making up stories about animals. Choose one of the animals from her article as the subject for a short story. Using the information in the article as a starting point, write a short story about the animal.

Chapter 7

Selection

Not Built with Mortal Hands
MacKinlay Kantor

Lesson

Selecting and Organizing Facts

About the Selection

"Not Built with Mortal Hands" is a magazine article that profiles an unusual man: Ed Snow. Unlike the famous individuals who are often profiled in magazines, Ed Snow was not known outside his own community. Nevertheless, he impressed everyone who knew him. What made Ed Snow remarkable was that he lived the same way as the people around him, only without the benefit of hands.

The title of MacKinlay Kantor's article, "Not Built with Mortal Hands," refers to what some people might consider Ed Snow's disability. The title can be understood on more than one level because of the two meanings of the word *mortal. Mortal* means human. It also means having human limitations. Ed Snow did not have hands. Yet he was not limited by his lack of hands. As you read the article, you will learn how Ed Snow lived a full life without hands.

MacKinlay Kantor grew up in Webster City, Iowa, where Ed Snow was county superintendent of schools. Kantor first saw Snow in about 1914. As Kantor points out in the article, good artificial limbs did not exist then. Ed Snow accomplished what he did without help from today's medical technology.

MacKinlay Kantor is the author of forty-three books. Many of them are novels about the Civil War. One popular novel, *Andersonville*, describes life in a Confederate prisoner of war camp. Kantor won a Pulitzer

Prize for that book. But Kantor himself admitted that for a time he made his living by writing for detective and crime magazines. He said, "I was well aware that the stuff I wrote had little value, except that in most cases it made entertaining narrative. Yet I don't think my rather complicated talents were harmed in the least."

MacKinlay Kantor was born in 1904. His father, unwilling to accept family responsibilities, deserted his wife and two children. Kantor's mother eventually became the editor of the local newspaper. She was the first person to publish her son's work—some of his poems.

As a boy, Kantor had no ambition to become a writer. He wanted to be an entomologist—a scientist who studies insects. His special interests were butterflies and moths. When Kantor was fourteen, his father showed new concern for his children. He took them to live with him in Chicago. Although they were supposed to go to school there, young MacKinlay soon found himself having to work to put food on the table. Eventually, he and his sister returned to Webster City.

By that time, he was three years behind in his schooling, but he was determined to finish high school. While in school, he worked on his mother's newspaper, and after graduating, he worked as a reporter before returning to Chicago. There, he took a job in a department store. In his spare time he wrote stories for crime and detective magazines.

In Chicago Kantor married. He and his wife moved to New York City in 1932. By that time, Kantor was struggling to make a living as a writer. With his fourth novel, published in 1934, he won recognition, and his financial struggles were over.

During World War II, MacKinlay Kantor worked as a war correspondent. He also flew eleven missions as a machine gunner in a bomber squadron. During the Korean War, he flew another six combat missions. He was later awarded the Medal of Freedom for his service in the United States Air Force.

As a writer, Kantor was known for his careful research. Once, when he wanted to write a novel about police life, he spent a year patrolling the streets with New York City police officers. On other occasions, he gathered material for books by traveling as a hobo throughout the Midwest. MacKinlay Kantor died in 1977 at the age of seventy-three.

Lesson Preview

The lesson that follows "Not Built with Mortal Hands" focuses on the author's selection and organization of facts. "Not Built with Mortal Hands" is a magazine profile of Ed Snow. MacKinlay Kantor wanted to give as complete a picture of Ed Snow as was possible in a short space. To do that, he had to limit the number of facts in the article. He then had to organize those facts in a way that would give the reader a clear idea of Ed Snow's character.

The questions that follow will help you understand Kantor's approach to his subject. As you read, think about how you would answer these questions.

1 What facts do you learn about Ed Snow? What kinds of facts about his life are not mentioned?

2 What picture do you get of Ed Snow's character? How does MacKinlay Kantor let you know what he thinks of Snow?

3 What do you think is the main idea of the article?

4 Think about the information that Kantor gives you at the beginning of the article, in the middle, and at the end. Why do you think he organized the material in this way?

Vocabulary

Here are some difficult words that appear in the selection that follows. Study the words and their definitions, as well as the sentences that show how the words are used. This will help you get the most from your reading.

proficiency skillfulness; expertise. *We admired the proficiency of the skilled concert pianist.*

facility ease or skill in doing something. *Because she has spent several years in Italy, Sue can speak Italian with great facility.*

resolute determined; unyielding. *Despite her sore throat, the singer was resolute about giving her performance as scheduled.*

jaunty lively; sprightly. *With jaunty steps, the excited vacationers walked up the gangway of the cruise ship.*

emitted sent out. *The parrot emitted a screech of anger.*

tremulous trembling; quivering. *The child's tremulous voice told us how nervous she was.*

stout strong; sturdy. *The elderly woman leaned on her son's stout arm when they crossed the street.*

Not Built with Mortal Hands

MacKinlay Kantor

Eternal house, not built with mortal hands! . . .

—DRYDEN

When I was a boy in Webster City, Iowa, I would go out of my way to watch Mr. Ed Snow drinking a glass of milk, signing a receipt, or tipping his hat to the ladies. So would any other boy in town.

Ed Snow was our County Superintendent of Schools, which title we children considered an accolade[1] bestowed upon him not so much for executive proficiency in educational matters, as for his remarkable facility at gardening, penmanship, and automobiling.

By the way, I neglected to mention that Ed Snow had no hands.

He never had had any hands, insofar as little folks knew.

Certain older people could remember when the Snows lived in a house out on the prairie where the old-fashioned Illinois Central trains trumpeted their way to Fort Dodge and Sioux City. It seemed, according to an anecdote with which we became familiar in time, that Ed Snow

---

1. **accolade:** recognition of merit; an award.

Selecting and Organizing Facts

had indeed possessed hands, up until the age when he could first toddle away from the door-stoop through prairie flowers native to the railroad right-of-way.

He had wandered onto the tracks, and there he had encountered a passenger train—no matter with what urgency the engineer applied his brakes. Little Eddie was conveyed to town for such repairs as might be managed, while weeping passengers aboard the train shook their heads and declared that the infant would be better off dead.

Scraps of the upper arms left to him seemed inadequate for the struggle ahead. Surgeons did the best they could; but when the wounds were finally healed, Eddie was missing one arm close to the shoulder, and the other just above the elbow.

A modest sum of money was paid the parent Snows for damages to Eddie, and the world forgot him until he grew up. Then the world observed him again: a resolute blond-haired stripling intent on earning a college education, and taking orders as a book salesman in order to do it.

"It was too easy," he chuckled, long afterward. "So I had to quit selling books. I was a phenomenal success—too phenomenal."

"But why did you quit, if—?"

"Oh," he said, "I know why I was selling so many books. The books weren't the greatest books in the world, nor the most necessary ones, nor the most inviting; and few of the people who were buying from me could be called well off. They were just sorry for me. I didn't like that."

The active brain of the maimed young student soon hit upon a better plan. He got hold of a horse and wagon, hired a boy for the driving and harnessing, and spent the next summer trekking from farm to farm through the more remote countryside of that region, collecting abandoned iron, copper, and other fragments of cast-off metals.

An old engine axle here, a flywheel there, a set of cogs from some abandoned mill—things like those were not worth the time and labor for busy farmers, if they tried to transport them across the long miles to the junk yards themselves.

Ed Snow used his imagination and his knowledge of rural geography and equipment, and his energies paid a handsome profit. I don't think he was ever really worried about how to get along in the world from that time forth.

His education was adequate when he started his life's work in earnest. He taught school and did a few other jobs so well that it was no surprise to anyone when he achieved practically a lifetime tenure on the office of County Superintendent.

Other people have gotten by without hands before and since Ed Snow, and some have done it brilliantly. But I always experience a severe attack of rapid eye-winking when I witness their jaunty courage.

There is Harold Russell, the handless veteran who played the handless veteran in *The Best Years of Our Lives,* the movie made from my novel, *Glory for Me.* I remember our first meeting on a Hollywood set.

"Rus," I asked, "what are you planning to do after you finish your work in this picture?"

Harold Russell flashed his easy grin—and his prosthetic hooks[2]—before my eyes.

"Look," he said, "I'm not worried. I can always get a job picking poison ivy."

It must be remembered that Ed Snow's injury was incurred a couple of generations or so before World War II. Artificial arms and hooks and clamps being as crude as they were in those days, it is easy to understand why Mr. Snow never bothered with them. He preferred to let the mighty stump of one arm perform the lion's share of necessary manual activity, and let his active intelligence and merry nature do the rest.

He married, because he was affectionate and home-loving and gregarious—he married a pretty little woman with bright eyes, and Alice Snow swore forever that there were only two things she had to do for Ed: (1) cut his meat at table, and (2) put the brass collar-buttons in the old-fashioned stiff collars he liked to wear.

2. **prosthetic hooks:** artificial devices used to replace missing hands.

Take the very ordinary matter of manners on the street. It disgusted Ed to note how slovenly some men were in their observance of an etiquette that offered spice and pride to his soul. It was fun to march down the street with him on a busy morning. He wore a derby in cold weather, and a stiff-brimmed straw hat in summer. It had to be a stiff-brimmed hat—that was the kind of hat he could handle.

"*Good* morning, Mrs. McAdow!" and the hardy stump of his arm would reach aloft. In some miraculous fashion the hat would be tossed from his head, caught and whirled by the stump as he bowed, and set evenly and trimly back again on top of his head, so that he might have the joy of saluting another lady, ten paces farther on. "*Good* morning, Mrs. Hunter! . . . *Good* morning, Miss Frank!" and the hat would be off and on twenty times before he reached the corner of Second Street.

Ed and his wife were members of the church which my grandmother attended, and I frequently had the pleasure of watching him eat and drink at picnics or suppers. He wore a broad leather strap buckled around the stump, and under this strap the spoon or fork or fountain pen or pencil or whatever other implement he wanted to use would be thrust, with lightning rapidity, by a brief shake of Ed Snow's head and a quick pressure of his strong white teeth. I never saw him spill a thing, and I don't think anyone else ever did, either.

I remember accompanying a friend of my mother's down Willson Avenue one day. She was a woman from out-of-town who was unfamiliar with the skills of our Ed Snow. There was a rattle of old springs and Ed passed us—buzzing by in his old Ford roadster. I waved after him, and my mother's friend stood gaping.

"That man!" she gasped. "He was driving—"

"Yes," I told her. "That's Mr. E. F. Snow, the County Superintendent of Schools."

"County Superintendent of Fiddlesticks!" the woman cried. "He hasn't got any hands. Why, he'll kill somebody! He'll—"

The whole task of explanation seemed too much for me. To explain how, on a Model-T Ford such as Ed Snow piloted, you did your braking and gear-shifting with your feet . . . how he had a strong steel ring fastened to the steering wheel, into which he could cement the sinewy wad that grew from his shoulder; how—

I do recall being able to say to the lady: "It may interest you to know that Mr. Snow has driven a hundred and fifty thousand miles without an accident. He won a certificate for his safe driving."

It was a toss-up whether we young people were more entranced when watching Ed breezily guiding his vehicle along our streets, or when estimating the wonder of the pen-and-ink marvels he could achieve. He was an avid student of what was known as "the Palmer Method" of penmanship. Besides long scrolls, loops and double-loops, he could make elegant roosters or pictures of Abraham Lincoln or Heaven knew what else, all contrived with the circular manipulation of his sharp-pointed pen.

Still I think it was in the homely phases of his life—the long, bustling years spent with Alice (there were just the two of them. A child came to them once, but there was only a tiny grave in the cemetery to show for all their hopes and longing) that Ed Snow found the supreme realization of his dream to be a man like all others.

It happened casually, but when it happened I think that Ed Snow felt a pride that rarely comes to men, even when a hundred thousand hands are applauding them, even when the medals are pinned on.

The Snows had been having the woodwork in their home newly painted, and Alice was vastly pleased with the snowy coating which lay upon old doors and banisters. But on the second day after the paint had dried, little Mrs. Snow emitted a snarl that brought her husband on the run.

"Ed Snow," she was commanding in no uncertain tone, "you come right here! See what you've done!"

He stood beside her and saw how the fresh ivory on a doorjamb had been sullied by the print of several very dirty fingers.

"We're entertaining the Sunday school class tonight," Alice cried, "and I wanted everything to look nice, and now just look what you've done!"

Ed Snow gazed down at her. "Alice, do you really think I made those finger marks on the doorjamb?"

"Well, if you didn't, I don't know who did!"

"Alice. On your honor, now. Do you really think I made those marks?"

His wife stared up at him for a long moment, and then—as he told it a hundred times afterward—"She just sort of collapsed. . . . Laugh? I don't know when we've ever laughed like that before."

It is quite apparent, when one views the life of Ed Snow, that hands are not a necessary implement in the building of either laughter or tears. And tears did come to the Snows, as I have remarked. There was that little grave. . . .

Alice was very ill when the baby was born, and only Ed might stand in tremulous awe before the small quiet shape which had slept so soundly and permanently before it ever drew a breath of life.

He told Alice later; and in time she told my grandmother through a blur of tears as she recited what Ed Snow had said.

"Alice," he whispered. There was a wistful smile on his big shiny face. "The baby had *hands*."

She gave his smile back to him, though her cheeks were as wet as his. "Ed, did you actually think it wouldn't have hands?"

Ed Snow shrugged the powerful shoulder with which he had managed to build a better life than many people have been able to build with eight stout fingers and two thumbs. "Well," he said, "you know— I couldn't *help* wondering. . . ."

Reviewing the Selection

Answer each of the following questions without looking back at the selection.

Recalling Facts

1. When did Ed Snow lose his hands?
   - ☐ a. as a young child
   - ☐ b. in high school
   - ☐ c. in World War I
   - ☐ d. when he was in college

Understanding Main Ideas

2. Ed Snow gave up his job as a book salesman because he
   - ☐ a. disliked traveling.
   - ☐ b. was ashamed of having no hands.
   - ☐ c. did not want to be pitied.
   - ☐ d. found a better-paying job.

Placing Events in Order

3. After Ed Snow stopped selling books, he next earned a living as a
   - ☐ a. schoolteacher.
   - ☐ b. collector of scrap metal.
   - ☐ c. county superintendent of schools.
   - ☐ d. store clerk.

Finding Supporting Details

4. Ed Snow loved Alice because she
   - ☐ a. never argued with him.
   - ☐ b. took care of him.
   - ☐ c. was hardworking.
   - ☐ d. never treated him as an incomplete person.

Selecting and Organizing Facts

5. "He stood beside her and saw how the fresh ivory on a doorjamb had been <u>sullied</u> by the print of several very dirty fingers." In this context *sullied* means
   ☐ a. painted.
   ☐ b. soiled.
   ☐ c. removed.
   ☐ d. decorated.

Interpreting the Selection

Answer each of the following questions. You may look back at the selection if necessary.

6. How do you think Alice Snow felt about her husband?
   ☐ a. She felt sorry for him.
   ☐ b. She often wished he had hands.
   ☐ c. She loved and respected him.
   ☐ d. She was frequently annoyed with him.

7. The incidents in the article show that the people who knew Ed Snow
   ☐ a. admired him.
   ☐ b. felt sorry for him.
   ☐ c. tried to help him.
   ☐ d. could never forget his lack of hands.

8. In the author's opinion Ed Snow
   - ☐ a. had driven 150,000 miles without an accident.
   - ☐ b. led a fuller life than many other people.
   - ☐ c. was determined to prove that he was better than other people.
   - ☐ d. sold a lot of books.

*Identifying Cause
and Effect*

9. Ed Snow did not use artificial arms and hooks because
   - ☐ a. they were too expensive.
   - ☐ b. he did not want to frighten children.
   - ☐ c. they were clumsy and awkward.
   - ☐ d. they had not yet been invented.

*Drawing
Conclusions*

10. Ed Snow considered having no hands to be a
    - ☐ a. punishment for wandering away from home.
    - ☐ b. way to entertain people.
    - ☐ c. way to get sympathy.
    - ☐ d. challenge to his inventiveness.

Selecting and
Organizing Facts

In the article you just read, MacKinlay Kantor gives only selected details about Ed Snow. He does not tell you when Snow was born, what he looked like, or how he spent most of his time. Kantor does not tell you those things because he is interested primarily in Ed Snow's character.

Kantor could have written a biography of Ed Snow. He could have interviewed people who worked with him. He could even have collected Snow's own memories of his childhood and youth. With all those facts, Kantor could have given a detailed account of Ed Snow's life. But that was not his goal. He wanted to write a profile of Ed Snow that could be published as a magazine article.

As you learned in Chapter 3, a profile is a short biography that focuses on one or two aspects of a person's character. In popular magazines you will find profiles of outstanding sports figures and powerful political leaders. Like Kantor, the writers of those profiles have the space to include only a few facts. Yet they want you to know what the people they are profiling are like.

When writing profiles for magazines, writers must select facts carefully. They must then organize those facts in a way that will not only make a point about their subject but also interest you. In this lesson you will learn how MacKinlay Kantor selected and organized facts in "Not Built with Mortal Hands."

Choosing Facts

One way to analyze how a writer has chosen facts is to notice what has been left out. The missing information may tell you something about the author's plan in writing the article.

In a profile you usually expect to learn what the subject was like as a young person. MacKinlay Kantor does not provide that information about Ed Snow. He describes only one incident connected to Ed Snow's childhood—the accident in which "Little Eddie" lost his hands. Kantor ends his description of that episode by saying, "A modest sum of money was paid the parent Snows for damages to Eddie, and the world forgot him until he grew up." Kantor also leaves Eddie until he has grown up. He chooses to overlook the years in which the injured child learned to live without hands.

Kantor could have discussed how Snow's parents treated Eddie as a boy, how Snow's character developed, and what made him so determined. But he was not interested in showing how Ed Snow got to be who he was. Instead, Kantor focuses on the adult Ed Snow—the man Kantor knew when he was growing up.

1. What other information about Ed Snow's life is missing from the article? What do the missing facts tell you about Kantor's plan for the article?

By examining the information that Kantor left out, you probably have begun to notice what information he included. Much of the article is based on incidents that Kantor witnessed himself. When he concentrates on those incidents, Kantor follows the advice given to many writers: Write about what you know.

Information that comes straight from the author's own experience is called <u>primary information</u>. A writer can use primary information to make a scene lively and realistic. Yet if Kantor had relied only on primary information, his profile of Ed Snow would have been limited. So he supplemented his own memories by talking to other people. When Kantor tells stories about Ed Snow that are based on others' memories, he uses secondary information—information that does not come from the author's own experiences.

2. Read the following list of incidents mentioned in Kantor's profile of Ed Snow. Identify which use primary information and which use secondary information. Suggest who might have given Kantor each piece of information. Why do you think Kantor included the secondary information?

> a. *Eddie's accident on the railroad tracks*
> b. *Ed Snow's job as a book salesman*
> c. *Ed Snow's job collecting junk metal*
> d. *Ed Snow tipping his hat to the ladies he met*
> e. *Ed Snow eating neatly at church suppers*
> f. *The out-of-town visitor's reaction to Snow's driving*
> g. *Alice Snow's accusation about the fingerprints on the new paint*
> h. *Ed Snow's response to the birth of his child*

Organizing the Facts

While MacKinlay Kantor was selecting facts to include in the profile of Ed Snow, he was also thinking about ways to organize them. As you learned in Chapter 6, writers organize information by using main ideas and supporting details. In "That Amazing Creator—Nature," you learned how Jean George clearly stated her main idea in a thesis statement. As you will recall, the thesis of an article is not always stated directly. Sometimes it is implied, or suggested. You then have to examine the facts and ask yourself, What is the thesis, or main idea, of the article?

MacKinlay Kantor does not state his thesis directly, but he clearly suggests it. The thesis of "Not Built with Mortal Hands" might be stated like this: Ed Snow lived an independent, fulfilled life despite having lost both hands as a child. If that thesis statement is correct, then the information that MacKinlay Kantor gives you about Ed Snow should support it.

3. Review the list of incidents in question 2. How does each incident support the thesis mentioned in the previous paragraph?

The Order of Facts. A thesis provides an overall organization for an article. The author then has to decide in what order to present the information. In biographies authors frequently use chronological order—the arrangement of events in the order in which they occur. Yet in a profile chronological order is not necessarily useful, because the author is highlighting a person's character rather than giving the full story of the person's life. As you can see, Kantor ignores chronology in "Not Built with Mortal Hands." He chooses instead to organize the facts so that they spark your interest.

Like most writers of articles, Kantor starts with a lead paragraph intended to catch your attention. An effective lead paragraph can contain an unusual fact, a question, or a surprising statement that makes you curious to know more about the subject. Read the first paragraph of "Not Built with Mortal Hands":

> When I was a boy in Webster City, Iowa, I would go out of my way to watch Mr. Ed Snow drinking a glass of milk, signing a receipt, or tipping his hat to the ladies. So would any other boy in town.

Kantor makes a straightforward statement about his boyhood, but the statement raises a curious question: Why did he and the other boys in town want to watch Ed Snow doing such ordinary things? That question makes you want to read the next paragraph. There, Kantor relates some facts about Ed Snow. At the end of that paragraph, you are still left asking, Why does he bother to watch the man so closely? In the third paragraph Kantor finally reveals an unusual fact about Ed Snow: He had no hands.

4. Read the single sentence that makes up the third paragraph. What is the effect of the words "By the way"?

Flashback and Digression. Kantor begins the article by describing his boyhood reaction to the adult Ed Snow. He then uses a flashback to reveal how Ed Snow lost his hands. A flashback is a scene, a

Selecting and Organizing Facts

conversation, or an event that interrupts the present action to show something that happened in the past. Writers use flashbacks to give you information about past events and to add interest to the present action of the story.

5. Kantor could have begun his article by telling you about young Eddie Snow's accident. Why do you think he chose to give that information in a flashback? Is the flashback effective? Why?

The flashback is one way that writers interrupt the straight chronological ordering of facts. Another device that interrupts the forward flow of facts is digression. In Chapter 5 you learned how James Thurber used digressions to create humorous effects. In "Not Built with Mortal Hands," MacKinlay Kantor also uses a digression to reveal his feelings about his subject.

6. Reread the paragraphs in which Kantor discusses Harold Russell. How does Kantor make the transition between talking about Ed Snow and talking about Harold Russell? Why do you think he includes that digression?

Although Kantor uses flashbacks and a digression, he still organizes his facts around a main idea. In the middle of the article, he describes the clever methods that Ed Snow invented to perform everyday tasks. Near the end of the profile, Kantor introduces a secondary idea that supports his thesis:

> Still I think it was in the homely phases of his life—the long, bustling years spent with Alice (there were just the two of them. A child came to them once, but there was only a tiny grave in the cemetery to show for all their hopes and longing) that Ed Snow found the supreme realization of his dream to be a man like all others.

Up to that point, Kantor has shown Ed Snow only in his public life. Now he focuses on his life at home with Alice. Kantor shows that both in public and in private Ed Snow led a fulfilling life.

7. What anecdote does Kantor use to show "that Ed Snow found the supreme realization of his dream to be a man like all others"? What does that anecdote reveal about both Ed and Alice Snow?

You might expect Kantor to end the profile by telling about Snow's old age or death. In his conclusion, however, Kantor uses another flashback. He recounts a story told to his grandmother by Alice Snow. The flashback shows Ed Snow's reaction to the birth of his child.

8. Why do you think Kantor ends the profile with that anecdote? What new information does it reveal about Ed Snow? What effect did it have on you?

Author's Attitude and the Selection of Facts

Why did MacKinlay Kantor choose to write about Ed Snow? The answer is obvious throughout the article. The author greatly admired Ed Snow. More than that, he was moved by Snow's energetic and determined attitude toward life. Kantor makes his feelings clear in statements such as the following:

> Other people have gotten by without hands before and since Ed Snow, and some have done it brilliantly. But I always experience a severe attack of rapid eye-winking when I witness their jaunty courage.

> Ed Snow shrugged the powerful shoulder with which he had managed to build a better life than many people have been able to build with eight stout fingers and two thumbs.

Besides stating his own views directly, Kantor also expresses his attitude toward his subject through facts that support his feelings. Recall the anecdote about Ed Snow taking off his hat to the women he passed in the street. The author uses that story for at least two reasons. First, it shows how Ed Snow managed difficult maneuvers without hands. Second, it supports Kantor's admiration for Snow's cheerful approach to life.

9. Reread the story about Ed Snow driving a car. What does it reveal about Kantor's attitude toward the county superintendent of schools?

Questions for Thought and Discussion

The questions and activities that follow will help you explore "Not Built with Mortal Hands" in more depth and at the same time develop your critical thinking skills.

1. **Interpreting.** Think about the title of the article, "Not Built with Mortal Hands." In what way might Ed Snow's lack of hands be considered an asset, or advantage, rather than a liability, or limitation?

2. **Making Inferences.** Read the quotation that Kantor included at the beginning of his article. John Dryden was a British poet and playwright who lived in the 1600s. To what do you think the "eternal house" refers? How do you think the quotation relates to the life of Ed Snow?

3. **Analyzing Character.** From the evidence given in the profile, what kind of person do you think Alice Snow was? Give specific facts to support your ideas.

4. **Comparing.** Compare Ed Snow to someone you know or have read about who has overcome a great hardship. You could even choose Frederick Douglass or Susan B. Anthony, both of whom you read about in earlier chapters. Describe similarities or differences between Ed Snow and the person you have chosen.

Writing About Literature

Several suggestions for writing projects follow. You may be asked to complete one or more of these projects. If you have any questions about how to begin a writing assignment, review Using the Writing Process, beginning on page 341.

1. **Analyzing the Article.** MacKinlay Kantor's main purpose in writing this article was to present a portrait of Ed Snow's character. Review Chapter 3 in which you learned about the techniques that writers use to show a subject's character. Then write several paragraphs discussing

which techniques of character development MacKinlay Kantor used to portray Ed Snow. Find specific examples from the article to show how he used the various techniques of character development.

2. **Writing a Self-Profile.** Write a brief profile of yourself as though someone else were describing you. Use "Not Built with Mortal Hands" as a model. Develop an inviting lead paragraph. Then use anecdotes that another person might tell to reveal your character.

3. **Giving an Interview.** Imagine that you are Ed Snow. A newspaper reporter has asked you for your impressions of the young MacKinlay Kantor who is now a well-known author. Use the information about Kantor provided in the article and in About the Selection as a starting point. Write what Ed Snow might have told the reporter about MacKinlay Kantor as a youth.

Chapter 8

Selection *The Icing of the Cream*
BECKY RUPP

Lesson *Author's Purpose*

About the Selection

"The Icing of the Cream" is an article about homemade ice cream. Like most articles, "The Icing of the Cream" is informative. It presents information about the history and science of making ice cream. You will learn, for example, about the earliest forms of ice cream and why salt is essential to making ice cream. The article is also instructional; that is, it teaches you how to make ice cream.

If you are used to buying ice cream in a store, you may wonder why anyone would want to know how to make it at home. Yet some people believe that homemade ice cream is better than anything you can buy in a store. Of course, there was a time when people had no choice but to make their own. Neither homes nor stores had freezers in which to store frozen food. So people made ice cream at home and ate it immediately. Making ice cream took time and effort. Because of the work involved, people did not often make it.

After refrigeration was invented, companies began to manufacture ice cream for sale. To the next generation of children, store-bought ice cream was the *only* kind of ice cream. Still, some people remembered the delicious taste of homemade ice cream. Others looked back on the fun of churning ice cream. Today, homemade ice cream has become popular again among ice-cream lovers.

"The Icing of the Cream" first appeared in *Country Journal* magazine. The people who read *Country Journal* are interested in topics related to

Author's Purpose

life in small towns or on farms. Sometimes the magazine has instructional articles on practical subjects, but other articles are intended simply to entertain readers. "The Icing of the Cream" is both instructional and entertaining.

Becky Rupp, who wrote "The Icing of the Cream," began her writing career in 1983. Since then, she has published many magazine articles. Her life shows the indirect way in which writers sometimes develop their careers. Rupp was born in 1948 in Burlington, Vermont. She says that she knew she wanted to be a writer as early as the third or fourth grade. Without delay, she wrote a novel about pioneers crossing America. It was her first and last attempt at fiction.

In college Becky Rupp found that she was interested in science. She majored in biology and eventually received an advanced degree in cell biology and biochemistry. For eight years, she worked as a research cell biologist. She satisfied her urge to write by preparing articles for scientific journals.

After the birth of her first child, Becky Rupp wanted to work at home. She and a business partner made candles and pottery and sold them at fairs. Then one day she decided to return to writing. She contacted the editors at *Country Journal*, asking if they wanted to buy an article she was writing about squirrels. When they said yes, Rupp's writing career was established. The topics she has written about include sleigh bells, butter, kites, home-schooling, scarecrows, tree houses, and blue jeans.

Becky Rupp says that what she likes best about writing articles is the research. "I like trivia," she says, "and learning about little chunks of stuff." Some of her research is done in the library with reference books. But more and more, she finds that she is telephoning people for information. At first she was shy about calling strangers. Then she discovered that people are eager to talk about their interests. Now she enjoys doing research by telephone.

Rupp gets many ideas for articles from things she wants to learn more about. Once she has an idea, she proposes it to a magazine editor. If the magazine agrees to buy the article, she begins the research. It usually takes her about three weeks to plan, research, and write an article.

Because Becky Rupp works at home, her husband and three children sometimes get involved in the testing phase of her work. The family has made butter, peanut butter, and ice cream. In fact, one of the children poured rock salt right into the first batch of ice cream they made, instead of layering it around the outside of the churn. "It doesn't work," says Becky Rupp.

Lesson Preview

The lesson that follows "The Icing of the Cream" focuses on an author's purpose in writing. A person may have a number of reasons for writing a magazine article. He or she may write to give you information, to teach you how to do something, to persuade you to think or behave in a certain way, or to entertain you. A writer often has more than one purpose in mind for a particular article. The purpose is based on who the writer thinks will read the article.

The questions that follow will help you identify Becky Rupp's purposes in writing the article. As you read, think about how you would answer these questions.

1 What examples, if any, can you find of the author's intention to give information, to teach, to persuade, or to entertain?

2 In general, what kind of information does the author provide?

3 Does the author teach you anything in the article? If so, what?

4 Do you find any parts of the article humorous? If so, why are they funny?

5 What effect does the author's informal language have on the article?

Vocabulary

Here are some difficult words that appear in the selection that follows. Study the words and their definitions, as well as the sentences that show how the words are used. This will help you get the most from your reading.

patent secure the exclusive right to produce or sell an invention or process. *The company will patent the product to keep other companies from copying it.*

unscrupulous dishonest. *Some unscrupulous store owners sell poorly made goods for very high prices.*

fluctuating wavering; changing. *The temperature is fluctuating around the freezing point.*

credo statement of a belief or principle. *Sue's credo of hard work and concentrated studying paid off when she won the scholarship.*

The Icing of the Cream

BECKY RUPP

Americans eat twice as much ice cream as anybody else in the world. On a regional basis, some of us eat even more than that. The top United States ice cream consumers, who live in Alaska and New England, slurp up something on the order of seven gallons apiece annually—nearly twice the national average. Chances are that at least half of what they eat is vanilla, the all-time national flavor favorite. The second most popular is chocolate, followed by strawberry. After that just about anything goes: coffee is a biggie in Rhode Island, inhabitants of western Massachusetts like butter pecan, and Midwesterners are said to pitch for Rocky Road. I like peppermint stick, which, though far down on the national list of preferred ice cream flavors, is a great way to get rid of candy canes left over from Christmas. Still, as homemade ice cream makers, our family tends to stick to vanilla, chocolate, and strawberry. There's a lot to be said for sure bets.

Author's Purpose

Early Ice Cream

Chocolate of a sort may have been among the earliest ice cream flavors. Legend has it that the Aztec emperor Montezuma ate an ice-cream-like dish of hot chocolate poured over snow. Early Mexican chocolate, however, was mixed with chili peppers and vanilla, and dyed orange—hardly the delectable dark-brown sweet we all know and love. The ancient Chinese ate a frozen rice-and-milk dessert flavored with camphor,[1] a possible relative of the ice cream brought back to Venice by Marco Polo in 1295. And the Romans ate fruit juice mixed with snow brought down by runners from the Alps.

Early ice cream was fairly sloppy stuff. It only became fully freezable in 1550 when Blasius Villafranca, an inventive Spanish doctor living in Rome, discovered that the freezing point of water could be lowered by adding salt to ice. Using the salt technique, the Italians became the world's first large-scale producers of ice cream and busily set about promoting their new treat all over Europe. Initially, ice cream was reserved for the nobility, and methods for making it were jealously guarded. Charles I of England went so far as to execute a loose-lipped palace chef who revealed the royal recipe.

Nothing, however, remains safe from the peasants for long. Ice cream made it to the uncivilized wilds of America by the mid-1700s, probably along with immigrants from France. Its first official colonial mention was in a letter written in 1744 by William Black, who had been served some strawberry ice cream while a guest of the governor of Maryland. George Washington was an ice cream lover, as was Thomas Jefferson, who brought an ice cream machine home with him from France in 1789, along with a recipe so outrageously complicated that it required eighteen separate operations from start to frozen finish. (Jefferson liked his ice cream encased in warm pastry crust, perhaps the first Baked Alaska.[2]) Mad Anthony Wayne ate ice cream to celebrate his

---

1. **camphor:** a fragrant substance obtained from an evergreen tree.
2. **Baked Alaska:** a dessert consisting of ice cream surrounded by a meringue which is quickly browned in an oven.

victory over the Indians at the Battle of the Fallen Timbers, and Dolley Madison[3]—"The First Lady of Ice Cream"—served a mountain of it (pink) at her husband's second inaugural ball, made with cream from the president's own dairy.

The Ingredients

The original ice creams, like the best homemade varieties today, contained only cream, sugar, flavorings, and occasionally eggs. The prime ingredient was and still is cream. The kind of cream used determines the richness of the final product. The most spectacular ice creams are made from heavy whipping cream (about 35 per cent butterfat); lesser grades are made with light cream (20 per cent), half-and-half (12 per cent), or combinations of the above. Unfortunately, cream is also the most expensive ingredient, and the richer the cream, the more expensive it is. Cheaper ice creams can be made from substitutes such as condensed milk, and the ice cream industry uses a whole battery of noncream dairy products, including dried cheese whey. None of these ingredients tastes as good as cream, however, and the consensus is that if you're going to ice something, ice the real thing.

The sweetener of choice, home ice cream makers generally agree, is granulated sugar. Alternatives such as corn syrups and artificial sweeteners alter ice cream flavors, sometimes unpleasantly. Recipes vary, but the rule of thumb is 3 to 4 tablespoons of sugar per 2½ cups of cream. It's best not to stray too far from this formula, because sugar also functions as an antifreeze: too little and the ice cream will be too hard; too much and it will be slush.

Some ice cream recipes call for eggs. Generally speaking the custard-type ice creams contain eggs, and the Philadelphia-style ice creams do not. French vanilla, which many people consider the richest vanilla on the face of the earth, is a custard ice cream. The eggless Philadelphia-style ice creams traditionally contain only pure cream, sugar and flavorings.

---

3. **Mad Anthony Wayne:** an officer in the American Revolution, called "mad" because of his daring deeds.
   Dolley Madison: wife of James Madison, the fourth President of the United States.

Author's Purpose

The name dates from the nineteenth century, when Philadelphia, with nearly fifty ice cream factories, was considered the ice cream capital of the world. (Today Pennsylvania is still one of the top ice-cream-producing states in the country, along with California and New York.)

Both types of ice cream recipes often require that the cream or custard base be cooked. In those cases, the ingredients should be cooled before adding flavorings because heat sometimes alters taste. This is particularly true of alcohol-based flavors: bottled vanilla extract, for example, which contains about 30 per cent alcohol; liquors; and liqueurs.[4]

There are hundreds, even thousands, of different flavors of ice cream. On the market at one time or another have been banana daiquiri, bubble gum, casaba melon, eggnog, ginger fig, green tea, jellybean, maple, mincemeat, papaya, peanut-butter-and-jelly, prune, pumpkin, rhubarb, sunflower seed, truffle,[5] and violet—enough to make Baskin Robbins's famous thirty-one flavors (which, to be fair, vary from year to year) look positively pale. With a little imagination you can do it all at home. A good flavor to start with, fitting right in there between truffle and violet, is the all-American favorite, vanilla.

Real Beans

According to ice cream connoisseurs, the best vanilla ice creams are made not with bottled extracts, but with genuine vanilla beans. Vanilla beans are the fruit of a Central American orchid, an immense plant with vines up to 350 feet long. When ripe and ready for picking, the beans are 4 to 12 inches long and gold-yellow in color, stuffed full of the minuscule seeds that form the black specks in top-notch vanilla ice creams. Processing turns the original yellow pods into the skinny black beans sold in supermarkets and specialty shops. Vanilla was introduced to this country by Thomas Jefferson, who came across it during his diplomatic tour of duty in France. When he settled in as secretary of state in Philadelphia in 1790, Jefferson was appalled to learn that the City of

---

4. **liqueurs:** liquor that has been flavored with some fragrant substance and usually sweetened.
5. **truffle:** a rare fungus used as a food and a flavoring.

Brotherly Love lacked vanilla beans. He promptly ordered a packet of fifty from Paris, perhaps then and there starting Philadelphia on the road to world-famous ice cream.

Most vanilla today comes from Madagascar. The beans cost about $1.50 apiece and can be used over and over until the flavor is depleted or can be slit open at once to release the seeds. It takes about three inches of bean to flavor a quart of ice cream. Unlike extract, the bean should be added to the cream or custard base while cooking, then fished out before freezing, rinsed, and stored for the next time around. If you can't lay your hands on real beans, at least make sure your vanilla extract is the natural product—it's distinctly better than the artificial vanilla now on the market, which is a benzaldehyde derivative. (The most commonly used vanilla substitute in ice creams is vanillin, a compound commercially derived from wood pulp treated with sulfuric acid.) Coffee, chocolate, and fruit purées can also be stirred in at the cooking stage. Fruit chunks, chopped nuts, raisins, and crushed candies should be tossed in later, part way through the freezing process when the mix is semisoft. These additions all lower the freezing point of the ice cream, which means that if added too early they slow down the whole process.

Ice Cream Machines

Ice cream freezers fortunately have improved a good deal since their early days. Martha Washington had to make do with a pair of pewter ice cream "pots," or interlocking bowls: the smaller, containing the ice cream mixture, was rapidly twirled within the larger, which held ice and salt. Ice cream making remained at this awkward stage until 1846, when Nancy Johnson invented the hand-cranked freezer, a machine not too different in design from models on the market today. (She didn't patent it, but two years later an alert entrepreneur named William Young did. He kindly called the machine the Johnson Patent Ice Cream Freezer.) The basic ice cream freezer has three major parts: a metal can for the ice cream ingredients, a larger insulating wooden bucket to hold the can and its surrounding layers of salt and ice, and inside the can a multipaddled

Author's Purpose

"dasher" or beater turned by a hand crank. In modern freezers the dasher is operated by an electric motor.

When you're ready to freeze, chill the ice cream mix, metal can, and dasher for at least an hour in the refrigerator. Once the mix is cold, transfer it to the metal can, filling it no more than three-quarters full. Ice cream expands as it freezes, partly because water expands as it solidifies and partly because the churning motion of the dasher whips air into the mix. Homemade ice cream usually expands only about 25 per cent, which means that it is generally solider than the average store-bought product. Commercial ice creams are frozen in huge continuous-flow factory freezers which use liquid ammonia instead of rock salt and ice. In these, mixes solidify inside of 30 seconds, and air is subsequently pumped in mechanically, increasing the volume of the ice cream by as much as 50 per cent. It was once common practice among unscrupulous manufacturers to balloon ice cream investments by pumping enormous amounts of air into their product. Today the Food and Drug Administration regulates the weight of commercial ice cream. By law, a half-gallon of ice cream must weigh at least 2 pounds, 4 ounces, and the better brands weigh twice that amount or more.

Place the can filled with ice cream mix inside the outer bucket of the ice cream freezer and pack the intervening spaces with alternating layers of rock salt and ice. The salt-and-ice trick works because salt effectively lowers the temperature of ice water to 16–18°F, in contrast to the 32°F of unsalted water. Ordinary ice cubes will work here if enough of them come in contact with the sides of the metal container. Unfortunately, since ice cubes don't pack too well, enough of them usually don't. This in turn slows the freezing time, which can be a real problem, because if the cream mixture is churned too long you'll end up with butter. For efficient freezing, it's better to use crushed ice, easily produced by smashing ice cubes in a burlap bag with a baseball bat. (Snow also works well for winter ice cream making.) The salt of choice is rock salt, the chunky gray stuff used to sprinkle sidewalks in February. It is sometimes sold as "ice cream salt." Ice and salt should be layered into the bucket in a ratio of about 4 parts ice to 1 part salt. Some ice cream makers cut this ratio down to 8 to 1. One source recommends a 2-inch layer of crushed ice topped with a ¼-inch layer of rock salt, repeated to a point above the level of the ice cream mixture inside the can (not much higher, however; you don't want cold salt water in your ice cream). It's tempting to consider adding even more salt to further speed up the freezing process, but this is a trap: too much salt lowers the temperature too much, leading to uneven freezing inside the can. Only the stuff next to the walls, where it is coldest, freezes rapidly, while the mix in the middle remains soupy. It makes for lousy ice cream.

It should take about 20 to 30 minutes of churning, cranking at a rate of about 60 turns per minute, to freeze a quart of ice cream. At this point, according to one ice cream expert, the mix should be about the consistency of stiff whipped cream—or even a little thicker, on the order of mashed potatoes. It must then be hardened, either by repacking the ice-salt layers and letting the mix sit, covered, in the shade for two or three hours, or by transferring it to the freezer compartment of the refrigerator (be sure to remove the dasher first). Some authorities feel that ice cream tastes better if it is allowed to "ripen" overnight, but we've never managed to wait that long.

A note of warning: once the ice cream is finished, be sure to clean the freezer thoroughly. Rock salt and ice is a corrosive mixture and eventually will do the same awful things to the metal parts of your ice cream freezer that it does every winter to the underside of your car.

If you're not lucky enough to have grandma's old ice cream freezer, you can still buy one, hand crank and all, for about $20. Electric equivalents are somewhat more expensive, on the order of $30 to $50. Also available are even fancier models that can be filled with ice cream mix and placed directly in the freezer compartment of the refrigerator: no rock salt or crushed ice required. One drawback to these machines is that they generally have a much smaller capacity than the bucket-type freezers—

usually only one quart, while the buckets hold four or six. Also they're a little too tidy for our taste. The really prime ice creams are made out in the back yard.

Fancy Ice Creams

At the frozen stage ice cream can be rippled or ribboned, which is a nice touch, particularly if you feel like being fancy. This is easiest to do if the ice cream is hardened in flat containers like loaf pans. It works only if the mix has set quite solidly and is hard enough to slice. To ripple you simply pour warm—not hot—rippling sauce in strips across the top of the ice cream and cut it deeply into the frozen block with a knife. Then rechill. The most common rippling sauce is chocolate fudge, but good also are fruit syrups and sauces, butterscotch sauce, and coffee syrup.

In the Freezer

If you don't have an ice cream freezer, passable ice cream can still be made in shallow pans or trays in a standard freezer. The ingredients are the same, but the trick is to take the mix out periodically once it begins to set and beat it thoroughly, preferably with an electric mixer or blender. One ice cream maker suggests doing this every 30 minutes until the freezing is complete. The beating, like the constant churning of conventional ice cream freezers, prevents the formation of ice crystals which make the finished ice cream granular or sandy in texture. These same crystals turn old ice cream unpleasantly grainy. In this case the crystals accumulate as a result of "heat shock," an effect brought on by fluctuating temperatures caused, for example, by frequently opening and closing the refrigerator door. Heat shock causes the tiny ice crystals in ice cream to melt and refreeze, each time becoming bigger and grittier. Crystals any bigger than one thousandth of an inch can be detected by oral touch receptors, causing ice cream to give an awful-feeling crunch when eaten. To prevent this, commercial ice creams contain stabilizers such as guar gums and carrageen, substances much more benign than they sound. In the absence of stabilizers, you can either learn to live with an occasional crunch or you can eat your ice cream in one fell swoop. In the latter case, recommended by many, it's often helpful to point out that you are not a pig, just a texture purist.

Dish, Cone, or Soda?

Homemade ice cream freezes harder than the commercial varieties and is best thawed somewhat before serving. For half a gallon, fifteen to twenty minutes usually does the trick. The best scooping temperature for ice cream is 8°F, at which point you're all set for a dandy dish, cone, soda, or sundae. I've always preferred the cone, because there's nothing left over to wash up afterward. No one is certain who invented the ice cream cone, although everybody agrees that it first appeared at the St. Louis World's Fair in 1904. Among the rival contestants are the unnamed girl-friend of an ice cream salesman, a souvenir-stand owner named Abe Doumar, and a Syrian waffle maker named Ernest Hamwi. Hamwi, the story goes, had set up shop next door to an ice cream dealer who ran out of dishes, and Hamwi offered him some rolled waffles to use in their place. Two years later ice cream cones—called World's Fair cornucopias[6]—were on sale at Coney Island,[7] and by 1924, when a machine to mass-produce cones finally came along, Americans were eating more than 200 million a year. One of the advantages of the cone, along with its convenience (you can take it with you on the roller coaster), is that it's easy to lick. Licking is the best way to consume ice cream because the taste buds for sweetness are located at the tip of the tongue.

If you want your ice cream in fancier form than the simple cone, there are ice cream sodas and ice cream sundaes, ever-popular examples of our irresistible urge to improve upon a good thing. The traditional ice cream soda contains, in sequence, two tablespoons of flavored syrup, soda water, and a scoop of ice cream. You're not supposed to spoon it, but sip it slowly through a straw. One of the all-time soda greats is the Brown Cow: two tablespoons of chocolate syrup, Coca-Cola, and a scoop of

6. **cornucopia:** horn of plenty, traditionally a goat's horn filled with fruits to symbolize abundance.
7. **Coney Island:** a popular amusement area in Brooklyn, New York.

195

Author's Purpose

vanilla. There's also a Black Cow, made with root beer. If sodas are too tame for your taste, the next step up is the sundae, which began its career as a soda-less ice cream soda. It was invented in the 1890s to circumvent a law prohibiting the sale of "stimulating beverages" on the Sabbath; the name is said to be a deliberate misspelling of "Sunday." Recipes for sundaes consist of ice cream decked out with syrups, fruits, nuts, candies, marshmallows, whipped cream, and anything else calorically disastrous that comes to mind. The champion sundae of all time was a 26,000-pound spectacular assembled and eaten in St. Albans, Vermont, in the glorious summer of 1983. It contained 3,000 gallons of ice cream topped with peaches, pineapples, strawberries, chocolate chips, peanuts from Jimmy Carter's[8] farm, and—you'll never guess—maple syrup.

While the caloric value of the average sundae is something only to be gingerly guessed at, the nutritional content of ice cream is a matter of record. Vanilla ice cream contains about 280 calories a cup, about twice as many as whole milk. Half of those calories come from butterfat. Commercial ice cream is required by law to contain at least 10 percent butterfat, but deluxe brands crank this up to 15 or 16 per cent, and home-made ice cream is even richer, around 18 per cent. While none of this bodes well for the dieter, there are some compensations. Vanilla ice cream is a reasonably good source of Vitamin A (twice as much as whole milk), calcium (about two thirds as much as milk), and protein (about half as much as milk). It also contains thiamine, riboflavin, and Vitamin B12— it's not *all* sin.

In the early 1800s, the aged, the delicate, and the very young were warned to abstain from ice cream in the belief that it brought on potentially dangerous digestive upsets. This credo, like much of nineteenth-century medicine, has long since fallen by the wayside. It's common knowledge nowadays that ice cream is an excellent treatment for practically everything, from mild depression to heat prostration.

And they say there's no such thing as progress.

8. **Jimmy Carter:** President of the United States from 1977–1981.

The recipe below makes about one quart of ice cream. You can increase it as necessary to suit the size of your ice cream freezer.

VANILLA ICE CREAM

1	quart light or heavy cream
1½	tablespoon vanilla extract or seeds from 3 inches of vanilla bean
¾	cup sugar
¼	teaspoon salt

Scald cream and seeds from vanilla bean. Remove from heat. Add sugar and salt while cream is still warm, stirring to dissolve. Chill in refrigerator for at least one hour. If using vanilla extract, add after the mix has cooled. Transfer to prechilled ice cream freezer and freeze as described in text.

Reviewing the Selection

Answer each of the following questions without looking back at the selection.

Recalling Facts

1. The most popular ice cream flavor in the United States is
   - ☐ a. chocolate.
   - ☐ b. vanilla.
   - ☐ c. peppermint stick.
   - ☐ d. strawberry.

Understanding Main Ideas

2. The discovery that made real ice cream possible was the
   - ☐ a. invention of the electric freezer.
   - ☐ b. discovery that cream becomes stiff when whipped.
   - ☐ c. invention of electricity.
   - ☐ d. discovery that salt lowers the freezing point of water.

Placing Events in Order

3. The first step in making ice cream is
   - ☐ a. adding flavorings.
   - ☐ b. churning the mixture in an ice cream freezer.
   - ☐ c. layering ice and salt in the freezer.
   - ☐ d. choosing the kind of cream to use.

Details

4. Which of the following is *not* an example of an ancient civilization that had a form of frozen dessert?
   - ☐ a. Greek
   - ☐ b. Aztec
   - ☐ c. Chinese
   - ☐ d. Roman

5. "The beans cost about $1.50 apiece and can be used over and over until the flavor is <u>depleted</u> or can be slit open at once to release the seeds." In this context *depleted* means
   ☐ a. used up.
   ☐ b. improved.
   ☐ c. restored.
   ☐ d. blended.

Interpreting the Selection

Answer each of the following questions. You may look back at the selection if necessary.

6. Based on the article, you can infer that in the years ahead ice cream is likely to
   ☐ a. remain popular.
   ☐ b. be made with fewer ingredients.
   ☐ c. be eaten more by children than by adults.
   ☐ d. be made mostly by people at home.

7. People who make ice cream at home agree that
   ☐ a. sundaes are better than sodas or cones.
   ☐ b. artificial sweeteners are just as good as granulated sugar.
   ☐ c. vanilla beans should be the only flavoring.
   ☐ d. cream is the key ingredient to the whole product.

8. Which of the following statements is a fact?
   ☐ a. The best vanilla ice cream is made with vanilla beans, not extract.
   ☐ b. Salt lowers the freezing point of water.
   ☐ c. Adding more air makes better ice cream.
   ☐ d. Ice cream is an excellent treatment for mild depression.

9. According to the author, licking is the best way to eat ice cream because
   ☐ a. it is the least messy.
   ☐ b. the tongue is sensitive to hot and cold.
   ☐ c. the taste buds for sweetness are on the tip of the tongue.
   ☐ d. the ice cream lasts longer.

10. From this article, you can conclude that the author
    ☐ a. has probably made ice cream more than once.
    ☐ b. prefers to make vanilla ice cream.
    ☐ c. never eats commercially made ice cream.
    ☐ d. likes ice cream sodas better than sundaes.

Author's Purpose

Whether or not you like ice cream, you probably learned a lot about it by reading "The Icing of the Cream." That was Becky Rupp's purpose— to teach you some facts about ice cream, including how to make it. You may also have found the article entertaining. That was another of the author's purposes. Perhaps you have even decided to try making ice cream some day. If so, then the author achieved a third goal—to persuade you that making ice cream can be fun and easy.

Authors usually have several purposes in mind when they begin to write. One purpose might be to give an opinion about a subject. Phyllis McGinley's essay "Keeping Up with the Joneses, Jr." is an example of that purpose.

Another purpose of nonfiction writing might be to relay information. Jean George did that in "That Astounding Creator—Nature." Or a writer may want to explain how to do something as Becky Rupp does in "The Icing of the Cream."

Some writers try to persuade you to accept their opinions. Others want to entertain or amuse you. James Thurber, for example, wanted to entertain you when he wrote "The Dog That Bit People."

In this lesson you will not only explore Becky Rupp's purposes in writing "The Icing of the Cream" but also study how she achieved those purposes.

Author's Purpose: To Inform

Before reading "The Icing of the Cream," did you know that the ancient Chinese ate a flavored frozen dessert made of milk and rice? Did you know that George Washington and Thomas Jefferson loved ice cream? Those are just two of the many facts contained in Becky Rupp's article. By including such facts, Rupp provides information about the history of ice cream.

When you read factual information, you might wonder if it is accurate. Unless you have reason to suspect the author's motives in writing or to believe that the author was careless, you can usually assume that the information is accurate. You still might ask how or where the author could have acquired that information. Some authors reveal their sources of information. Others may not want to burden you with those details.

After reading this selection, you might wonder how Becky Rupp knew that George Washington loved ice cream. You might reason that George Washington could have written about ice cream in a letter or a journal that Rupp read. Perhaps someone who knew Washington wrote about the president's taste for ice cream. Of course, you do not know where Rupp found her information. But you can determine that such information might exist somewhere.

1. Reread the first paragraph of the article. Make a list of the facts contained in that paragraph. Then think about where Becky Rupp might have learned those facts. Next to each fact, write a possible source for her information.

Author's Purpose: To Instruct

In "The Icing of the Cream" Rupp teaches you how to make ice cream at home. Instruction is a special kind of information. Instruction tells you how to do or make something. Cookbooks offer instruction. So do books and articles on computer programming, woodworking, and sewing.

There are three standards you can use to judge instructions. First, they should be clear. They should tell you exactly what to do in simple, straightforward language. Second, they should be complete. They should not leave out even the most obvious step. Third, the steps in the process should be given in the order in which they must be done.

2. Read the following excerpt from the article. Explain how it meets the three standards for instruction.

When you're ready to freeze, chill the ice cream mix, metal can, and dasher for at least an hour in the refrigerator. Once the mix is cold, transfer it to the metal can, filling it no more than three-quarters full.

3. Now skim the whole article. Make a list of all the steps in making ice cream. Do you think you could make ice cream from these instructions? Explain your answer.

Author's Purpose: To Entertain

Magazines stay in business only if they satisfy their readers. For general-interest magazines, such as *Country Journal*, that usually means entertaining as well as informing readers. People want information, but they also expect to get some pleasure from reading an informative article.

Think about how Becky Rupp entertains you in "The Icing of the Cream." One method she uses is including interesting facts. Many people have learned about Marco Polo's visit to China, but how many people know that he returned to Venice with a recipe for making ice cream? Even when Rupp is describing the process of making ice cream, she includes entertaining bits of information. You do not need to know that information to make ice cream. Its purpose is simply to add to the enjoyment of reading the article.

Rupp also entertains you by using a light and personal tone. Tone, you will recall, is a writer's attitude toward his or her subject or toward the audience. It is created by a writer's choice of words, use of formal or informal language, and selection of details. Becky Rupp takes an amusing attitude toward making ice cream. She uses informal language. She talks about her own preferences, as well as those of her family. "I like peppermint stick," she declares early in the article after listing the general preferences of people in the United States.

Two other methods that Rupp uses to make her article enjoyable are talking directly to you and sharing her own experiences. She helps you feel her excitement and enthusiasm for making ice cream. By sharing her experiences and those of her family, she reassures you that you too can have fun. Like her, you can trust your own instincts when you make ice cream.

Rupp explains, for example, that according to some experts, once the ice cream is made it "tastes better if it is allowed to 'ripen' overnight, but we've never managed to wait that long." Clearly, the ice cream made in her home is too good to be left uneaten for a day. So she and her family happily ignore the experts and eat it up as soon as it is made.

4. Skim the article to find an example of: (a) a fact that seems to be included simply to entertain the reader, (b) the author's informal and entertaining language, (c) the author's personal preference, (d) the author talking directly to you.

Organization and Author's Purpose

Like most articles, "The Icing of the Cream" begins with a lead paragraph that is meant to capture your interest. The lead paragraph lets you know that Rupp intends to inform and interest you. "The Icing of the Cream" also contains a device of organization that the other two articles you read in this book did not have: The article has subheads—short titles within an article that identify the beginning of each new topic.

5. Make a list of the subheads in the article. What do they tell you about how the article is organized?

As you have learned, an instructional article must be organized in a straightforward way. The steps must be explained in the correct order or you cannot finish the project successfully. In "The Icing of the Cream" Rupp follows the standard order of what must be done first, second, third, and so on. She also combines many facts with the instructions.

Rupp could have organized the article in another way. She could have given all the interesting bits of information about ice cream in the beginning of the article. Then, she could have given you a numbered list of the steps to follow in making ice cream. Why didn't the author organize the article in that way?

One answer is that by mixing factual information with the instructions, she makes the article more interesting. Another answer is that some facts help explain why a step has to be completed exactly as she describes. Knowing why something must be done in a certain way helps you decide what to do if anything goes wrong.

6. *Read the following passage about how much sugar to add to the ice cream mix. Then describe how the facts help explain the instructions.*

> *Recipes vary, but the rule of thumb is 3 to 4 tablespoons of sugar per 2½ cups of cream. It's best not to stray too far from this formula, because sugar also functions as an antifreeze: too little and the ice cream will be too hard; too much and it will be slush.*

Language and Author's Purpose

As you have learned, "The Icing of the Cream" is written in informal language. Many words and phrases are colloquial expressions that are mainly used in conversation. Some of Rupp's words are slang. Slang is even more informal than colloquial language. Slang consists of newly created words, such as *nerd,* or variations of everyday words, such as *biggie.* Some slang expressions develop in a particular region or among a small group of people. Rupp's use of informal language gives the article its light, entertaining tone.

7. *Read the two passages that follow. How does the language in them differ? What purpose does each passage serve?*

> a. *Ice cream expands as it freezes, partly because water expands as it solidifies and partly because the churning motion of the dasher whips air into the mix.*

> b. *For half a gallon, fifteen to twenty minutes usually does the trick.*

Rupp uses language in other ways to make her article more entertaining. At times, she uses alliteration. As you learned in Chapter 1, alliteration is the close repetition of similar sounds at the beginnings of words. "Early ice cream," Rupp writes, "was fairly sloppy stuff." You can almost feel the texture of that "sloppy stuff." Rupp's alliteration adds a cheerful tone to her article.

8. Find another example of alliteration in the article. Explain what effect the alliteration has on you.

Author Becky Rupp also uses figurative language to make her article more entertaining. As you have learned, figurative language involves using words and phrases in unusual ways to create strong, vivid images, to focus attention on certain ideas, or to compare things that are basically different. When words or phrases are used figuratively, they have meanings that differ from their usual, or literal, meanings. One figure of speech that you studied was hyperbole, which exaggerates the truth in order to express an idea or feeling.

Think about this description that Rupp gives: "Dolley Madison— 'The First Lady of Ice Cream'—served a mountain of it (pink) at her husband's second inaugural ball. . . . " The word *mountain* does not actually refer to an elevated piece of land. Instead, it means that Dolley Madison served an enormous amount of ice cream. Rupp deliberately compares the ice cream the First Lady served to a mountain in order to cast an amusing light on the scene.

9. Choose a sentence or paragraph in the article that you think best captures the author's purposes to instruct, to entertain, and to persuade. Explain how the language in the passage you chose reflects the author's purposes.

Questions for Thought and Discussion

The questions and activities that follow will help you explore "The Icing of the Cream" in more depth and at the same time develop your critical thinking skills.

1. **Applying Knowledge.** In the article Becky Rupp says that salt lowers the freezing point of water. Given that information, explain why rock salt is spread on icy and snowy roads.

2. **Forming a Theory.** Scientists and social scientists observe events and form theories to explain those events. They then test their theories through research and experimentation. Form a theory about why

people in the United States eat twice as much ice cream as people in any other nation do. Base your theory on what you know about the history, economy, technology, and culture of the United States.

3. **Analyzing an Author's Organization.** Find the section in "The Icing of the Cream" that begins with the subhead *The Ingredients.* Identify the topic sentence in each paragraph of that section. Explain how the topic sentences relate to the subhead.

Writing About Literature

Several suggestions for writing projects follow. You may be asked to complete one or more of these projects. If you have any questions about how to begin a writing assignment, review Using the Writing Process, beginning on page 341.

1. **Writing an Instructional Article.** Write a brief instructional article about a process that you know well. For example, you might write an article about how to prepare a certain food, how to ice skate, or how to win at video games. Make your article as informative, instructive, and entertaining as possible by using the techniques that Becky Rupp used in "The Icing of the Cream."

2. **Expressing a Personal View.** Write an essay in praise of ice cream or some other food that you like. Describe what you like about the food. Use details, descriptive language, and anecdotes that will help your readers see, smell, taste, and hear the food. Include anecdotes or factual information about the food you have chosen.

3. **Using Language to Establish a Tone.** As you have learned, Becky Rupp uses informal language to create a light tone in her article. Choose an experience that you have had recently, such as forgetting your keys, meeting an old friend, or finding five dollars. First describe the experience in a light, amusing tone. Then take the same story and present it in a different tone. For example, you might use a mournful, threatening, or sarcastic tone. In each case, think about how you can use language to create your tone.

Diaries, Letters, and Speeches

*T*he selections in Unit Three represent three types of nonfiction that have one thing in common: they were orginally meant for a specific audience different from the one they now have. In this unit you will read excerpts from a diary, a sampling of letters written by two well-known people, and three complete speeches.

When you read diaries, letters, and speeches, you need first to identify the audience for whom they were orginally intended. A diary is a daily record of a person's experiences and thoughts. A letter is usually written from one person to another. Speeches are talks addressed to a particular audience, and they are meant to be heard, not read. Some diaries, letters, and speeches are published because they are of interest to a wider audience.

Because of their varied purposes, different standards must be used to evaluate diaries, letters, and speeches than are used to judge other forms of writing. Writers of diaries and personal letters generally do not revise and polish their works. Although they are, in a sense, only "first drafts," some diaries and letters contain powerful messages.

Speeches are different from diaries and letters. Some speeches are intended to entertain, others to persuade, still others to honor a person or an occasion. Though some speeches have been revised and polished, they are still missing an important element—the sound of the speaker's voice and the power of the speaker's personality.

When you read a speech, you cannot hear the speaker's voice bringing the words to life. Nor can you see the speaker's facial expressions and body movements. So when you read the speeches that are included in Unit Three, try to imagine how each speaker looked and sounded.

In the lessons in Unit Three, you will learn how authors communicate their thoughts and feelings in ways that affect larger audiences than they might ever have intended.

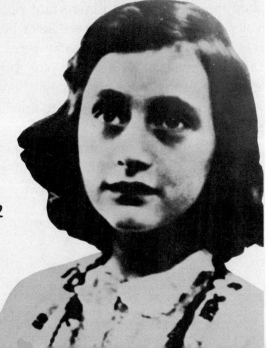

Dit is een foto, zoals
ik me zou wensen,
altijd zo te zijn.
Dan had ik nog wel
een kans om naar
Holywood te komen.

Anne Frank.
10 Oct. 1942

"This is a photo as I would wish myself
to look all the time. Then I would maybe
have a chance to come to Hollywood."

Anne Frank, Oct. 10, 1942

Chapter 9

Selection

Life in Hiding
Excerpts from
The Diary of a Young Girl

ANNE FRANK

Lesson

Facts, Feelings, and Thoughts

About the Selection

Anne Frank was a thirteen-year-old schoolgirl in Holland when she was given a diary. She soon began to record her thoughts and feelings about the events in her life. Less than a month after she started her diary, her life suddenly changed. She and her family were forced to hide from the Nazis because they were Jewish. For more than two years, Anne kept a record in her diary of her family's life in hiding.

A diary is a special form of nonfiction writing—a daily record of a person's thoughts, experiences, and feelings. Most diarists consider their writing private, and some keep their diaries hidden. Many ordinary people who would never think of writing for publication keep diaries. Some famous people have confided their thoughts to diaries. And a few people, such as Anne Frank, have become well known simply because their diaries were published and widely read.

Anne Frank was born in Frankfurt, Germany, in 1929. Her father, Otto, was a respected businessman. A few years after Anne's birth, Adolf Hitler rose to power in Germany. Hitler believed that Germans belonged to a "master race" that was destined to rule the world. He considered other races inferior. He particularly hated Jews, blacks, gypsies, and people with physical disabilities.

In the years before Hitler gained power, he and his followers in the

Nazi party promoted anti-Semitism, or hatred of Jews. Once in power, he began to persecute Jews. He expelled them from government positions and forbade them to teach in the universities.

Otto Frank felt that life could only get worse for his family under Hitler's rule. In 1934 he moved his family to Amsterdam, Holland, and began a business there. For five years, Anne led a normal life divided between family, school, and friends. Then in 1939 Germany invaded Poland, sparking World War II. By 1940, Germany had occupied Holland, Belgium, and France. Like all the Jews in occupied Europe, the Franks were threatened by Hitler's anti-Semitism.

All Jews were required to wear a yellow star on their outer garments so they could be easily identified. Jews were not allowed to own businesses, so Mr. Frank had to resign from his business. He left its management to his partner, who was not Jewish. Jews were forbidden to attend school with Christians, so Anne had to leave her school and go to a special Jewish school.

During the war, Hitler formulated his "final solution" to what he called "the Jewish problem." The solution was the destruction of the Jews. All over Europe, Jews were rounded up and transported to extermination camps. To escape that fate, Mr. Frank made plans to take his family into hiding. On July 5, 1942, Margot, Anne's older sister, was called up for deportation. The Franks immediately gathered a few belongings and went into hiding. Their hiding place was on the upper floor of Mr. Frank's place of business. A bookcase concealed the entrance to the staircase that led to their hideout.

Mr. Frank's partner and a few employees knew of the hiding place. For two years, at great risk to themselves, they supplied the refugees with food and other necessities, as well as news of the outside world. Eventually, the Franks were joined by four other people—Mr. and Mrs. Van Daan, their son Peter, and Mr. Dussel, an elderly dentist.

Life was difficult in the "Secret Annexe," as the hiding place was called. Food was scarce. The eight refugees had to remain perfectly quiet during business hours to avoid arousing the suspicion of workers in the office below. Harder still was the problem of eight people, each with his or her own personality, crowded into a very small space. Their arguments and disagreements were frequent subjects for Anne's diary entries.

In June 1944 the residents of the Secret Annexe learned that the Allies had liberated France from the Germans and were marching toward Germany. They began to hope that the war would end soon, and that they would survive. On August 4, 1944, however, Hitler's secret police, the Gestapo, discovered the hiding place. All eight residents were sent to concentration camps. Mr. Frank was the only one who survived. Anne died in a camp in Belsen, Germany, probably in early March 1945, just two months before the war in Europe ended.

Friends of the Franks discovered Anne's diary in the Secret Annexe. When Mr. Frank returned to Holland after the war, they gave it to him. He circulated a few copies to friends as a memorial to his family. His friends urged him to let the world see Anne's diary. *The Diary of a Young Girl* was published in Holland in 1947 and in the United States in 1952. It has since been published in more than thirty countries.

Anne Frank has become known around the world because of her diary. Yet she never intended the diary to be read by anyone. It was a record of her private thoughts. In her diary Anne addresses an imaginary friend whom she calls Kitty. Anne opens her heart freely to Kitty. Her diary is the expression of an ordinary person caught up in extraordinary circumstances. Anne's naturalness and honesty are the qualities that have attracted millions of readers to her story.

Lesson Preview

The lesson that follows "Life in Hiding" focuses on the facts, feelings, and thoughts in Anne Frank's diary. Like most diarists, Anne Frank kept a diary for her own personal satisfaction. In it she recorded facts, feelings, and thoughts about her life. She did not, however, consciously divide her diary into those categories.

One way for you to appreciate a diarist's work is to examine its various elements. Are the facts Anne records accurate? Is she honest about her feelings? How clearly does she express her thoughts?

The questions that follow will help you find that information in Anne Frank's diary. As you read, think about how you would answer these questions.

1 What facts about wartime Holland do you learn from the diary? Do you think those facts can be trusted?

2 What different feelings does Anne express in her diary entries?

3 What conclusions does Anne draw about her life before and after her family went into hiding?

Vocabulary

Here are some difficult words that appear in the selection that follows. Study the words and their definitions, as well as the sentences that show how the words are used. This will help you get the most from your reading.

insufferable intolerable; unbearable. *My headache was so insufferable that I had to take an aspirin and lie down.*

impertinent rude; insolent. *The speaker was insulted by his opponent's impertinent questions.*

despondency dejection; depression. *The writer's despondency about life is reflected in his depressing novels.*

embryonic not fully developed. *George's idea for the science fair was still in the embryonic stage when he realized he had only one week left to complete the project.*

nonchalance casualness; unconcern. *Sue, nervous about remembering her lines, was angry at Tom's nonchalance and lack of concern about their audition.*

Life in Hiding

Excerpts from

The Diary of a Young Girl

ANNE FRANK

The first two diary entries that you will read were written in January 1943, about six months after the Franks went into hiding. The third and fourth entries were written in March 1944, after twenty months in hiding.

Wednesday, 13 January, 1943

Dear Kitty,

Everything has upset me again this morning, so I wasn't able to finish a single thing properly.

It is terrible outside. Day and night more of those poor miserable people are being dragged off, with nothing but a rucksack and a little money. On the way they are deprived even of these possessions. Families are torn apart, the men, women, and children all being separated. Children coming home from school find that their parents have disappeared. Women return from shopping to find their homes shut up and their families gone.

The Dutch people are anxious too, their sons are being sent to Germany. Everyone is afraid.

And every night hundreds of planes fly over Holland and go to German towns, where the earth is plowed up by their bombs, and every hour hundreds and thousands of people are killed in Russia and Africa. No one is able to keep out of it, the whole globe is waging war and although it is going better for the Allies, the end is not yet in sight.

And as for us, we are fortunate. Yes, we are luckier than millions of people. It is quiet and safe here, and we are, so to speak, living on capital.[1] We are even so selfish as to talk about "after the war," brighten up at the thought of having new clothes and new shoes, whereas we really ought to save every penny, to help other people, and save what is left from the wreckage after the war.

The children here run about in just a thin blouse and clogs; no coat, no hat, no stockings, and no one helps them. Their tummies are empty; they chew an old carrot to stay the pangs,[2] go from their cold homes out into the cold street and, when they get to school, find themselves in an even colder classroom. Yes, it has even got so bad in Holland that countless children stop the passers-by and beg for a piece of bread. I could go on for hours about all the suffering the war has brought, but then I would only make myself more dejected. There is nothing we can do but wait as calmly as we can till the misery comes to an end. Jews and Christians wait, the whole earth waits; and there are many who wait for death.

Yours, Anne

Saturday, 30 January, 1943

Dear Kitty,

I'm boiling with rage, and yet I mustn't show it. I'd like to stamp my feet, scream, give Mummy a good shaking, cry, and I don't know

---

1. **living on capital:** capital is accumulated wealth. Anne probably meant that they were not struggling to maintain existence like so many others.
2. **stay the pangs:** stop the hunger pains.

what else, because of the horrible words, mocking looks, and accusations which are leveled at me repeatedly every day, and find their mark, like shafts from a tightly strung bow, and which are just as hard to draw from my body.

I would like to shout to Margot, Van Daan, Dussel—and Daddy too—"Leave me in peace, let me sleep one night at least without my pillow being wet with tears, my eyes burning and my head throbbing. Let me get away from it all, preferably away from the world!" But I can't do that, they mustn't know my despair, I can't let them see the wounds which they have caused, I couldn't bear their sympathy and their kind-hearted jokes, it would only make me want to scream all the more. If I talk, everyone thinks I'm showing off; when I'm silent they think I'm ridiculous; rude if I answer, sly if I get a good idea, lazy if I'm tired, selfish if I eat a mouthful more than I should, stupid, cowardly, crafty, etc., etc. The whole day long I hear nothing else but that I am an insufferable baby, and although I laugh about it and pretend not to take any notice, I *do* mind. I would like to ask God to give me a different nature, so that I didn't put everyone's back up. But that can't be done. I've got the nature that has been given to me and I'm sure it can't be bad. I do my very best to please everybody, far more than they'd ever guess. I try to laugh it all off, because I don't want to let them see my trouble. More than once, after a whole string of undeserved rebukes, I have flared up at Mummy: "I don't care what you say anyhow. Leave me alone: I'm a hopeless case anyway." Naturally, I was then told I was rude and was virtually ignored for two days; and then, all at once, it was quite forgotten, and I was treated like everyone else again. It is impossible for me to be all sugar one day and spit venom[3] the next. I'd rather choose the golden mean[4] (which is not so golden), keep my thoughts to myself, and try for *once* to be just as disdainful to them as they are to me. Oh, if only I could!

Yours, Anne

---

3. **venom:** poison.
4. **golden mean:** the happy medium between two extremes.

Dear Kitty,

If I think now of my life in 1942, it all seems so unreal. It was quite a different Anne who enjoyed that heavenly existence from the Anne who has grown wise within these walls. Yes, it was a heavenly life. Boy friends at every turn, about twenty friends and acquaintances of my own age, the darling of nearly all the teachers, spoiled from top to toe by Mummy and Daddy, lots of sweets, enough pocket money, what more could one want?

You will certainly wonder by what means I got around all these people. Peter's word "attractiveness" is not altogether true. All the teachers were entertained by my cute answers, my amusing remarks, my smiling face, and my questioning looks. That is all I was—a terrible flirt, coquettish and amusing. I had one or two advantages, which kept me rather in favor. I was industrious, honest, and frank. I would never have dreamed of cribbing[5] from anyone else. I shared my sweets generously, and I wasn't conceited.

Wouldn't I have become rather forward with so much admiration? It was a good thing that in the midst of, at the height of, all this gaiety, I suddenly had to face reality, and it took me at least a year to get used to the fact that there was no more admiration forthcoming.

How did I appear at school? The one who thought of new jokes and pranks, always "king of the castle," never in a bad mood, never a crybaby. No wonder everyone liked to cycle with me, and I got their attentions.

Now I look back at that Anne as an amusing, but very superficial girl, who has nothing to do with the Anne of today. Peter said quite rightly about me: "If ever I saw you, you were always surrounded by two or more boys and a whole troupe of girls. You were always laughing and always the center of everything!"

-----

5. **cribbing:** cheating.

What is left of this girl? Oh, don't worry, I haven't forgotten how to laugh or to answer back readily. I'm just as good if not better, at criticizing people, and I can still flirt if . . . I wish. That's not it though, I'd like that sort of life again for an evening, a few days, or even a week; the life which seems so carefree and gay. But at the end of that week, I should be dead beat and would be only too thankful to listen to anyone who began to talk about something sensible. I don't want followers, but friends, admirers who fall not for a flattering smile but for what one does and for one's character.

I know quite well that the circle around me would be much smaller. But what does that matter, as long as one still keeps a few sincere friends?

Yet I wasn't entirely happy in 1942 in spite of everything; I often felt deserted, but because I was on the go the whole day long, I didn't think about it and enjoyed myself as much as I could. Consciously or unconsciously, I tried to drive away the emptiness I felt with jokes and pranks. Now I think seriously about life and what I have to do. One period of my life is over forever. The carefree schooldays are gone, never to return.

I don't even long for them any more; I have outgrown them, I can't just only enjoy myself as my serious side is always there.

I look upon my life up till the New Year, as it were, through a powerful magnifying glass. The sunny life at home, then coming here in 1942, the sudden change, the quarrels, the bickerings. I couldn't understand it, I was taken by surprise, and the only way I could keep up some bearing was by being impertinent.

The first half of 1943: my fits of crying, the loneliness, how I slowly began to see all my faults and shortcomings, which are so great and which seemed much greater then. During the day I deliberately talked about anything and everything that was farthest from my thoughts, tried to draw Pim[6] to me; but couldn't. Alone I had to face the difficult task of changing myself, to stop the everlasting reproaches, which were so oppressive and which reduced me to such terrible despondency.

---

6. **Pim:** Anne's nickname for her father.

Things improved slightly in the second half of the year, I became a young woman and was treated more like a grownup. I started to think, and write stories, and came to the conclusion that the others no longer had the right to throw me about like an india-rubber ball. I wanted to change in accordance with my own desires. But *one* thing that struck me even more was when I realized that even Daddy would never become my confidant over everything. I didn't want to trust anyone but myself any more.

At the beginning of the New Year: the second great change, my dream. . . . And with it I discovered my longing, not for a girl friend, but for a boy friend. I also discovered my inward happiness and my defensive armor of superficiality and gaiety. In due time I quieted down and discovered my boundless desire for all that is beautiful and good.

And in the evening, when I lie in bed and end my prayers with the words, "I thank you, God, for all that is good and dear and beautiful," I am filled with joy. Then I think about "the good" of going into hiding, of my health and with my whole being of the "dearness" of Peter, of that which is still embryonic and impressionable and which we neither of us dare to name or touch, of that which will come sometime; love, the future, happiness and of "the beauty" which exists in the world; the world, nature, beauty and all, all that is exquisite and fine.

I don't think then of all the misery, but of the beauty that still remains. This is one of the things that Mummy and I are so entirely different about. Her counsel when one feels melancholy is: "Think of all the misery in the world and be thankful that you are not sharing in it!" My advice is: "Go outside, to the fields, enjoy nature and the sunshine, go out and try to recapture happiness in yourself and in God. Think of all the beauty that's still left in and around you and be happy!"

I don't see how Mummy's idea can be right, because then how are you supposed to behave if you go through the misery yourself? Then you are lost. On the contrary, I've found that there is always some beauty left—in nature, sunshine, freedom, in yourself; these can all help you. Look at these things, then you find yourself again, and God, and then you regain your balance.

And whoever is happy will make others happy too. He who has courage and faith will never perish in misery!

Yours, Anne

Sunday, 12 March, 1944

Dear Kitty,

I can't seem to sit still lately; I run upstairs and down and then back again. I love talking to Peter, but I'm always afraid of being a nuisance. He has told me a bit about the past, about his parents and about himself. It's not half enough though and I ask myself why it is that I always long for more. He used to think I was unbearable; and I returned the compliment; now I have changed my opinion, has he changed his too?

I think so; still it doesn't necessarily mean that we shall become great friends, although as far as I am concerned it would make the time here much more bearable. But still, I won't get myself upset about it— I see quite a lot of him and there's no need to make you unhappy about it too, Kitty, just because I feel so terrible.

On Saturday afternoon I felt in such a whirl, after hearing a whole lot of sad news, that I went and lay on my divan for a sleep. I only wanted to sleep to stop myself thinking. I slept till four o'clock, then I had to go into the living room. I found it difficult to answer all Mummy's questions and think of some little excuse to tell Daddy, as an explanation for my long sleep. I resorted to a "headache," which wasn't a lie, as I had one . . . but inside!

Ordinary people, ordinary girls, teenagers like myself, will think I'm a bit cracked with all my self-pity. Yes, that's what it is, but I pour out my heart to you, then for the rest of the day I'm as impudent, gay, and self-confident as I can be, in order to avoid questions and getting on my own nerves.

Margot is very sweet and would like me to trust her, but still, I can't tell her everything. She's a darling, she's good and pretty, but she lacks the nonchalance for conducting deep discussions; she takes me so seriously, much too seriously, and then thinks about her queer little sister for a long time afterwards, looks searchingly at me, at every word I say, and keeps on thinking: "Is this just a joke or does she really mean it?" I think that's because we are together the whole day long, and that if I trusted someone completely, then I shouldn't want them hanging around me all the time.

When shall I finally untangle my thoughts, when shall I find peace and rest within myself again?

Yours, Anne

Reviewing the Selection

Answer each of the following questions without looking back at the selection.

Recalling Facts

1. Before her family went into hiding, Anne
   - ☐ a. had many friends.
   - ☐ b. was unpopular at school.
   - ☐ c. argued constantly with her sister.
   - ☐ d. was in love with Peter Van Daan.

Understanding Main Ideas

2. Anne believed that life in hiding
   - ☐ a. made her more even-tempered.
   - ☐ b. could be bearable if she were alone.
   - ☐ c. brought out her serious side.
   - ☐ d. made her appreciate other people.

Placing Events in Order

3. Anne usually argued with her mother after
   - ☐ a. her mother tried to get her to work.
   - ☐ b. Anne spent time with Peter.
   - ☐ c. her mother criticized her unfairly.
   - ☐ d. Margot complained about Anne to her mother.

Finding Supporting Details

4. One thing that upset Anne was
   - ☐ a. the silence in their hiding place.
   - ☐ b. the suffering of people on the "outside."
   - ☐ c. Peter's desire to escape.
   - ☐ d. people's asking to read her diary.

Facts, Feelings, and Thoughts

5. "That is all I was—a terrible flirt, <u>coquettish</u> and amusing." In this context *coquettish* means
   - ☐ a. troublemaking.
   - ☐ b. acting like a flirt.
   - ☐ c. acting serious.
   - ☐ d. entertaining.

Interpreting the Selection

Answer each of the following questions. You may look back at the selection if necessary.

6. In her two years in hiding Anne learned
   - ☐ a. how to get what she wanted from people.
   - ☐ b. that she did not like her father.
   - ☐ c. that Margot was jealous of her.
   - ☐ d. that her feelings about people could change.

7. A word that could be used to describe Anne as she was in March 1944 is
   - ☐ a. thoughtful.
   - ☐ b. frivolous.
   - ☐ c. angry.
   - ☐ d. immature.

Recognizing Fact and Opinion

8. Which of the following statements based on the diary is an opinion?
   - ☐ a. Every night many planes flew over Holland.
   - ☐ b. Anne felt wounded by the criticism of others.
   - ☐ c. Anne had many friends at her school.
   - ☐ d. Margot took Anne too seriously.

Identifying Cause and Effect

9. Things improved somewhat for Anne in 1943 after she
   - ☐ a. began to keep her diary.
   - ☐ b. stopped thinking about Peter all the time.
   - ☐ c. was treated more like an adult by her family.
   - ☐ d. made her father her confidant.

Drawing Conclusions

10. Before going into hiding, the Franks
    - ☐ a. were very poor.
    - ☐ b. had a comfortable middle-class life.
    - ☐ c. had few friends in their community.
    - ☐ d. argued constantly with one another.

Facts, Feelings, and Thoughts

Diaries are different from other types of nonfiction because they are not written for an audience. Most diary writers are not concerned about the effect their diaries will have on others. They do not expect anyone to read what they have written. Of course, some celebrities who keep diaries may plan to publish them. Even Anne Frank, after she had been in hiding for some time, began to think that she might publish her diary after the war. Still, diarists write mainly for themselves.

Since diaries are not written for a general audience, why do people read them? Most people read diaries to get a glimpse into another person's life and to understand that person's character. They expect to get a clearer understanding of what the person is, or was, like.

Through reading about others, you also learn more about yourself. You may compare your thoughts and feelings to those of the diarist. From Anne Frank's diary, you get an intimate and revealing view of what it was like to be a Jew in hiding in German-occupied Europe. You get a glimpse not only of Anne Frank's daily struggles but also of the people with whom she shared her hideout.

A diary is a record told in the first person. The subject of the diary is the author. By reading "Life in Hiding," you see Anne as she sees herself. She confides a lot of information to her imaginary friend, Kitty.

But it is up to you to distinguish the different types of information she reveals. From that information you can decide what the diary shows about Anne. In this lesson you will examine the facts, feelings, and thoughts in Anne Frank's diary.

The Diarist's Facts

Like other kinds of writers, the diarist is selective about the facts that he or she records. When Anne Frank confided in her diary, she wrote about the events that were most important to her. She did not, of course, record every event that took place during her two years in hiding.

Although Anne's diary contains many facts about her life in the Secret Annexe, she was also concerned with what was going on "outside." Anne probably got most of this information from her friends in the office downstairs. These trusted friends visited the Franks daily. They brought the Franks food and other necessities. Just as important, they brought news of the outside world. The news made a great impression on Anne.

In her diary entry of January 13, 1943, Anne paints a picture of the outside world. How well does she describe that world? Remember that a good factual description gives as much specific information as possible. Anne uses secondary information. She did not witness the hardships she records here. Yet she faithfully includes the specific details that her sources must have described.

1. Read the following passage and list at least three facts that Anne includes. Then summarize the picture of life in wartime Holland that you get from these facts.

> *The children here run about in just a thin blouse and clogs; no coat, no hat, no stockings, and no one helps them. Their tummies are empty; they chew on an old carrot to stay the pangs, go from their cold homes out into the cold street and, when they get to school, find themselves in an even colder classroom. Yes, it has even got so bad in Holland that countless children stop the passers-by and beg for a piece of bread.*

The Diarist's Feelings

Beyond the facts revealed in a diary, the feelings that are expressed give you an insight into the diarist's life and character. Anne's world—a hiding place in wartime Holland—is very different from the world of most young people today. Yet Anne's feelings are interesting because they are not so different from those of many teenagers.

As you have learned, diarists are free to express their true feelings openly and honestly. They do not concern themselves with whether or not an audience will respond critically to their feelings. In "Life in Hiding" Anne Frank confides a variety of feelings to her diary.

2. Skim each of the four diary entries. List at least one feeling that Anne expresses in each entry.

Anne does not simply say, I felt sad or depressed or happy. Rather, she shows how she felt by giving specific details. Read this passage from Anne's diary entry for January 30, 1943:

> I'm boiling with rage, and yet I mustn't show it. I'd like to stamp my feet, scream, give Mummy a good shaking, cry, and I don't know what else, because of the horrible words, mocking looks, and accusations which are leveled at me repeatedly every day, and find their mark, like shafts from a tightly strung bow, and which are just as hard to draw from my body.

Notice the figures of speech that Anne uses to describe her feelings. She says that she is "boiling with rage." That phrase is an example of hyperbole. It gives a much better picture of Anne's feelings than if she had simply said, I'm so angry. The word *boiling* is an exaggeration. Yet it suggests that feelings are about to bubble out of her in an uncontrollable way. It also suggests the physical heat that an angry person often feels.

Anne uses figurative language to describe the impact "of the horrible words, mocking looks, and accusations" of others. She says such criticisms are "like shafts." Like arrows, they wound her deeply and she cannot easily forget them. When Anne compares the words and looks of others to arrows, she is using a figure of speech called a simile. A <u>simile</u>

is a direct comparison between two unlike things that are connected by *like, as,* or *resembles* or the verb *appears* or *seems.* As with other kinds of figurative language, the purpose of a simile is to give you a vivid new way of looking at one of the things.

In the passage just cited, Anne creates a clear picture of her feelings by using figurative language. She also shows her feelings by telling how she would like to stamp her feet, scream, shake her mother, and cry.

3. Reread the first two paragraphs of the diary entry for March 12, 1944. What feelings does Anne describe? How does she make those feelings vivid?

The Diarist's Thoughts

Thinking is different from feeling. Feelings are spontaneous, or unplanned, reactions to events. They cannot really be controlled, although you can control how you express them. Thinking, on the other hand, is a conscious act. When you think, you choose to examine something in a rational, logical way.

Some diarists do not think clearly about their lives. Anne Frank, however, makes a conscious effort to think clearly about the events she witnesses and about her own feelings. People use many methods to help themselves think rationally. Anne Frank uses at least three.

Reviewing the Facts. First, Anne reviews the facts. On March 7, 1944, she looked back on her life in 1942. As she did so, she reviewed the facts in this way.

> Yes, it was a heavenly life. Boy friends at every turn, about twenty friends and acquaintances of my own age, the darling of nearly all the teachers, spoiled from top to toe by Mummy and Daddy, lots of sweets, enough pocket money, what more could one want?

Anne may sound boastful or conceited, but remember that she was writing just for herself. Remember, too, the circumstances of her life in hiding—she may have been trying to cheer herself by recalling a time when her life was "heavenly." Yet even as she lists the facts, she is also judging them.

4. *What facts does Anne give you about her life in 1942? What judgments does she make about those facts?*

Using Objectivity. The second method for rational thinking that Anne uses is objectivity. <u>Objectivity</u> means putting aside personal feelings and prejudices when looking at events. It is not always easy to tell if a writer is being objective. But a writer who examines both the positive and the negative sides of a situation or a person shows some objectivity. You can also judge a writer's objectivity by comparing what the writer says with what he or she does.

5. *Read the following passage from Anne Frank's diary. Do you think Anne is being objective here? Give reasons for your answer.*

All the teachers were entertained by my cute answers, my amusing remarks, my smiling face, and my questioning looks. That is all I was—a terrible flirt, coquettish and amusing. I had one or two advantages, which kept me rather in favor. I was industrious, honest, and frank. I would never have dreamed of cribbing from anyone else. I shared my sweets generously, and I wasn't conceited.

Using Perspective. The third method of clear thinking that Anne Frank uses is perspective. <u>Perspective</u> means examining things, people, or events in as general a way as possible to determine their true relationship to each other. Allowing time to pass is one way of achieving perspective. You can usually understand a situation more clearly if you study it after some time has gone by. For example, a conversation that made you furious three months ago may seem much less important today. Anne Frank uses the perspective of time when she looks back on her life before she and her family went into hiding.

Examining a situation from another person's point of view is a second way of achieving perspective. That is not always easy to do, but it is possible to imagine how others view you. Anne Frank tries to look at herself from the point of view of other people when she writes: "How did I appear at school? The one who thought of new jokes and pranks, always 'king of the castle,' never in a bad mood, never a crybaby."

6. *Reread paragraphs 5 through 8 of Anne's diary entry for March 7, 1944. Find at least one example in which Anne (a) shows objectivity, (b) uses the perspective of time, and (c) uses the perspective of another person's point of view.*

The Diary as a Self-Portrait

Anne Frank did not set out to paint a picture of her character. Yet the diary is a self-portrait. By understanding her feelings and thoughts, you get to know her character. She is a person whose emotions are in turmoil, and she is someone who has deep feelings.

7. *Read the following passages. What does each tell you about Anne Frank's character?*

a. *And as for us, we are fortunate. Yes, we are luckier than millions of people. It is quiet and safe here, and we are, so to speak, living on capital.*

b. *And in the evening, when I lie in bed and end my prayers with the words, "I thank you, God, for all that is good and dear and beautiful," I am filled with joy. Then I think about "the good" of going into hiding, of my health and with my whole being of the "dearness" of Peter, of that which is still embryonic and impressionable and which we neither of us dare to name or touch, of that which will come sometime; love, the future, happiness and of "the beauty" which exists in the world; the world, nature, beauty and all, all that is exquisite and fine.*

Diarists often write about their lives in an attempt to understand themselves. As they record facts, feelings, and thoughts, they try to draw conclusions. Conclusions must be based on evidence. After looking back on her life in 1942, Anne Frank was ready to draw some conclusions about herself before and after she went into hiding.

8. Skim the diary entry for March 7, 1944. Explain at least one conclusion that Anne Frank draws about herself.

Questions for Thought and Discussion

The questions and activities that follow will help you explore "Life in Hiding" in more depth and at the same time develop your critical thinking skills.

1. **Comparing and Contrasting.** Compare the Anne Frank of 1942 with the Anne Frank of 1944. How are they similar? How are they different? Do you think Anne would have changed in the same way if the war had not forced the Franks into hiding? Explain your answer.

2. **Interpreting.** In the diary entry for March 7, 1944, Anne refers to "the 'dearness' of Peter" and "that which is still embryonic and impressionable and which we neither of us dare to name or touch." What do you think she means by those words?

3. **Expressing an Opinion.** Review the last three paragraphs of the diary entry for March 7, 1944, in which Anne compares her mother's ideas on unhappiness with her own. With whom do you agree? Why?

4. **Speculating.** Some diarists begin their entries with "Dear Diary." Others just give the date and start writing. Why do you think Anne begins each entry "Dear Kitty" and signs "Yours, Anne"?

Writing About Literature

Several suggestions for writing projects follow. You may be asked to complete one or more of these projects. If you have any questions about how to begin a writing assignment, review Using the Writing Process, beginning on page 341.

1. **Keeping a Diary.** Keep a diary for at least a week. Write an entry every day. Try to record events that are important to you, as well as your feelings and thoughts about those events.

2. **Taking Another Point of View.** Describe Anne from the point of view of Mrs. Frank, Peter, or Margot. Use incidents in the excerpts you read as the basis on which to write about Anne.

3. **Analyzing Character.** Write a letter to a new friend in which you compare the person you were two or three years ago to the person you are today. You might describe changes both in your physical appearance and in your character. Try to be objective and to use perspective in your description.

4. **Describing an Interview.** Imagine that Anne Frank had lived and you were able to interview her soon after the war. Write an article describing your interview with Anne. Include both description and dialogue to show what Anne was like, what you thought of her, and what issues you discussed.

Chapter 10

Selection *The President Visits Panama*
Excerpts from
**Theodore Roosevelt's Letters
to His Children**

THEODORE ROOSEVELT

Lesson *Author's Viewpoint and Frame of Reference*

About the Selection

Letters are addressed to a particular audience—the person to whom the letter is written. Like other kinds of writing, they contain the thoughts, ideas, and opinions of the writer.

There are several kinds of letters. The letters you write to friends are personal letters. Like diaries, most personal letters are not written for publication. Rather, they are communications between friends or family members. This kind of letter is informal. It often sounds like conversation, and the writer may use sentence fragments and colloquial language.

Certain other letters, such as business letters, letters of appeal, and letters to the editor, are different. They are usually addressed to a larger, public audience. They tend to be written in more formal language and to use complete sentences.

The letters in this chapter were written by a public figure, President Theodore Roosevelt. But because they are addressed to his sons, they are personal letters.

In 1906 President Roosevelt and his wife sailed to Panama, in Central America. A few years earlier, the United States had started to build the Panama Canal, and Roosevelt had a great interest in the project.

Roosevelt's policies had helped the United States gain the right to build the Panama Canal. He had encouraged the people of Panama to revolt against their Colombian rulers. Once Panama became independent, it signed a treaty giving the United States rights to the canal zone.

Roosevelt was severely criticized for his backing of the revolt in Panama. But he ignored the criticism. He considered the canal essential. He knew that in order for the United States to be a world power its navy and merchant ships had to be able to move swiftly from the Atlantic to the Pacific Ocean. So he made sure that the canal could be built.

Building the Panama Canal was a difficult project. In the 1880s a French company had tried but failed. The project involved difficult engineering tasks. It was complicated by the tropical diseases that killed many workers. When the American builders had problems and Congress refused to act, Roosevelt used his presidential powers to reorganize the project. He then put the United States in charge of the construction.

Because Roosevelt realized both the difficulty and the importance of building the canal, he decided to visit Panama in 1906. He wanted to see the work in progress and judge the problems himself. During the visit, he wrote letters to his four sons, some of which you will read. No letters to his daughters Alice and Ethel have survived.

Roosevelt was a devoted father who never let official duties prevent him from enjoying his children. If he could not be with them, then he wrote to them. *Theodore Roosevelt's Letters to His Children* is a collection of the letters he wrote to his children between 1898 and 1911. The book does not, however, contain any letters to Alice, his oldest child, perhaps because she did not want them to be published or possibly because they have been lost.

Roosevelt seemed to find his children more interesting than he found many adults. His interest in them probably stemmed from the fact that in many ways he was like a child himself. A good friend once said of Roosevelt: "You must always remember that the President is about six years old." The friend meant that Theodore Roosevelt loved fun, adventure, and strenuous physical activity.

As president, Roosevelt's enthusiasm startled many official visitors. He frequently led politicians and visiting dignitaries on what he called point-to-point walks. He had originally invented such walks for the children. The rule was that you had to get from the beginning to the end of the walk by going in a straight line over, under, and through—but never around—any obstacle. Officials sometimes returned to the White House covered with mud. No one, except for the president, was very happy about it!

But Theodore Roosevelt also had a serious side. He had great pride in his country and believed that it was his duty to watch over its moral as well as its physical well-being. He was not afraid to speak out if he felt the United States had made a mistake.

Roosevelt's family enlivened the White House. Roosevelt had six children. His first wife died two days after giving birth to their daughter Alice, in 1884. His second wife, Edith, had five children: Theodore in 1887, Kermit in 1889, Ethel in 1891, Archibald in 1894, and Quentin in 1897.

The children inherited their father's enthusiasm for life. As a young woman, Alice scandalized the country by smoking cigarettes in public and driving a car at twenty-five miles an hour, an outrageous speed in the early 1900s. The younger children kept the White House staff off balance by roller-skating in the basement, walking on stilts in the high-ceilinged rooms, and harboring an assortment of pets. On one occasion, Quentin wanted to cheer up Archie, who was sick in bed. So he arranged to take a pony in a freight elevator to his brother's room.

The Roosevelts, however, were not all noise and bustle. They enjoyed quiet moments and pursued serious interests as well. In the letters that you will read, Roosevelt writes about some of the family's interests: animals, history, natural history, and the progress of the nation. At the time that these letters were written, Ted was nineteen, Kermit seventeen, Archie twelve, and Quentin nine.

Lesson Preview

The lesson that follows "The President Visits Panama" focuses on an author's viewpoint and frame of reference. Every author writes from a particular viewpoint, which reflects his or her feelings, opinions, and experiences. An author's viewpoint affects what facts are included, which are emphasized, and which are left out. You can often discover an author's viewpoint by examining his or her language. Writers are also influenced by their <u>frame of reference</u>—the social and historical conditions in which they live.

The questions that follow will help you identify Theodore Roosevelt's viewpoint and understand his frame of reference. As you read, think about how you would answer these questions.

1 What is Roosevelt's attitude toward the *Louisiana,* the ship on which he traveled to Panama? How does he let you understand his attitude?

2 What feelings does Roosevelt have about the history of Central America? How can you tell?

3 What is the author's attitude toward the builders from the United States who are working on the canal? How can you tell?

4 Which of Roosevelt's many interests are reflected in his letters?

5 Notice that the letters are addressed to different children. How does each letter differ depending on the person to whom it is written?

Vocabulary

Here are some difficult words that appear in the selection that follows. Study the words and their definitions, as well as the sentences that show how the words are used. This will help you get the most from your reading.

raft large number. *The petting zoo had a raft of friendly animals to play with.*

fare food. *The guidebook recommends the excellent fare and comfortable rooms at this inn.*

flinch shrink away; wince. *Although his cavity was painful, the man tried not to flinch as the dentist examined it.*

abject wretched; miserable. *The organization is trying to improve the abject living conditions in this poor neighborhood.*

galleon a large Spanish ship of the 1400s and 1500s with three or four decks at the stern. *The Spanish galleon was used both as a warship and as a trading vessel.*

advent a coming or arrival. *With the advent of electrical power, many homes changed their gas lights to electric lights.*

dominion rule. *Although India was once under Great Britain's dominion, today it is a free country.*

epic heroic. *The poet Homer wrote about the epic deeds of the Greek heroes.*

feat remarkable deed. *For Mary, who had struggled so hard in her English class, receiving an A on her exam was a remarkable feat.*

The President Visits Panama

Excerpts from

**Theodore Roosevelt's
Letters to His Children**

THEODORE ROOSEVELT

On Board U.S.S. *Louisiana,*
On the Way to Panama.
Sunday, November 11, 1906.

Blessed Quentin:

You would be amused at the pets they have aboard this ship. They have two young bulldogs, a cat, three little raccoons, and a tiny Cuban goat. They seem to be very amicable with one another, although I think the cat has suspicions of all the rest. The coons clamber about everywhere, and the other afternoon while I was sitting reading, I suddenly felt my finger seized in a pair of soft black paws and found the coon sniffing at it, making me feel a little uncomfortable lest it might think the finger something good to eat. The two puppies play endlessly. One of them belongs to Lieutenant Evans. The crew will not be allowed ashore at Panama or else I know they would pick up a whole raft of other pets there. The jackies[1] seem especially fond of the little coons. A few minutes

1. **jackies:** slang for sailors.

ago I saw one of the jackies strolling about with a coon perched upon his shoulder, and now and then he would reach up his hand and give it a small piece of bread to eat.

On Board U.S.S. *Louisiana,*
Sunday, November 11, 1906.

Blessed Archie:

I wish you were along with us, for you would thoroughly enjoy everything on this ship. We have had three days of perfect weather, while this great battleship with her two convoys, the great armored cruisers, *Tennessee* and *Washington,* have steamed steadily in column ahead south-ward through calm seas until now we are in the tropics. They are three as splendid ships of their class as there are afloat, save only the English Dreadnaught. The *Louisiana* now has her gun-sights[2] and everything is all in good shape for her to begin the practice of the duties which will make her crew as fit for man-of-war's work as the crew of any one of our other first-class battleships. The men are such splendid-looking fellows, Americans of the best type, young, active, vigorous, with lots of intel-ligence. I was much amused at the name of the seven-inch guns, which include *Victor, Invincible, Peacemaker,* together with *Skidoo,* and also one called *Tedd* and one called *The Big Stick.*[3]

On Board U.S.S. *Louisiana,*
Nov. 14.

Dear Ted:

I am very glad to have taken this trip, although as usual I am bored by the sea. Everything has been smooth as possible, and it has been

---

2. **gun-sights:** devices for guiding the eye in aiming a weapon.
3. **The Big Stick:** although this is the name of a gun, it was amusing to Roosevelt who often quoted an African saying, "Speak softly and carry a big stick."

lovely having Mother along. It gives me great pride in America to be aboard this great battleship and to see not only the material perfection of the ship herself in engines, guns and all arrangements, but the fine quality of the officers and crew. Have you ever read Smollett's[4] novel, I think "Roderick Random" or "Humphrey Clinker," in which the hero goes to sea? It gives me an awful idea of what a floating hell of filth, disease, tyranny, and cruelty a war-ship was in those days. Now every arrangement is as clean and healthful as possible. The men can bathe and do bathe as often as cleanliness requires. Their fare is excellent and they are as self-respecting a set as can be imagined. I am no great believer in the superiority of times past; and I have no question that the officers and men of our Navy now are in point of fighting capacity better than in the times of Drake and Nelson;[5] and morally and in physical surroundings the advantage is infinitely in our favor.

It was delightful to have you two or three days at Washington. Blessed old fellow, you had a pretty hard time in college this fall; but it can't be helped, Ted; as one grows older the bitter and the sweet keep coming together. The only thing to do is to grin and bear it, to flinch as little as possible under the punishment, and to keep pegging steadily away until the luck turns.

U.S.S. *Louisiana,*
At Sea, November 20, 1906.

Dear Kermit:

Our visit to Panama was most successful as well as most interesting. We were there three days and we worked from morning till night. The

---

4. **Smollett:** the Scottish novelist Tobias Smollett (1721–1771) who wrote about the sea in his novel *The Adventures of Roderick Random.*
5. **Drake and Nelson:** Sir Francis Drake (1540–1596) was an admiral of the English fleet that defeated the Spanish Armada in 1588. Horatio Nelson (1758–1805) was a British naval hero whose greatest victory was at the battle of Trafalgar in 1805.

second day I was up at a quarter to six and got to bed at a quarter of twelve, and I do not believe that in the intervening time, save when I was dressing, there were ten consecutive minutes when I was not busily at work in some shape or form. For two days there [were] uninterrupted tropic rains without a glimpse of the sun, and the Chagres River rose in a flood, higher than any for fifteen years; so that we saw the climate at its worst. It was just what I desired to do.

It certainly adds to one's pleasure to have read history and to appreciate the picturesque. When on Wednesday we approached the coast, and the jungle-covered mountains looked clearer and clearer until we could see the surf beating on the shores, while there was hardly a sign of human habitation, I kept thinking of the four centuries of wild and bloody romance, mixed with abject squalor and suffering, which had made up the history of the Isthmus until three years ago. I could see Balboa crossing at Darien,[6] and the wars between the Spaniards and the Indians, and the settlement and the building up of the quaint walled Spanish towns; and the trade, across the sea by galleon, and over land by pack-train and river canoe, in gold and silver, in precious stones; and then the advent of the buccaneers, and of the English seamen, of Drake and Frobisher and Morgan,[7] and many, many others, and the wild destruction they wrought. Then I thought of the rebellion against the Spanish dominion, and the uninterrupted and bloody wars that followed, the last occurring when I became President; wars, the victorious heroes of which have their pictures frescoed on the quaint rooms of the palace at Panama City, and in similar palaces in all capitals of these strange, turbulent little half-caste civilizations. Meanwhile the Panama railroad had been built by Americans over a half century ago, with appalling loss of life, so that it is said, of course with exaggeration, that every sleeper[8] laid represented

6. **Balboa crossing at Darien:** Darien was a Spanish settlement at the eastern end of the Isthmus of Panama. Vasco Nuñez de Balboa (1475–1519) was a Spanish explorer who crossed the isthmus from east to west. He was the first European to see the Pacific Ocean from the shores of America.
7. **Frobisher and Morgan:** Sir Martin Frobisher (?1539–1594) was an English explorer who searched for the Northwest Passage. Sir Henry Morgan (1635–1688) was a Welsh buccaneer who plundered Spanish ships and settlements in the New World.
8. **sleeper:** a tie supporting a railroad track.

the death of a man. Then the French canal company started work, and for two or three years did a good deal, until it became evident that the task far exceeded its powers; and then to miscalculation and inefficiency was added the hideous greed of adventurers, trying each to save something from the general wreck, and the company closed with infamy and scandal.

Now we have taken hold of the job. We have difficulties with our own people, of course. I haven't a doubt that it will take a little longer and cost a little more than men now appreciate, but I believe that the work is being done with a very high degree both of efficiency and honesty; and I am immensely struck by the character of American employees who are engaged, not merely in superintending the work, but in doing all the jobs that need skill and intelligence. The steam shovels, the dirt trains, the machine shops, and the like, are all filled with American engineers, conductors, machinists, boiler-makers, carpenters. From the top to the bottom these men are so hardy, so efficient, so energetic, that it is a real pleasure to look at them. Stevens, the head engineer, is a big fellow, a man of daring and good sense, and burly power. All of these men are quite as formidable, and would, if it were necessary, do quite as much in battle as the crews of Drake and Morgan; but as it is, they are doing a work of infinitely more lasting consequence. Nothing whatever remains to show what Drake and Morgan did. They produced no real effect down here, but Stevens and his men are changing the face of the continent, are doing the greatest engineering feat of the ages, and the effect of their work will be felt while our civilization lasts. I went over everything that I could possibly go over in the time at my disposal. I examined the quarters of married and single men, white men and negroes. I went over the ground of the Gatun and La Boca dams; went through Panama and Colon, and spent a day in the Culebra cut, where the great work is being done. There the huge steam-shovels are hard at it; scooping huge masses of rock and gravel and dirt previously loosened by the drillers and dynamite blasters, loading it on trains which take it away to some dump, either in the jungle or where the dams are to be built. They are eating steadily into the mountain, cutting it down and down. Little tracks are laid on the side-hills, rocks blasted out, and the great ninety-five ton steam-shovels work up like mountain howitzers[9] until they come to where they can with advantage begin their work of eating into and destroying the mountainside. With intense energy men and machines do their task. It is an epic feat, and one of immense significance.

The deluge of rain meant that many of the villages were knee-deep in water, while the flooded rivers tore through the tropic forests. It is a real tropic forest, palms and bananas, breadfruit trees, bamboos, lofty ceibas,[10] and gorgeous butterflies and brilliant colored birds fluttering among the orchids. There are beautiful flowers, too.

All my old enthusiasm for natural history seemed to revive, and I would have given a good deal to have stayed and tried to collect specimens. It would be a good hunting country too; deer, and now and then jaguars and tapir,[11] and great birds that they call wild turkeys; there are alligators in the rivers. One of the trained nurses from a hospital went to bathe in a pool last August and an alligator grabbed him by the legs and was making off with him, but was fortunately scared away, leaving the man badly injured.

I tramped everywhere through the mud. Mother did not do the roughest work, and had time to see more of the really picturesque and beautiful side of the life, and really enjoyed herself.

P.S. The Gatun dam will make a lake miles long, and the railroad now goes on what will be the bottom of this lake, and it was curious to think that in a few years great ships would be floating in water 100 feet above where we were.

9. **howitzers:** short cannons.
10. **ceibas:** tropical trees.
11. **tapir:** a hoofed, hoglike mammal found in the tropics.

Reviewing the Selection

Answer each of the following questions without looking back at the selection.

Recalling Facts

1. President Roosevelt wrote these letters from
   - ☐ a. Panama City.
   - ☐ b. Washington.
   - ☐ c. a United States ship.
   - ☐ d. a ship sailing through the Panama Canal.

Understanding Main Ideas

2. While he was in Panama, Roosevelt spent most of his time
   - ☐ a. hunting and exploring.
   - ☐ b. inspecting the work on the canal.
   - ☐ c. writing letters.
   - ☐ d. negotiating treaties with officials.

Placing Events in Order

3. Which of the following events took place first?
   - ☐ a. The United States built the Panama railroad.
   - ☐ b. President Roosevelt visited Panama.
   - ☐ c. The United States began building the Panama Canal.
   - ☐ d. The French tried to build a canal through Panama.

Finding Supporting Details

4. To show how naval life has improved, Roosevelt mentions the
   - ☐ a. private sleeping quarters of the men.
   - ☐ b. animals aboard ship.
   - ☐ c. shorter tours of duty.
   - ☐ d. cleanliness of the men.

Recognizing Words in Context

5. "The <u>deluge</u> of rain meant that many of the villages were knee-deep in water, while the flooded rivers tore through the tropic forests." In this context *deluge* means

   ☐ a. lack.
   ☐ b. sound.
   ☐ c. downpour.
   ☐ d. lightness.

Interpreting the Selection

Answer each of the following questions. You may look back at the selection if necessary.

Making Inferences

6. In Roosevelt's letter to Ted, the president refers to the boy's "hard time in college last fall." The "hard time" probably had something to do with Ted's

   ☐ a. poor performance in some subject.
   ☐ b. lack of money.
   ☐ c. being ill.
   ☐ d. loneliness without his family.

Generalizing

7. A good word to describe Roosevelt's attitude toward his children is

   ☐ a. stern.
   ☐ b. indifferent.
   ☐ c. negligent.
   ☐ d. affectionate.

8. In Roosevelt's opinion the work on the canal
   ☐ a. was seriously behind schedule.
   ☐ b. should have been finished by
         the French.
   ☐ c. was almost finished.
   ☐ d. was being done with efficiency
         and honesty.

9. As a result of two days of heavy rain,
   ☐ a. Roosevelt's visit to Colon was canceled.
   ☐ b. Mrs. Roosevelt stayed on the ship.
   ☐ c. some villages were flooded.
   ☐ d. all work on the canal stopped.

10. Roosevelt enjoyed the trip to Panama
    because he
    ☐ a. liked sea voyages more than other
          kinds of travel.
    ☐ b. had a good time hunting alligators.
    ☐ c. collected many new specimens
          of animals.
    ☐ d. saw that progress was really being
          made on the canal.

Author's Viewpoint
and Frame of Reference

The letters you have just read are personal messages from a father to his children. They are informal and instructive. Theodore Roosevelt wants to teach his children about the people, places, and things that he is seeing.

The letters are of more interest to a general audience than most family letters. The author is the president of the United States. He is a well-read and opinionated man. His knowledge and opinions shape his interpretation of the events that he is describing. In his letters he expresses his <u>viewpoint</u>—the feelings, opinions, and experiences that affect his outlook on life.

As you have learned, nonfiction writing tells about actual events or gives factual information. When people read nonfiction, they tend to accept the author's statements as true. Generally, authors do try to present the truth. Few authors deliberately lie. But when reading any nonfiction work, it is important to identify the author's viewpoint because a person's viewpoint affects not only how he or she sees the facts but also which facts are included.

In this lesson you will examine the interests, beliefs, and experiences that affected Theodore Roosevelt's viewpoint. You will also learn how his viewpoint determined what facts he noticed and how he interpreted those facts.

The Author's Interests and Beliefs

Theodore Roosevelt was a man of varied interests. Among them were history, natural history, and hunting. The affect of those interests on his viewpoint is especially clear when you read about the subjects he discusses in his letters to his sons. Roosevelt himself acknowledges the importance of his interests when he writes to Kermit, "It certainly adds to one's pleasure to have read history and to appreciate the picturesque."

In that letter his interest in history is evident. He gives Kermit a summary of the history of Panama from the early Spanish explorers to the present. Later in the same letter, he talks about the natural history of Panama and the plants and animals that he saw there. Another Roosevelt interest—hunting—also colors his viewpoint.

1. Imagine that you had accompanied Roosevelt on his trip. What subjects would you have written about in your letters to your family? How do those subjects reflect your interests and beliefs?

As president of the United States, Roosevelt was interested in the building of the canal. Critics at home had attacked his policies with regard to the canal. So while in Panama, Roosevelt looked for evidence of the project's success. That interest affected his views about the project. In his letters to his sons, the president's concern about the success of the canal is clear.

2. Find an example of how Roosevelt's desire to have the Panama Canal project succeed influenced his viewpoint.

Roosevelt's beliefs were another influence on his viewpoint. Roosevelt was a strong patriot who believed that the United States was superior to other nations. In his letter to Ted he writes:

> I am no great believer in the superiority of times past; and I have no question that the officers and men of our Navy now are in point of fighting capacity better than in the times of Drake and Nelson. . . .

Notice that Roosevelt offers no proof of the validity of his statement. He admits that the statement depends on his belief that the present is superior to the past.

Roosevelt had strong moral beliefs that also affected his viewpoint. His father had taught him that service to humanity was a nobler goal than the pursuit of personal pleasure or gain. That moral outlook influenced the way the president reported certain events to his sons.

3. Read the following passage about the French company that tried to build a canal through Panama. What moral judgment does Roosevelt make here?

> *Then the French canal company started work . . . until it became evident that the task far exceeded its powers; and then to miscalculation and inefficiency was added the hideous greed of adventurers, trying each to save something from the general wreck, and the company closed with infamy and scandal.*

The Author's Situation in Life

Besides interests and beliefs, an author's situation in life can influence his or her viewpoint. Someone who is poor and struggling to make a living might have a different viewpoint about spending money, for example, than a person who has inherited wealth or gained a position of power.

The author of these letters had a very special situation in life. He was the president of the United States. That position affected Roosevelt's viewpoint. As president, he was traveling on a United States Navy ship, and he looked with pride on the *Louisiana* and its escorts.

Even more significant than the president's attitude toward the navy is his viewpoint toward the canal project. Roosevelt had pushed the country into building the canal, bypassing Congress's decision about the project. To Roosevelt, therefore, it was extremely important that the canal be a successful venture.

Of course, Roosevelt did not have to justify his actions to his sons. But like most fathers, he probably wanted them to think that what he had done was right.

4. Find a passage in one of Roosevelt's letters that reflects his viewpoint about the canal. Summarize the passage in your own words.

The Author's Frame of Reference

Every writer is affected by the attitudes and outlook of the historical period in which he or she lives. Some authors reject those attitudes, while others agree with them. But in either case, the author's viewpoint is related to his or her frame of reference, the social and historical conditions in which the author lives.

To understand Theodore Roosevelt's viewpoint about certain topics, you need to examine the attitudes that were common in the United States in the early 1900s. For example, Roosevelt refers to the countries of Central America as "these strange, turbulent little half-caste civilizations." His words carry a negative judgment about those countries. He considers them peculiar and backward compared with the United States. His judgment reflects the opinions of many people in the United States.

Roosevelt's frame of reference also affects his enthusiasm about machines, a subject he mentions in his letter to Kermit. At the time Roosevelt was president, many new machines were beginning to replace human laborers. Like Roosevelt, Americans were excited and optimistic about industrial growth in the United States. They felt that machines and industry would help to make the United States a world power.

5. Skim Theodore Roosevelt's letters. Find another example of how Roosevelt's frame of reference affected his viewpoint.

The Audience's Interests

President Roosevelt writes a different kind of letter to each of his sons. Like all writers, Roosevelt is well aware of his audience's interests. A letter is usually meant for an audience of one, so it is important for the letter-writer to consider that person's interests.

Theodore Roosevelt realized that his sons had different interests and experiences. He was aware, too, of their age differences. Notice how he begins his letters. He addresses the two younger boys, Quentin and Archie, as "Blessed." They are still children, and he can use affectionate language with them. To the two older boys, Ted and Kermit, he writes "Dear."

The letters to the two younger boys are shorter and simpler than those to the two older boys. Roosevelt also considered the different interests of his four sons. To Quentin, the youngest, he writes about the animals aboard ship. To Archie, age twelve, he writes about the ship itself, including the names of the guns.

His letter to Ted, a college student at the time, mentions a book that Ted might have read. Roosevelt also comments on some problems Ted was having at school. To Kermit, who shared Roosevelt's interest in hunting and natural history, Roosevelt describes the plants and animals of Panama, as well as the history of the area.

Roosevelt acknowledges the differences among his sons in another way. His language and the length of his sentences vary in the different letters. Read the following examples and notice the differences in style. The first passage is from the letter to Quentin, age nine. The second is from the letter to Kermit, age seventeen.

The two puppies play endlessly. One of them belongs to Lieutenant Evans.

Then I thought of the rebellion against the Spanish dominion, and the uninterrupted and bloody wars that followed, the last occurring when I became President; wars, the victorious heroes of which have their pictures frescoed on the quaint rooms of the palace at Panama City, and in similar palaces in all capitals of these strange, turbulent little half-caste civilizations.

Not only are the sentences in Quentin's letter shorter and simpler but the words are also easier. Roosevelt was clearly aware of the different reading abilities of Quentin and Kermit.

6. Read the following passage from another letter that Roosevelt wrote on his trip to Panama. The letter is not one of those you read. To which of his sons do you think the letter was addressed? Keep in mind the sentence length and vocabulary. If you cannot decide, try to narrow the choice to the younger boys or the older boys. Give reasons for your answer.

> *All the forenoon we had Cuba on our right and most of the forenoon and part of the afternoon Haiti on our left; and in each case green, jungly shores and bold mountains—two great, beautiful, venomous tropic islands.*

Questions for Thought and Discussion

The questions and activities that follow will help you explore "The President Visits Panama" in more depth and at the same time develop your critical thinking skills.

1. **Finding Evidence.** In About the Selection you learned that Theodore Roosevelt was energetic, patriotic, and fond of his children. What evidence of those qualities do you find in his letters to his children? What other character traits are evident in his letters?

2. **Evaluating.** What kind of parent do you think the letters in this chapter show Theodore Roosevelt to be? Give examples to support your evaluation.

3. **Analyzing.** In Chapter 8 you learned that an author writes for various purposes—to inform, to instruct, to entertain, and to persuade. Which of those purposes do you think Theodore Roosevelt had in writing to his sons? Give examples to support your answer. Do you see evidence in his writing of any other purposes? Explain your answer.

Writing About Literature

Several suggestions for writing projects follow. You may be asked to complete one or more of these projects. If you have any questions about

how to begin a writing assignment, review Using the Writing Process, beginning on page 341.

1. **Writing Letters.** Choose a topic that interests you—a hobby, a sport, or a place you have visited. Write two letters about the topic to two separate people, each of whom has different interests or attitudes. You might write to a younger or older relative and to a friend your own age. As you write each letter, think about the interests of the person to whom you are writing. Consider what your audience might be interested in hearing about the topic.

2. **Maintaining the Same Viewpoint.** Imagine that you are Theodore Roosevelt and are writing a letter to one of your children. Choose a place or a topic that is in the news to discuss in your letter. Be sure to remember Theodore Roosevelt's attitudes, beliefs, and frame of reference as you write the letter. Keep in mind your audience, as well as his or her age and interests.

3. **Reporting on Research.** Theodore Roosevelt's views on history and important people of the past may have influenced his actions as president. In the letters to his children that you read, Roosevelt mentions a number of historical figures, including Drake, Nelson, Balboa, Frobisher, and Morgan. Use library sources to find out more about one of those men. Then prepare a written or an oral report in which you explain why that person is remembered and why Roosevelt might have admired him.

Chapter 11

Selection

A Letter Home
Excerpt from
West from Home: Letters of Laura Ingalls Wilder
to Almanzo Wilder, San Francisco, 1915

LAURA INGALLS WILDER

Lesson

Description

About the Selection

The selection in this chapter is a single letter written by Laura Ingalls Wilder to her husband, Almanzo—or Manly, as she called him. Like the letters of Theodore Roosevelt to his children, Wilder's letter gives a personal view of the author's travels. It, too, is a written communication between family members.

Laura Ingalls Wilder is well known as the author of *Little House on the Prairie*. That book is one of a series of novels about pioneer life during the late 1800s. Laura and Almanzo Wilder had been farming in Missouri for a long time before Laura began to write her nine "Little House" books.

In 1915, when this letter was written, Laura Wilder traveled alone to San Francisco to visit her daughter, Rose. At the time, Rose was working as a journalist for a San Francisco newspaper. Besides wanting to see Rose, Laura Wilder thought she might learn about writing from her daughter.

Another attraction in San Francisco at that time was the Panama-Pacific International Exposition. It was held to celebrate the completion of the Panama Canal, which you read about in Theodore Roosevelt's letters in Chapter 10. The Panama Canal greatly improved trade for cities on the West Coast. The exposition was called "The Dream City." It extended along two miles of San Francisco's waterfront, offering a spectacular array of towers, palaces, obelisks, gardens, sculpture, and fountains. Twenty-eight countries built pavilions, and thirty of the forty-eight states contributed replicas of their most famous landmarks for the exposition.

In 1915 electricity was still a fairly recent development. The exposition's designers took full advantage of the invention. By night two hundred hidden searchlights played over the fairgrounds. A device called a scintillator, located in San Francisco Bay, caused flashes of light to dance above the exposition.

Before the exposition closed on December 4, 1915, about eighteen million people had visited the many exhibits. Among the visitors was Laura Ingalls Wilder. She stayed in San Francisco with her daughter and son-in-law for two months, enjoying a city that was very different from her farm in the Ozark Mountains of Missouri.

Although the trip was Laura Ingalls Wilder's first visit to the Pacific Coast, she had traveled widely in her lifetime. Laura Ingalls was born in 1867 in a log cabin in Wisconsin. She and her family journeyed by covered wagon through Kansas and Minnesota to the Dakota Territory. There, her father established a homestead.

At the age of fifteen, Laura Ingalls started teaching school. Three years later, she married Almanzo Wilder. Together, they established a farm near De Smet, Dakota Territory. After suffering much bad fortune—storms, drought, fire, and locusts—they moved to Mansfield, Missouri. At first, they could not earn a living from the new farm, so both Manly and Laura worked for an oil company. Manly became a salesman, and Laura did his bookkeeping.

They eventually made their farm prosperous and Laura, Manly, and Rose, their only child, enjoyed a happy life. Laura helped her husband build the farmhouse. She raised chickens and made butter. Despite her many activities, she found time to write articles about rural life. She wrote a regular column, called "As a Farm Woman Thinks," for the *Missouri Ruralist*. She later became home editor for the *Ruralist* and poultry editor for the St. Louis *Star*.

In 1930, at the age of sixty-three, Laura Ingalls Wilder began writing the "Little House" books. Rose had suggested that her mother's early life on the frontier would make good reading. Although the books are fictional, they are based on Laura's life.

Little House in the Big Woods describes the life of a frontier family who built a log cabin in the Wisconsin woods. In *Little House on the Prairie* the same family establishes a homestead in Indian Territory but is forced by the government to leave. *On the Banks of Plum Creek* takes the family to Minnesota, where they suffer from a plague of grasshoppers. The family's arrival in Dakota Territory is portrayed in *By the Shores of Silver Lake*.

In Wilder's fifth book, *The Long Winter*, she describes the severe winter of 1881, which the family spent in the town of De Smet. *Little Town on the Prairie* covers Laura's teenage years, and *These Happy Golden Years* tells of her teaching career and her courtship by Almanzo. In another book, *Farmer Boy*, Laura tells of Almanzo's childhood and youth on a large farm in New York.

The letter that you will read in this chapter was written before either Laura or Rose won fame for their writing. Mother and daughter were eager to see each other in 1915. Since it was impossible for both Laura and Manly to leave the farm, Manly insisted that Laura go to San Francisco. She agreed, promising to be Manly's eyes as she crossed the country by train and explored San Francisco. It was a promise she was well suited to keep. In childhood Laura had served as the eyes for her blind sister.

Laura's letters to Manly were kept bundled together among her belongings for years. Rose found them after Laura died in 1957, but they were not published until after Rose's death in 1968. In the letter you will read, Laura describes her first days in San Francisco.

Lesson Preview

The lesson that follows "A Letter Home" focuses on the author's use of description. Laura Ingalls Wilder's letter to her husband is full of descriptions of new sights and experiences. Like any good writer, Wilder makes her descriptions vivid by appealing to all the senses—sight, sound, taste, touch, and smell. By doing that, she gives you a feeling of what it was

Description

like to be at the exposition. She chooses her words carefully to give you a clear picture of her experiences.

The questions that follow will help you notice how Wilder creates effective descriptions. As you read, think about how you would answer these questions.

1 How does Wilder appeal to your five senses in her descriptions? How does that make a description stronger?

2 What words or phrases make the author's descriptions vivid? What images does she create in her descriptions?

3 As you know, Laura Wilder wrote this letter to her husband. How do you think that fact affected what she chose to describe?

Vocabulary

Here are some difficult words that appear in the selection that follows. Study the words and their definitions, as well as the sentences that show how the words are used. This will help you get the most from your reading.

schooner a two-masted sailing ship. *When the wind caught its sails, the schooner sped quickly across the water.*

foliage the leaves of plants. *Vermont is famous for its beautiful autumn foliage.*

inset something set in or inserted into something else. *The wooden writing desk was inset with ceramic tiles.*

ramparts protective barriers. *After climbing to the top of the tower, we leaned over the ramparts and looked at the view.*

cornices a decorative molding that projects off the top of a building. *The architect had designed very elaborate cornices for the statehouse.*

A Letter Home

Excerpt from

**West from Home:
Letters of Laura Ingalls Wilder to
Almanzo Wilder, San Francisco, 1915**

LAURA INGALLS WILDER

San Francisco
Sunday, August 29, 1915

Manly Dear,

As you of course know I arrived safely in San Francisco. As I walked down the walk from the train toward the ferry, Rose stepped out from the crowd and seized me.

On the ferry we sat out on the upper deck and well in front, but a fog covered the water so I did not see much of the bay except the lights around it. I was so tired anyway I could not realize I was really here. Gillette [Rose's husband] met us as we stepped off the ferry and we took a streetcar nearly home and climbed a hill the rest of the way. I went to bed soon and have been resting most of the time since.

It took all the first day to get the motion of the cars out of my head. Yesterday afternoon I went with Rose and Gillette down to the beach. We walked down the hill—all paved streets and walks and lovely buildings—to the car-line and took a car to Land's End, from six to ten miles all the way through the city except for a few blocks at the last.

At Land's End I had my first view of the Pacific Ocean. To say it is beautiful does not half express it. It is simply beyond words. The water is such a deep wonderful blue and the sound of the waves breaking on the beach and their whisper as they flow back is something to dream about. I saw a lumber schooner coming in and another going out as they passed each other in the Golden Gate. They sail between here and Seattle, Washington. We walked from Land's End around the point of land and came to the Cliff House and Seal Rocks but the seals would not show themselves.

We took a side path into the parks of the Sutro Estate, which has been turned over to the city as a public park under certain conditions as to its use. The lodge near the gates and the old mansion itself were built with materials brought around the Horn[1] in sailing ships about a hundred years ago. We went through the massive arched gateway made of stone with a life-sized lion crouched at each side and through a beautiful park of about forty acres. I don't mean we walked over it all, but we walked miles of it. The soil in these grounds was all brought to them, for originally the surface was just sand. The forest trees were all planted by this first Sutro. At every turn in the paths we came upon statues of stone, figures of men and women and animals, and birds, half hidden among the foliage of flowering plants, or peeping out from among the trees.

The house itself is built at the top of the hill. The whole front and side of the house is glass so that one would have the view from every point. The pillars of the balcony have porcelains inset, as do the posts of the stone fence around the house. They are small squares as smooth

---

1. **Horn:** Cape Horn, at the tip of South America.

and glossy as my china, with quaint old-fashioned pictures of children and animals, instead of the flowers on my dishes. Just think, they have stood there for a hundred years exposed to the sun and wind and weather without a stain or a crackle. Close beside the house is a very tall slender building, an observatory with a glass room at the top where the family used to go to watch the ships come in through the Golden Gate. The building is so old that it is considered unsafe and no one is allowed to go in it now.

We went from there out on the edge of the cliff where there are seats and statues around the edge and one can sit or stand and look over the ramparts across the blue Pacific. An American eagle in stone stands screaming on the edge at one side. Two cannon were in place pointing out to sea and there were several piles of cannon balls. I kicked one to be sure it was real—and it was. The winds off the ocean are delightful.

We went down on the beach where the waves were breaking. There were crowds of people there and some of them were wading. I wanted to wade. Rose said she never had but she would, so we took off our shoes and stockings and left them on the warm sand with Gillette to guard them and went out to meet the waves. A little one rolled in and covered our feet, the next one came and reached our ankles, and just as I was saying how delightful, the big one came and went above our knees. I just had time to snatch my skirts up and save them and the wave went back with a pull. We went nearer the shore and dug holes in the sand with our toes. We went out to meet the waves and ran back before the big one caught us and had such a good time.

The salt water tingled my feet and made them feel so good all the rest of the day, and just to think, the same water that bathes the shores of China and Japan came clear across the ocean and bathed my feet. In other words, I have washed my feet in the Pacific Ocean.

The ocean is not ugly. It is beautiful and wonderful.

We went from the beach to the Coast Guard or life-saving station and saw the lifeboat. Then we went to see the "Gjöa," the only boat that has ever gone around the continent through the Northwest Passage.[2] It is battered and worn but strong-looking still. The ship was made in Norway in 1878 and with a crew of six men and the captain was three years and four months making the journey from Norway through the Northwest Passage to San Francisco. The government of Norway and the Norwegians of California gave the ship to this city and left it here.

By this time I was tired, very tired, so we took a car back to the city and stopped for dinner at a restaurant. The waiter was an Alsatian, which is a cross between a Frenchman and a German. The dinner was delicious. French bread and salmon steak and tenderloin of sole, delicious fish. I could hardly tell which was the best. Then there was some kind of an Italian dish which I liked very much, and a French strawberry pie or "tarte" which was fresh berries in a pastry shell with some kind of rich syrup poured over. There was music in the restaurant and I heard "It's a Long, Long Way to Tipperary" for the first time.[3]

Believe me, I was tired after seeing all this in one afternoon and we have been loafing all today. We went out on the walk before the house and saw Niles [an exhibition aviator] fly this afternoon. The Tower of Jewels is in sight from there too. Niles flew up and up and up, then dropped like an autumn leaf, floating and drifting and falling. He turned over, end over end, he turned over sideways both ways, then righted himself and sailed gracefully down.

Christopherson was flying at the beach yesterday and Rose says I shall have a flight before I go home. Gee, if it can beat wading in the ocean it will be some beat, believe me.

You know I have never cared for cities but San Francisco is simply the most beautiful thing. Set on the hills as it is with glimpses of the bay here and there and at night with the lights shining up and down the hills

---

2. The Norwegian explorer Roald Amundsen bought the *Gjöa* and turned it into a laboratory for scientific work in the Arctic. After several winters aboard the *Gjöa* in northern Canada, he made his way west into open water. He soon realized that he had unintentionally crossed through the often searched-for Northwest Passage. The *Gjöa* was displayed in San Francisco's Golden Gate Park until 1972, when it was returned to Norway.

3. "It's a Long, Long Way to Tipperary" was a popular song during World War I, which began in Europe in August 1914.

and the lights of ships on the water, it is like fairyland. I have not seen any of the Exposition yet. San Francisco itself would be wonderful enough for a year, but we will begin this week to go to the Fair. You must not expect me to see it all for it has been figured out that it would cost $500 just to see the five-cent, ten-cent and twenty-five-cent attractions.

Rose and Gillette have a dandy little place to live with a fine view from the windows. It is up at the very top of a hill, with the bay in sight.

Just here Rose called to come quick and go see the fireworks at the Fair. We put on our heavy coats and went out to the walk before the house and just a little way along it and sat down on a stone curb. The white Tower of Jewels is in sight from there. The jewels strung around it glitter and shine in beautiful colors. The jewels are from Austria and cost ninety cents each and they decorate all the cornices on the high, fancifully built tower. A searchlight is directed on the tower at night to show it off and it is wonderful.

As we looked, the aeroscope rose above the tops of the buildings. It is a car that can hold five hundred people. Its outlines are marked by electric lights. It is on the top of a more slender part and is lowered for the people to fill the car, then is raised high so they can look down on the whole Exposition at once. They have that instead of the Ferris Wheel. As it rises, it looks like some giant with a square head, craning his long neck up and up. I don't suppose it looks like that to anyone else, but that is the way it makes me feel.

Well, we sat and watched and soon a long finger of white light swept across the sky, then another and another of different colors, and then there was flashing and fading across the whole sky in that direction, the most beautiful northern-lights[4] effect you could imagine. I think you have seen them. Well, this was more brilliant, more colors and *very* much higher on the sky. All the colors of the rainbow and some shades that I never saw the rainbow have. I have used the word "beautiful" until

---

4. **northern-lights:** another name for the aurora borealis. These streamers of light arch across the night sky in Arctic regions. They are believed to be electrical in origin.

Description

it has no meaning, but what other word can I use? There are forty searchlights producing this effect. Forty men handle them, producing the flashes in a sort of drill, under direction and orders as a drill march is done. It costs $40 a minute to show these northern lights, in salary alone. What the lights themselves cost is not for common mortals to know.

After a little of this, rockets went shooting up the beams of light, burst and fell in showers of colored stars and strings of jewels. The different colors of the searchlights were played upon the steam, making most beautiful and fantastic cloud shapes of different colors after the shower of stars had fallen. I do not know how long it lasted, but at last the flashes stopped and there was left the wonderful Tower of Jewels shining and glowing in the light thrown on it, and the aeroscope craning its long neck for a look down on the grounds.

I will meet some of Rose's friends this week and begin to get a line on things. Rose gets $30 a week now and she says she is saving ten percent of it, absolutely salting it down. She says it is not much but it is making a start. Gillette has worked on extra jobs for the Call[5] since he came to the city, which leaves him at times without work but he has a promise of a good job as soon as a vacancy occurs, which is expected soon. Rose says they have $4,000 due them from their real estate work and that Gillette has made an assignment to us of what he owes us, but they do not know when they, or we, will get this money as the men who bought the land are unable to pay it now. The real estate business went all to smash and Stine & Kendrick[6] are resting till things turn.

I am so glad Mr. Nall came so soon and to get your letter. I do hope you and Inky are getting along comfortably. Take care of yourself and him, and I will look for us both as much as possible.

What a time you must have had with those chickens and that milk. I'm glad the pie was good and the thing to do was to put it in the oven. I hope you did not burn it.

---

5. **Call:** a San Francisco newspaper and the rival of Rose's paper, the *Bulletin*.
6. **Stine & Kendrick:** a real estate agency for which Rose and Gillette had worked.

Rose says tell you those fireworks are the best the world has ever known. It costs hundreds of thousands to produce them and they had experts from all over the world at work on them. She says there never was anything like them in the world except those Roman candles you got for her the last Fourth of July we were in De Smet. They surpassed them, she says.

Well, goodbye for this time. I'll go see some more to write you.

Lovingly,

Bessie[7]

---

7. **Bessie:** Laura's middle name was Elizabeth. She was called Bessie or Mama Bessie within the family to avoid confusion with Manly's sister, whose name was also Laura.

Reviewing the Selection

Answer each of the following questions without looking back at the selection.

Recalling Facts

1. To get to Rose's house, Laura took a
   - ☐ a. stagecoach and a ferry.
   - ☐ b. train and a ferry.
   - ☐ c. train, a ferry, and a streetcar.
   - ☐ d. train, a bus, and a streetcar.

Understanding Main Ideas

2. The main reason Laura wrote to Manly was to
   - ☐ a. let him know she had arrived safely.
   - ☐ b. ask him what was happening on the farm.
   - ☐ c. tell him about Rose's house in San Francisco.
   - ☐ d. describe her first days in San Francisco.

Placing Events in Order

3. As soon as Laura reached San Francisco, she went to
   - ☐ a. see the exposition.
   - ☐ b. watch the fireworks.
   - ☐ c. visit the Pacific Ocean.
   - ☐ d. rest at her daughter's house.

Finding Supporting Details

4. An example of a new experience for Laura was
   - ☐ a. wading in the Pacific Ocean.
   - ☐ b. eating in a Chinese restaurant.
   - ☐ c. visiting a city.
   - ☐ d. writing a letter.

5. "As it rises, it looks like some giant with a square head, <u>craning</u> his long neck up and up." In this context *craning* means

☐ a. holding.
☐ b. climbing.
☐ c. bending.
☐ d. stretching.

Interpreting the Selection

Answer each of the following questions. You may look back at the selection if necessary.

6. The fireworks that Laura Wilder saw were probably

☐ a. a regular nighttime event in San Francisco in the early 1900s.
☐ b. a special event connected with the exposition.
☐ c. the first fireworks Laura had ever seen.
☐ d. the only way of lighting the fairgrounds at night.

7. Laura's attitude toward San Francisco can best be described as

☐ a. enthusiastic.
☐ b. bored.
☐ c. disappointed.
☐ d. bewildered.

8. Which of the following statements expresses
    an opinion of Laura Wilder's?
    - ☐ a. "At Land's End I had my first view of
      the Pacific Ocean."
    - ☐ b. "I wanted to wade."
    - ☐ c. "The ocean is not ugly. It is beautiful
      and wonderful."
    - ☐ d. "By this time I was tired, very tired, so
      we took a car back to the city and
      stopped for dinner at a restaurant."

9. Laura told Manly that she would not be able
    to see all the exhibits at the exposition because
    - ☐ a. there was not enough time.
    - ☐ b. it would cost too much money.
    - ☐ c. some exhibits had already closed.
    - ☐ d. she was not interested in some of them.

10. From reading Laura Wilder's letter, you can
    conclude that she
    - ☐ a. would have liked to move to
      San Francisco.
    - ☐ b. thought the exposition was a waste
      of time.
    - ☐ c. enjoyed her visit to San Francisco.
    - ☐ d. thought flying was too dangerous
      to try.

Description

Good descriptions are clear and vivid. They make scenes come to life by focusing on details that will interest an audience. When you read a personal letter such as this one, remember that the intended audience was Laura Ingalls Wilder's husband. In writing to Almanzo Laura described what impressed her and what she thought would interest him. Her letter was not written for anyone else to read.

When Laura wrote her letters to Manly from San Francisco, she knew he would never see the Panama-Pacific International Exposition. He might never see San Francisco, either. So she wanted to show him those places through her letters.

In this lesson you will learn how Laura Ingalls Wilder describes for Manly the events and sights that she saw in San Francisco in 1915.

Sensory Impressions

When people describe experiences, they often begin by telling what they saw. Although you absorb many impressions through your eyes, you also experience life through your other senses—sound, smell, touch, and taste. When a writer tells about a place or experience, the more sensory details he or she includes, the more vivid the description will be.

Laura Ingalls Wilder is excited when she visits the Pacific Ocean for the first time. In her letter she describes her many sensory impressions:

> The water is such a deep wonderful blue and the sound of the waves breaking on the beach and their whisper as they flow back is something to dream about.

> The salt water tingled my feet and made them feel so good all the rest of the day. . . .

1. To what three senses does Wilder appeal when she describes these first impressions of the Pacific Ocean? To what other senses might she have appealed? Give examples.

Description and Action

Although descriptions focus on sensory impressions—what you can see, hear, smell, touch, and taste—they would not be as interesting without some action. In the following passage Laura Ingalls Wilder describes the *Gjöa*, a historic ship that she saw. To enliven the description, she tells a brief anecdote about the ship.

> It is battered and worn but strong-looking still. The ship was made in Norway in 1878 and with a crew of six men and the captain was three years and four months making the journey from Norway through the Northwest Passage to San Francisco. The government of Norway and the Norwegians of California gave the ship to this city and left it here.

The story of the ship's long journey from Norway to San Francisco encourages you to imagine how it became battered. Notice how Wilder gives the exact length of the voyage—three years and four months. That descriptive detail suggests the amount of hardship that the ship and its crew probably endured.

2. In the letter find another place in which Wilder blends sensory description and action. What does the action add to the description?

Descriptive Language

Like painters who use color and brush strokes to create images on canvas, writers use words to create images on paper. The more precise, lively, and colorful the words, the more vivid the images, or word pictures, become. Writers use specific nouns and strong verbs, as well as colorful adjectives and adverbs to create clear pictures for you.

Nouns are words that name people, places, or things. A good writer chooses the most specific nouns possible. For example, when Laura Ingalls Wilder visits the Sutro Estate, she names three buildings on the estate: the lodge, the mansion, and the observatory. Each noun gives you a specific idea of the building Wilder is describing. A lodge is a house on an estate set aside for a special purpose, such as a hunting base or a caretaker's home. A mansion suggests a large, elaborate residence. An observatory refers to a structure designed for observing the skies.

Some adjectives—such as *beautiful, fantastic,* and *splendid*—can be overused in descriptions. Even Wilder admits, "I have used the word 'beautiful' until it has no meaning, but what other word can I use?" An adjective like *beautiful* is too general. It does not create a clear image in your mind. *Beautiful* tells you that something is pleasing, but not how or why it is pleasing.

But Wilder also uses specific adjectives to paint clear pictures, as in the following passage.

> We went through the <u>massive</u> arched gateway made of stone with a <u>life-sized</u> lion crouched at each side and through a beautiful park of about forty acres.

The words *massive* and *life-sized* help you to imagine the arched stone gateway and the crouching lions. If Wilder had described the gateway as large and the lions as big, she would not have given as clear a picture of the scene.

3. Read the following passages. Then explain how the underlined word in each sentence helps to make the description vivid.

a. *At every turn in the paths we came upon statues of stone, figures of men and women and animals, and birds, half hidden among the foliage of flowering plants, or <u>peeping</u> out from among the trees.*

b. *The pillars of the balcony have porcelain insets, as do the posts of the stone fence around the house. They are small squares as smooth and <u>glossy</u> as my china, with quaint old-fashioned pictures of children and animals, instead of the flowers on my dishes.*

c. *We went from there out on the edge of the cliff where there are seats and statues around the edge and one can sit or stand and look over the <u>ramparts</u> across the blue Pacific.*

d. *An American eagle in stone stands <u>screaming</u> on the edge at one side.*

Figurative Language

In Chapter 1 you learned that figurative language involves using words and phrases in unusual ways to create strong, vivid images, to focus attention on certain ideas, or to compare things that are basically different. When words or phrases are used figuratively, they have meanings other than their usual, or literal, meanings. When describing people, places, and events, writers often use figurative language to give you a new way of looking at everyday things.

Laura Ingalls Wilder uses two figures of speech: similes and metaphors. A simile, you will recall, is a direct comparison between two unlike things connected by *like, as,* or *resembles* or the verb *appears* or *seems.* Wilder uses a simile to describe the stunt flyer: "Niles flew up and up and up, then dropped like an autumn leaf, floating and drifting and falling."

A metaphor is an imaginative implied comparison between two unlike things. It suggests that one thing *is* another thing. Wilder uses a metaphor to describe the fireworks: "After a little of this, rockets went shooting up the beams of light, burst and fell in showers of colored stars and strings of jewels."

"Rockets . . . fell in showers of colored stars and strings of jewels" is a metaphor. Of course, the rockets did not actually release stars and jewels. Wilder uses that metaphor to create an image of starlike and jewel-like fireworks showering from the sky.

4. Skim the selection to find another simile and another metaphor. Explain what image each creates.

Descriptions and the Author's Viewpoint

As you learned in Chapter 10, a writer's viewpoint affects his or her writing. Wilder's background, experiences, opinions, and beliefs certainly affected what she chose to describe and how she described it. In San Francisco Wilder saw the ocean for the first time. Naturally, her first letter to Manly focuses in large part on her impressions of the Pacific Ocean.

5. Read the following passages from Wilder's letter. What do you think they reveal about Wilder's viewpoint?

You must not expect me to see it all for it has been figured out that it would cost $500 just to see the five-cent, ten-cent and twenty-five-cent attractions.

It costs $40 a minute to show these northern lights, in salary alone. What the lights themselves cost is not for common mortals to know.

Rose says they have $4,000 due them from their real estate work and that Gillette has made an assignment to us of what he owes us, but they do not know when they, or we, will get this money as the men who bought the land are unable to pay now.

Description and Organization of Facts

As you learned in earlier chapters, authors organize their writing in different ways. Among the most common ways are chronological order, spatial order, and order of importance. Laura Ingalls Wilder uses all three methods in her letter to Manly.

Chronological order, you will remember from Chapter 7, refers to the arrangement of events in the order in which they occur. It is most useful for writing about a series of events. Spatial order refers to the order in which objects are arranged in space. Spatial order is often used to describe scenes. A writer might use spatial order to show a scene from the foreground to the background or from the left to the right. For example, a writer using spatial order might describe a party by telling you that some people were seated on a sofa to the right of the door, others were grouped around the stereo in one corner, and still others were standing by the food table in the middle of the room.

Order of importance refers to an ordering of topics or events based on the significance the writer places on each. For example, a writer may describe an unimportant idea first and work up to the most important idea. Or a writer might begin with the most important topic and work down to the least important.

In her letter Wilder describes her experiences in chronological order. By treating each event as it occurred, she lets Manly—and you—see how the events were related over time. The letter also follows order of importance. Wilder begins the letter by describing the exciting events of her trip. She ends by commenting on family business and responding to the news about Mr. Nall and the chickens, which Manly must have included in a letter to her. Those domestic matters probably seemed less important to her than the new experiences she was enjoying in San Francisco.

6. Review paragraphs 5 through 7 of Wilder's letter. How does Wilder use spatial order to describe the Sutro Estate? Why is spatial order suitable for the material Wilder is describing?

Questions for Thought and Discussion

The questions and activities that follow will help you explore "A Letter Home" in more depth and at the same time develop your critical thinking skills.

1. **Asking Questions.** In her letter Laura Ingalls Wilder describes her

experiences as completely as possible. Yet Manly might still wonder about her trip. Imagine that you are Manly. What questions about any of the experiences Laura mentions in her letter would you ask her?

2. **Making Inferences.** The last paragraphs of Wilder's letter concern domestic matters. Laura was probably responding to Manly's last letter to her, but you do not know exactly what he said. Make some educated guesses about who Mr. Nall was. Who do you think Inky was? What do you think Manly said about the chickens, milk, and pie?

3. **Analyzing Character.** Based on this letter, what kind of person do you think Laura Ingalls Wilder was? For each character trait you name, find evidence in her letter that supports that view of her.

4. **Comparing.** Compare Laura Ingalls Wilder's letter to her husband to Theodore Roosevelt's letters to his children. How are they similar? How are they different?

Writing About Literature

Several suggestions for writing projects follow. You may be asked to complete one or more of these projects. If you have any questions about how to begin a writing assignment, review Using the Writing Process, beginning on page 341.

1. **Writing a Postcard.** Imagine that you saw the fireworks with Laura, Rose, and Gillette. Write a postcard to a friend describing the scene in your own words. Use information from Wilder's letter, as well as your own ideas, to give a brief but vivid description of the scene.

2. **Writing a Description.** Think of an exciting event or experience in which you or a friend have recently been involved. Write a letter describing the event or experience. Use sensory impressions and choose your words carefully to make your description as realistic and as vivid as possible.

3. **Using Metaphors and Similes.** Prepare a diary entry about a school or vacation trip you have taken. In your diary entry use at least one metaphor and one simile to describe some aspect of the trip.

Chapter 12

Selection

Plymouth Rock and the Pilgrims
MARK TWAIN

Lesson

Style and Structure

About the Selection

"Plymouth Rock and the Pilgrims" is a speech. It was given by Mark Twain to a group called the New England Society of Philadelphia, on December 22, 1881.

Speeches are different from other forms of nonfiction writing because they are meant to be heard. They may be written before a speaking event to provide the speaker with an organized presentation, or they may be written down after the speech is given as a public record of the event.

The spoken version of a speech is seldom the same as the written version. Most good speakers do not read their speeches. Either they use notes to remind themselves of what they want to say, or they memorize the main points and add the details as they go along.

Even in the rare case when a speaker reads from a prepared text, the written copy does not show his or her facial expressions, hand gestures, or tone of voice. Those nonverbal elements are important because they affect the impact of the speech on an audience.

Speeches are given for many reasons and on many occasions. Some speeches, such as the opening and closing statements in debates, are formal and follow a set pattern. Others are more informal. Twain's speech "Plymouth Rock and the Pilgrims" was an after-dinner speech. That kind of speech may be formal or informal, depending on the purpose of the dinner and the personality of the speaker.

Mark Twain was one of the most popular speakers of his time. He had a sharp wit and did not hesitate to state his opinions. He is best known today as the author of *The Adventures of Tom Sawyer, The Adventures of Huckleberry Finn,* and *The Prince and the Pauper.* In his own time he was famous both as a writer and as a speaker.

Mark Twain was the pen name of Samuel Langhorne Clemens. A pen name is a name used by an author in place of his or her real name. Clemens was born in Florida, Missouri, in 1835. A few years later, his family moved to Hannibal, Missouri, on the banks of the Mississippi River. The river greatly influenced Clemens's life and writing.

As a boy, Samuel Clemens dreamed of becoming a Mississippi riverboat pilot. As a young man, he tried to fulfill that ambition by taking a job on a riverboat. The outbreak of the Civil War in 1861, however, put an end to piloting on the river. Clemens later wrote about his experiences in his book *Life on the Mississippi.* On the river, the phrase "mark twain" referred to a water depth of two fathoms. To pilots, this was considered "safe water." Clemens chose that riverboat term as his pen name.

Twain served briefly in the Confederate army, but his brother, who supported the Union cause, persuaded Twain to go west with him. There, Twain again turned to writing and soon his writing won national attention. In 1870 he married Olivia Langdon. The two eventually settled in Hartford, Connecticut, where Twain lived until his death in 1910.

Although Twain spent much of his life on the East coast, his two most famous books, *Tom Sawyer* and *Huckleberry Finn,* were inspired by his boyhood experiences in Hannibal, Missouri. Although both books are humorous, they also contain severe criticisms of various social evils, including slavery. While Twain was a humorist, he was also a man with a keen sense of justice. He frequently pointed out problems that he thought needed to be changed.

As a speaker, Mark Twain used his wit in the service of social justice. Twain's speaking career began in 1866 when he returned to California from a trip to the Sandwich Islands in the Pacific. He was short of money, so he agreed to give a lecture about his journey. The speech was a great success. Twain continued to give speeches throughout his career.

In the late 1800s speakers were in great demand. Neither radio, television, nor movies had yet been invented. So attending lectures—both educational and entertaining—was a popular leisure-time activity. Speeches were also popular at formal dinners. After dinner, one or more speakers would address the guests. Twain was often asked to give one of those after-dinner speeches.

Twain was critical of speakers who did not honor the art of public speaking. He himself was always carefully prepared. Before an engagement, he wrote, memorized, and rehearsed his speech. Once on the platform, however, he never used notes. His careful preparation gave the impression that he was speaking casually. He once said that it took at least four days to prepare a good speech.

People who heard Twain speak said that his manner was informal. Yet he had magnetism and charm. He spoke as if he were taking part in a conversation. If there was a lectern or other piece of furniture to lean on, he would lounge against it. Twain did not use elaborate gestures. He usually maintained a serious expression, fixing his eyes on the audience.

Although Twain wrote his speeches, modern researchers do not know exactly what he said or how he sounded. Sometimes he wrote more than one version of a speech. Often newspapers gave differing accounts of the same speech.

Newspaper accounts of Twain's speeches were not always accurate. After seeing one speech reprinted in a newspaper, Twain said, "You do not recognize the corpse. You wonder if this is really that gay and handsome creature of the evening before. You look him over and find that he certainly is those very remains. Then you want to bury him. You wish you could bury him privately."

The speech that you will read is a composite. That is, it combines several versions of the same speech.

Lesson Preview

The lesson that follows "Plymouth Rock and the Pilgrims" focuses on the author's style. As you learned in Chapter 5, style includes the kinds of words a writer chooses, as well as the kinds of images he or she creates. Every good writer has a personal style of writing. Style is what makes

Style and Structure

Mark Twain sound like Mark Twain and not like Frederick Douglass or Theodore Roosevelt.

A writer's style depends partly on his or her personality. It also depends on the writer's attitude toward his or her subject. The questions that follow will help you notice Mark Twain's style. As you read, think about how you would answer these questions.

1 What is Mark Twain's attitude toward the Pilgrims? Is it the same throughout his speech?

2 What words seem to show Twain's attitude toward his topic?

3 What parts of the speech do you find humorous? Why are they humorous?

4 What serious points does Twain make in his speech?

Vocabulary

Here are some difficult words that appear in the selection that follows. Study the words and their definitions, as well as the sentences that show how the words are used. This will help you get the most from your reading.

aggrandized praised highly. *They aggrandized the mayor's good work at the dinner given in his honor.*

intractable stubborn; unruly. *The intractable child refused to apologize for the noise he made.*

disputatious argumentative. *The disputatious family members rarely agreed on anything.*

predecessors people who came before. *After we bought the house, we realized that our predecessors had not made many repairs in it.*

rankles causes anger or irritation. *Because I am more qualified for the position, it still rankles to think of Sue's recent promotion.*

implacable   relentless. *The wolves were in implacable pursuit of the injured deer.*

pestiferous   annoying. *I finally killed the pestiferous mosquito that had been buzzing around my head.*

progenitors   ancestors. *A number of Celtic tribes were the progenitors of the people in modern Great Britain.*

laudation   praise. *The volunteer firemen deserve the town's laudation for the long hours and hard work they donate to the fire department.*

beguile   trick; lure. *Because the boy is so easy to trick, the other children beguile him into believing almost anything.*

prevaricating   lying. *Stop your prevaricating and tell the truth!*

opulent   rich; plentiful. *This opulent party is hosted by one of the wealthiest men in the city.*

Plymouth Rock and the Pilgrims

MARK TWAIN

First Annual Dinner, New England Society of Philadelphia,
December 22, 1881

I rise to protest. I have kept still for years, but really I think there is no sufficient justification for this sort of thing. What do you want to celebrate those people for?—those ancestors of yours, of 1620—the *Mayflower* tribe, I mean. What do you want to celebrate *them* for? Your pardon; the gentleman at my left assures me that you are not celebrating the Pilgrims themselves, but the landing of the Pilgrims at Plymouth Rock on the 22nd of December. So you are celebrating their landing. Why, the other pretext was thin enough, but this is thinner than ever; the other was tissue, tinfoil, fish bladder, but this is gold leaf.

Celebrating their landing! What was there remarkable about it, I would like to know? What can you be thinking of? Why, those Pilgrims had been at sea three or four months. It was the very middle of winter; it was as cold as death off Cape Cod, there. Why shouldn't they come ashore? If they hadn't landed there would be some reason in celebrating the fact. It would have been a case of monumental leatherheadedness which the world would not willingly let die. If it had been *you*, gentlemen, you probably wouldn't have landed, but you have no shadow of right to be celebrating, in your ancestors, gifts which they did not exercise, but only transmitted.

Why, to be celebrating the mere landing of the Pilgrims—to be trying to make out that this most natural, and simple, and customary procedure was an extraordinary circumstance—a circumstance to be amazed at and admired, aggrandized and glorified, at orgies like this for two hundred and sixty years—hang it, a horse would have known enough to land; a horse—pardon again; the gentleman on my right assures me that it was not merely the landing of the Pilgrims that we are celebrating, but the Pilgrims themselves. So we have struck an inconsistency here—one says it was the landing, the other says it was the Pilgrims. It is an inconsistency characteristic of your intractable and disputatious tribe, for you never agree about anything but Boston.

Well, then, what do you want to celebrate those Pilgrims for? They were a mighty hard lot—you know it. I grant you, without the slightest unwillingness, that they were a deal more gentle and merciful and just than were the peoples of Europe of that day; I grant you that they were better than their predecessors. But what of that?—that is nothing. People always progress. You are better than your fathers and grandfathers were (this is the first time I have ever aimed a measureless slander at the departed, for I consider such things improper). Yes, those among you who have not been in the penitentiary, if such there be, are better than your fathers and grandfathers were, but is that any sufficient reason for getting up annual dinners and celebrating you? No, by no means—by no means.

Well, I repeat, those Pilgrims were a hard lot. They took care of themselves, but they abolished everybody else's ancestors. I am a border ruffian from the state of Missouri. I am a Connecticut Yankee by adoption. I have the morals of Missouri and the culture of Connecticut, and that's the combination that makes the perfect man.

Style and Structure

But where are my ancestors? Whom shall I celebrate? Where shall I find the raw material? My first American ancestor, gentleman, was an Indian—an early Indian. Your ancestors skinned him alive, and I am an orphan. Not one drop of my blood flows in that Indian's veins today. I stand here, lone and forlorn, without an ancestor. They skinned him! I do not object to that, if they needed his fur; but alive, gentlemen—alive! They skinned him alive—and before company! That is what rankles. Think how he must have felt; for he was a sensitive Indian and easily embarrassed. If he had been a bird, it would have been all right, and no violence done to his feelings, because he would have been considered "dressed."[1] But he was not a bird, gentlemen, he was a man, and probably one of the most undressed men that ever was.

I ask you to put yourselves in his place. I ask it as a favor; I ask it as a tardy act of justice; I ask it in the interest of fidelity to the traditions of your ancestors; I ask it that the world may contemplate with vision unobstructed by disguising swallowtails and white cravats,[2] the spectacle which the true New England Society ought to present. Cease to come to these annual orgies in this hollow modern mockery—the surplusage of raiment.[3] Come in character; come in the summer grace, come in the unadorned simplicity, come in the free and joyous costume which your sainted ancestors provided for mine.

Later ancestors of mine were the Quakers, William Robinson, Marmaduke Stephenson, *et al.*[4] Your tribe chased them out of the country for their religion's sake; promised them death if they came back, for your ancestors had forsaken the homes they loved, and braved the perils of the sea, the implacable climate, and the savage wilderness, to acquire that highest and most precious of boons, freedom for every man on this broad continent to worship according to the dictates of his own conscience

---

1. **dressed:** an animal is said to be dressed after it has been killed, bled, and made ready for cooking.
2. **swallowtails and white cravats:** swallowtails refers to a man's dress jacket with two long tails in the back. A cravat is a necktie. A white cravat was worn for formal occasions.
3. **surplusage of raiment:** excess of clothing.
4. **William Robinson, Marmaduke Stephenson, *et al.*:** Robinson and Stephenson were hanged on Boston Common in 1659 for preaching Quaker beliefs. *Et al.* is a Latin abbreviation meaning "and others."

—and they were not going to allow a lot of pestiferous Quakers to interfere with it.

Your ancestors broke forever the chains of political slavery, and gave the vote to every man in this wide land, excluding none!—none except those who did not belong to the orthodox church. Your ancestors—yes, they were a hard lot; but, nevertheless, they gave us religious liberty to worship as they required us to worship, and political liberty to vote as the church required; and so I, the bereft one, I, the forlorn one, am here to do my best to help you celebrate them right.

The Quaker woman, Elizabeth Hooton,[5] was an ancestress of mine. Your people were pretty severe with her—you will confess that. But, poor thing! I believe they changed her opinions before she died, and took her into their fold; and so we have every reason to presume that when she died she went to the same place which your ancestors went to. It is a great pity, for she was a good woman. Roger Williams was an ancestor of mine. I don't really remember what your people did with him. But they banished him to Rhode Island, anyway. And then, I believe, recognizing that this was really carrying harshness to an unjustifiable extreme, they took pity on him and burned him. They were a hard lot!

All those Salem witches were ancestors of mine. Your people made it tropical for them. Yes, they did; by pressure and the gallows they made such a clean deal with them that there hasn't been a witch and hardly a halter[6] in our family from that day to this, and that is 189 years.

The first slave brought into New England out of Africa by your progenitors was an ancestor of mine—for I am of a mixed breed, an infinitely shaded and exquisite mongrel. I'm not one of your sham meerschaums[7] that you can color in a week. No, my complexion is the patient art of eight generations. Well, in my own time, I had acquired a lot of my kin—by purchase, and swapping around, and one way and another—and was

5. **Elizabeth Hooton:** sixty-year-old Quaker missionary in New England who was whipped and left to starve in a forest. She managed to escape, but the hardships probably hastened her death.
6. **halter:** noose.
7. **meerschaums:** tobacco pipes made of a light white clay. They became dark brown with use. Sham, or fake, meerschaums were colored and sold as used pipes.

Style and Structure

getting along very well. Then, with the inborn perversity of your lineage, you got up a war and took them all away from me. And so, again am I bereft, again am I forlorn; no drop of my blood flows in the veins of any living being who is marketable.

Oh my friends, hear me and reform! I seek your good, not mine. You have heard the speeches. Disband these New England societies—nurseries of a system of steadily augmenting laudation and hosannahing,[8] which, if persisted in uncurbed, may some day in the remote future beguile you into prevaricating and bragging. Oh, stop, stop while you are still temperate in your appreciation of your ancestors! Hear me, I beseech you; get up an auction and sell Plymouth Rock!

The Pilgrims were a simple and ignorant race. They had never seen any good rocks before, or at least any that were not watched, and so they were excusable for hopping ashore in frantic delight and clapping an iron fence[9] around this one. But you, gentlemen, are educated; you are enlightened; you know that in the rich land of your nativity, opulent New England, overflowing with rocks, this one isn't worth, at the outside, more than thirty-five cents. Therefore, sell it, before it is injured by exposure, or at least throw it open to the patent medicine[10] advertisements, and let it earn its taxes.

Yes, hear your true friend—your only true friend—list[11] to his voice. Disband these societies, hotbeds of vice, of moral decay—perpetuators of ancestral superstition. Here on this board I see water, I see milk, I see the wild and deadly lemonade. These are but steps upon the downward path. Next we shall see tea, then chocolate, then coffee—hotel coffee. A few more years—all too few, I fear—mark my words, we shall have cider!

Gentlemen, pause ere it be too late. You are on the broad road which

---

8. **laudation and hosannahing:** singing praises.
9. **iron fence:** by the 1800s, long after the Pilgrims had landed, an iron fence was set up around Plymouth Rock.
10. **patent medicine:** nonprescription medicine whose ingredients are protected, or secret. In Twain's day, patent medicines were often useless fakes.
11. **list:** poetic way of saying listen.

leads to dissipation, physical ruin, moral decay, gory crime and the gallows! I beseech you, I implore you, in the name of your anxious friends, in the name of your suffering families, in the name of your impending widows and orphans, stop ere it be too late. Disband these New England societies, renounce these soul-blistering saturnalia,[12] cease from varnishing the rusty reputations of your long-vanished ancestors—the super-high-moral old ironclads of Cape Cod, the pious buccaneers of Plymouth Rock—go home, and try to learn to behave!

However, chaff and nonsense aside, I think I honor and appreciate your Pilgrim stock as much as you do yourselves, perhaps; and I endorse and adopt a sentiment uttered by a grandfather of mine once—a man of sturdy opinions, of sincere make of mind, and not given to flattery. He said: "People may talk as they like about that Pilgrim stock, but, after all's said and done, it would be pretty hard to improve on those people; and, as for me, I don't mind coming out flat-footed and saying there ain't any way to improve on them—except having them born in Missouri!"

12. **saturnalia:** wild parties.

Reviewing the Selection

Answer each of the following questions without looking back at the selection.

Recalling Facts

1. At what time of year did the Pilgrims land at Plymouth Rock?
   - ☐ a. winter
   - ☐ b. spring
   - ☐ c. summer
   - ☐ d. fall

Understanding Main Ideas

2. When Twain says that the Pilgrims were "a hard lot," he means that they
   - ☐ a. could tolerate the New England climate.
   - ☐ b. survived the trip across the Atlantic.
   - ☐ c. were intolerant of people with different ideas.
   - ☐ d. did not allow themselves any luxuries.

Placing Events in Order

3. Twain says that his first American ancestor was
   - ☐ a. a Quaker.
   - ☐ b. a Pilgrim.
   - ☐ c. a Salem witch.
   - ☐ d. an Indian.

Finding Supporting Details

4. Twain criticizes the Pilgrims for
   - ☐ a. settling in a rocky area.
   - ☐ b. limiting political and religious freedom.
   - ☐ c. leaving England.
   - ☐ d. selling Plymouth Rock.

5. "I believe they changed her opinions before she died, and took her into their <u>fold</u>." In this context *fold* means
   - ☐ a. bend.
   - ☐ b. group.
   - ☐ c. ship.
   - ☐ d. confidence.

Interpreting the Selection

Answer each of the following questions. You may look back at the selection if necessary.

6. The part of Twain's speech about his ancestors was probably
   - ☐ a. based on research he had done.
   - ☐ b. an attempt to impress his audience.
   - ☐ c. not literally true.
   - ☐ d. told to him by his parents.

7. From Twain's speech, you can tell that he
   - ☐ a. wished he had been a Pilgrim.
   - ☐ b. thought the Pilgrims were great leaders.
   - ☐ c. felt the Pilgrims were overpraised.
   - ☐ d. believed the Pilgrims were overdressed.

8. Which of the following information in Twain's speech is a fact?
   - ☐ a. The Pilgrims abolished everyone else's ancestors.
   - ☐ b. The soil of New England is rocky.
   - ☐ c. The Pilgrims were simple and ignorant.
   - ☐ d. People are always better than their fathers or grandfathers.

9. Twain says that the landing of the Pilgrims at Plymouth Rock should not be celebrated because
   - ☐ a. landing was the only sensible thing to do.
   - ☐ b. the Pilgrims did not actually land on the rock.
   - ☐ c. others had landed before the Pilgrims.
   - ☐ d. the Pilgrims should have landed farther south.

10. Mark Twain was critical of the Pilgrims because they
    - ☐ a. were religious.
    - ☐ b. persecuted other people.
    - ☐ c. landed at Plymouth and not in Connecticut.
    - ☐ d. made the Indians wear formal clothes.

Style and Structure

In "Plymouth Rock and the Pilgrims," Mark Twain is both humorous and serious. Humor that makes a serious point is part of Mark Twain's style. As you have learned, style is the distinctive way in which a person writes. It does not refer to *what* is said but rather to *how* it is said.

Writers have different styles. Style is what makes each writer sound unique. A writer's style depends partly on his or her personality. In other words, the character of the writer is expressed in his or her writing. A writer's style is also expressed through the structure of a piece of writing. Structure is a writer's arrangement or overall design of a work. Structure refers to the way words, sentences, and paragraphs are organized to create a complete work.

Speeches, of course, are not only written in a specific style but also delivered in a unique speaking style. A good speech is written in such a way that it allows the speaker to make the most of his or her speaking style.

In this lesson you will study some of the ways in which "Plymouth Rock and the Pilgrims" reflects Mark Twain's style.

Elements of Style

For most authors, style grows naturally out of their approach to a subject. When they write, they make choices about tone—their attitude toward their subject or audience—and diction, a writer's choice and arrangement of words. Many other elements, such as imagery and sentence length, are also part of an author's style.

A writer's tone might be enthusiastic, hostile, critical, or indifferent. One clue to a writer's attitude toward a subject is the words or phrases that he or she uses. As you learned in Chapter 1, all words have a literal, or dictionary, meaning, called denotation. Some words also have connotations, the emotions that words arouse or the meanings that they suggest beyond their denotations.

A writer can express the same thought in many different ways. In his speech Mark Twain refers to the Pilgrims as "the *Mayflower* tribe." Instead of using the word *tribe,* he could have said "brave souls," "freedom seekers," "gang," or "fools." Each of those words or phrases suggests a different attitude toward the Pilgrims. By choosing the word *tribe,* Twain's tone suggests a close-knit group of people. He expresses a humorous and casual attitude toward the Pilgrims. *Tribe* also creates an association between the Pilgrims and the Indians that makes the Pilgrims' injustice to the Indians seem even more brutal. Twain is saying that the Pilgrims were no better or more spiritually advanced than the native Americans, many of whom the Pilgrims killed.

1. *Read the following passages from Twain's speech. For each passage, explain what the underlined word means, and what attitude toward the subject the word suggests. Then think of another word that would have suggested a different attitude.*

a. *If they hadn't landed there would be some reason in celebrating the fact. It would have been a case of monumental* <u>leatherheadedness</u> *which the world would not willingly let die.*

b. *Disband these New England societies—*<u>nurseries</u> *of a system of steadily augmenting laudation and hosannahing, which, if persisted in uncurbed, may some day in the remote future beguile you into prevaricating and bragging.*

The Structure of the Speech

In preparing "Plymouth Rock and the Pilgrims," Mark Twain had to decide not only what he was going to say but how he was going to structure his speech. How should he put his ideas together? The simplest way for you to examine his structure is to study the beginning, the middle, and the end of his speech.

The Beginning. How would you expect someone to begin a speech in honor of the Pilgrims' landing at Plymouth Rock? You usually hear first about the persecution the Pilgrims faced in England, then about the hardships of their voyage, and finally about their relief upon reaching land. Another way to begin a speech might be to describe the virtues and qualities for which the Pilgrims are remembered.

How does Twain begin his speech? His first words are "I rise to protest." Those words probably made his audience pay attention to him. Twain was clearly announcing that the audience would not hear a traditional speech about the Pilgrims.

2. Skim the first five paragraphs of Twain's speech. What reasons does Twain give for (a) not celebrating the landing of the Pilgrims, and (b) not celebrating the Pilgrims themselves?

In his opening paragraphs Twain lets his audience know that he is not going to repeat the expected anecdotes about the Pilgrims. In fact, he is going to try to persuade his audience that their celebration is based on false reasoning. Although he was invited to give a speech in honor of the Pilgrims, Twain has reversed that purpose.

The Middle. If Twain's purpose is to persuade his audience that the celebration of the Pilgrims' landing is foolish, then he must present strong arguments to support his view. The middle of the speech contains Twain's arguments.

3. Read the middle of the speech, paragraphs 6 through 16. What two main arguments for not celebrating the Pilgrims does Twain develop? Do you think that Twain wants those arguments to be taken seriously? Explain your answer.

The End. Twain begins the last paragraph of his speech by saying that everything he has said before was "chaff [jokes] and nonsense." He assures his audience that he honors and appreciates the Pilgrims as much as they do.

Does Twain really want his audience to believe that most of his speech was nonsense? He probably does not. He has certainly made some strong arguments against the Pilgrims. His audience should consider his ideas seriously. The purpose of his last paragraph is to end on a pleasant note. After all, the dinner is a social occasion, and the members of the society invited Twain as their guest speaker. Moreover, they are not responsible for the actions of their ancestors.

By organizing his speech in the way he did, Twain accomplished several purposes. He challenged his audience's acceptance of the traditional view of the Pilgrims. He then criticized the Pilgrims' behavior toward the Indians and Quakers. Finally, he softened his criticism by denying that he meant what he said.

How does the structure of Twain's speech relate to his style? Twain was an outspoken critic of social problems. His style was critical but humorous. The structure of his speech allows him to make his points about the Pilgrims and still end on a pleasant, humorous note.

4. Imagine that Twain had reversed the order of his speech, starting first with the ideas in the last paragraph and then criticizing the Pilgrims. How would that structure have changed the style of the speech?

Humor and Style

A central element of Mark Twain's style is his humor. He surrounds his sharp criticism with layers of humor. The technique is effective because people often absorb difficult truths if they can laugh in the process. Many comedians today encourage audiences to think about serious issues by making audiences laugh.

Twain uses several techniques to achieve his humorous style. One technique is repetition. He says the same idea in several ways, using different words each time. Consider this passage from his speech:

> What do you want to celebrate those people for?—those ancestors of yours, of 1620—the *Mayflower* tribe, I mean. What do you want to celebrate *them* for?

Notice that Twain finds three ways to refer to the Pilgrims: "those people," "those ancestors of yours," "the *Mayflower* tribe." The phrases are not flattering. Yet if Twain had simply said, "Why do you want to celebrate the Pilgrims?" the question would have sounded like an obvious attack. By using repetition, he makes his opening remarks more humorous and makes the speech more casual and natural.

5. Find another example of the use of repetition to achieve humor. Explain why the repetition is humorous.

Another technique of humor is irony. As you learned in Chapter 1, irony is the contrast between appearance and reality or what is expected and what actually happens. Notice Twain's use of irony when he speaks about the Pilgrims' treatment of the Indians.

> Your ancestors skinned him alive. . . . They skinned him! I do not object to that, if they needed his fur; but alive, gentlemen—alive! They skinned him alive—and before company!

Twain does not really mean that it would have been all right for the Pilgrims to have skinned the Indian "if they needed his fur." He is using irony to point out how unjustly the Pilgrims deprived the Indians of their land and heritage. Twain is also using two different meanings of the word *skinned*. To skin means (1) to remove the skin from, and (2) to cheat or swindle. In Twain's opinion both meanings apply to the Pilgrims' brutal treatment of the Indian.

6. Find another example of Twain's use of irony. Explain what is ironic about the words or phrases that Twain uses.

A third element of Twain's humor is the use of circumlocution. Circumlocution is an indirect way of saying something. It often involves using many more words than necessary to express an idea. Read the paragraph on page 288 that begins: "I ask you to put yourselves in his [the Indian's] place."

What is Twain actually saying in that paragraph? He is asking the people in the audience to put themselves in the place of the Indians (who were deprived of everything by the audience's ancestors) and come to their annual banquets naked. By using circumlocution, however, he turns a bitter accusation into a humorous suggestion.

7. In the following passage Twain uses circumlocution again. Explain what Twain is actually saying.

I believe they [the Pilgrims] changed her [Elizabeth Hooton's] opinions before she died, and took her into their fold; and so we have every reason to presume that when she died she went to the same place which your ancestors went to. It is a great pity, for she was a good woman.

Speaking Style

Every speaker has his or her own style of addressing an audience. Speakers often adjust their styles to their audiences or the occasion. For example, a comedian may speak quickly and use facial expressions and hand gestures to make a point. A preacher or public official usually speaks more slowly, with a concerned expression that shows his or her sincerity.

You do not know exactly how Mark Twain delivered his speech. But you can make some educated guesses. You know that he used the people on either side of him as props. That is, he pretended that they interrupted his speech to correct him about what was being celebrated. You can assume that he was pretending because Twain always planned his speeches ahead of time.

You can also make some guesses about Twain's delivery based on the punctuation. Exclamation points, for example, suggest emphasis, as do words printed in italics.

8. Based on the speech and what you know about Mark Twain, what style do you think he used in delivering "Plymouth Rock and the Pilgrims"? Was he formal or casual? Did he speak slowly or quickly? Do you think he gestured with his hands? Give reasons for your answers.

Questions for Thought and Discussion

The questions and activities that follow will help you explore "Plymouth Rock and the Pilgrims" in more depth and at the same time develop your critical thinking skills.

1. **Generalizing.** What groups of people does Mark Twain claim were his ancestors? What do all of those people have in common?

2. **Analyzing Humor.** A humorous technique used by Twain is exaggeration. Find at least two examples of exaggeration in the speech and explain what is humorous about each.

3. **Interpreting a Speech.** Divide the class into small groups. Each group should be assigned one or two paragraphs of Twain's speech. After reading the part, each group should choose a student to give that part of the speech. After each part is presented to the whole class, discuss its meaning and presentation. After you have discussed the entire speech, try to decide how Twain might have delivered "Plymouth Rock and the Pilgrims" on December 22, 1881.

Writing About Literature

Several suggestions for writing projects follow. You may be asked to complete one or more of these projects. If you have any questions about how to begin a writing assignment, review Using the Writing Process, beginning on page 341.

1. **Preparing a Newspaper Report.** Prepare a newspaper article reporting on Twain's speech the day after it was given. As part of the article, summarize the speech, give a few details about Mark Twain, and comment on Twain's presentation. You may make up details about the presentation.

2. **Writing a Speech.** Choose an actual event in history and write a humorous speech in honor of that event. Think about who your audience might be. Try to use some of the techniques that Mark Twain used. After you have written your speech, think about how you would deliver it. Possible topics include a local historical event, the signing of the Declaration of Independence, or Columbus's arrival in America.

3. **Explaining an Opinion.** Decide whether you agree or disagree with Mark Twain's view of the Pilgrims. Then write a short paper in which you explain your opinion as it relates to Twain's. Use examples from the speech to illustrate your views.

Chapter 13

Selection   *I Have a Dream*
MARTIN LUTHER KING, JR.

Lesson   *Persuasion*

About the Selection

"I Have a Dream" is one of the most powerful political speeches ever given. The Reverend Martin Luther King, Jr., gave the speech outside the Lincoln Memorial in Washington, D.C., on August 28, 1963. The occasion was the largest civil rights march ever held.

Martin Luther King, Jr., was an important force behind that march, which was called the March on Washington for Jobs and Freedom. The march was organized to show support for a civil rights bill that Congress was debating. The bill was designed to support the integration of public schools and other public facilities.

Civil rights leaders hoped to attract at least 100,000 marchers from all over the country. They were more than successful. A crowd estimated at 250,000 people joined the march. About 60,000 of the marchers were white.

Martin Luther King, Jr., was one of several prominent black leaders scheduled to speak at the rally after the march. The leaders had agreed that each person would speak for only eight minutes. King worked on his speech with several aides the night before. They wondered how he could possibly say all that needed to be said in just eight minutes. Finally, one of King's aides said, "Look, Martin, you let the Lord lead you. You go on and do what the Spirit say do."

The next day the crowd was already beginning to thin when A. Philip Randolph introduced King as the "moral leader of our nation."

King began to give the speech that he had written the night before. But as he sensed the support and enthusiasm of the crowd, he ignored his prepared text and spoke from the heart.

"I have a dream," he said. The crowd shouted, "Tell us! Tell us!" He continued, "I have a dream that one day on the red hills of Georgia, sons of former slaves and sons of former slave-owners will be able to sit down together at the table of brotherhood." "Yes! Yes! I see it," the crowd shouted.

The people responded as though they were in a church service. By listening to "the Spirit," King turned the political rally into a powerful emotional experience for the participants. As he neared the end of his speech, many in the crowd wept.

Martin Luther King, Jr., was born Michael Luther King, Jr., on January 15, 1929. His parents changed his name to Martin when he was six years old. At about the same time, his father changed his own name to Martin Luther. King's father was pastor of Ebenezer Baptist Church in Atlanta, Georgia. Young Martin grew up in a comfortable middle-class home. Still, he experienced the pain of segregation early in his life when two white friends were forbidden to play with him because he was black.

King attended segregated schools in Atlanta. He graduated from high school at the age of fifteen after skipping the ninth and twelfth grades. While still in college, he became an ordained minister and was appointed assistant pastor in his father's church.

In 1955 King became involved in the civil rights movement when he led protesters in a boycott of segregated buses in Montgomery, Alabama. During the boycott, King's philosophy of nonviolent protest received national attention. The philosophy was inspired by the teachings of Jesus Christ and Mohandas Gandhi. King's commitment to nonviolence was tested during the boycott when his house was bombed. When an angry crowd of blacks gathered outside his home after the bombing, he calmed them by saying that they too must fight violence with nonviolent protest.

In 1957 Dr. King and other black leaders formed the Southern Christian Leadership Conference (SCLC) to fight discrimination. King traveled extensively, making speeches and taking part in nonviolent protests. In 1964 he became the youngest person to win the Nobel Peace Prize.

In April 1968 King was assassinated in Memphis, Tennessee. Millions of people around the world mourned his death. Today, he is remembered as a man dedicated to equal rights for all people in the United States and as a believer in nonviolence.

Lesson Preview

The lesson that follows "I Have a Dream" focuses on the techniques of persuasion. A person usually gives a political speech to try to persuade an audience to think or act in a certain way. One way to persuade people is to present strong reasons for what you want others to do. Another way is to appeal to their emotions. In his speech Dr. King used both those methods.

The questions that follow will help you identify the persuasive techniques that King used. As you read, think about how you would answer these questions.

1 What reason does King give to show that blacks deserve better treatment?

2 How does he show that a civil rights bill is necessary?

3 How does he answer people who say that the civil rights movement should move more slowly?

4 What warning does he give to his followers?

5 What words and phrases does King use to appeal to his audience's emotions?

Vocabulary

Here are some difficult words that appear in the selection that follows. Study the words and their definitions, as well as the sentences that show how the words are used. This will help you get the most from your reading.

manacles restraints; shackles. *Adult education classes often help to break the manacles of illiteracy.*

desolate joyless and deserted. *The girl was desolate when she realized that her puppy was lost.*

degenerate decline; deteriorate. *I hope the debate will not degenerate into a petty argument.*

engulfed swallowed up; overwhelmed. *A new concern for health and fitness has engulfed many people in this country.*

tribulation great misery and distress. *The Pilgrims suffered great tribulation in their search for religious freedom.*

prodigious enormous; huge. *The Pacific Ocean contains a prodigious amount of water.*

I Have a Dream

MARTIN LUTHER KING, JR.

I am happy to join with you today in what will go down in history as the greatest demonstration for freedom in the history of our nation.

Fivescore[1] years ago, a great American, in whose symbolic shadow we stand today, signed the Emancipation Proclamation.[2] This momentous decree came as a great beacon light of hope to millions of Negro slaves who had been seared in the flames of withering injustice. It came as a joyous daybreak to end the long night of their captivity.

But one hundred years later, the Negro still is not free; one hundred years later, the life of the Negro is still sadly crippled by the manacles of segregation and the chains of discrimination; one hundred years later, the Negro lives on a lonely island of poverty in the midst of a vast ocean

---

1. **Fivescore:** one hundred; a score is twenty.
2. **Emancipation Proclamation:** an executive order, signed by Abraham Lincoln on January 1, 1863, during the Civil War. It abolished slavery in the Confederate states.

of material prosperity; one hundred years later, the Negro is still languished in the corners of American society and finds himself in exile in his own land.

So we've come here today to dramatize a shameful condition. In a sense we've come to our nation's capital to cash a check. When the architects of our republic wrote the magnificent words of the Constitution and the Declaration of Independence, they were signing a promissory note[3] to which every American was to fall heir. This note was the promise that all men, yes, black men as well as white men, would be guaranteed the unalienable rights of life, liberty, and the pursuit of happiness.

It is obvious today that America has defaulted[4] on this promissory note in so far as her citizens of color are concerned. Instead of honoring this sacred obligation, America has given the Negro people a bad check; a check which has come back marked "insufficient funds." We refuse to believe that there are insufficient funds in the great vaults of opportunity of this nation. And so we've come to cash this check, a check that will give us upon demand the riches of freedom and the security of justice.

We have also come to this hallowed spot to remind America of the fierce urgency of now. This is no time to engage in the luxury of cooling off or to take the tranquilizing drug of gradualism.[5] Now is the time to make real the promises of democracy; now is the time to rise from the dark and desolate valley of segregation to the sunlit path of racial justice; now is the time to lift our nation from the quicksands of racial injustice to the solid rock of brotherhood; now is the time to make justice a reality for all God's children. It would be fatal for the nation to overlook the urgency of the moment. This sweltering summer of the Negro's legitimate discontent will not pass until there is an invigorating autumn of freedom and equality.

Nineteen sixty-three is not an end, but a beginning. And those who hope that the Negro needed to blow off steam and will now be content,

3. **promissory note:** a note that promises to pay a debt.
4. **defaulted:** failed to do something required by duty or law.
5. **gradualism:** the policy of approaching a goal by gradual steps.

will have a rude awakening if the nation returns to business as usual.

There will be neither rest nor tranquility in America until the Negro is granted his citizenship rights. The whirlwinds of revolt will continue to shake the foundations of our nation until the bright day of justice emerges.

But there is something that I must say to my people who stand on the warm threshold which leads into the palace of justice. In the process of gaining our rightful place we must not be guilty of wrongful deeds.

Let us not seek to satisfy our thirst for freedom by drinking from the cup of bitterness and hatred. We must forever conduct our struggle on the high plane of dignity and discipline. We must not allow our creative protest to degenerate into physical violence. Again and again we must rise to the majestic heights of meeting physical force with soul force.

The marvelous new militancy which has engulfed the Negro community must not lead us to a distrust of all white people, for many of our white brothers, as evidenced by their presence here today, have come to realize that their destiny is tied up with our destiny and they have come to realize that their freedom is inextricably bound to our freedom. We cannot walk alone.

And as we walk, we must make the pledge that we shall always march ahead. We cannot turn back. There are those who are asking the devotees of civil rights, "When will you be satisfied?" We can never be satisifed as long as the Negro is the victim of the unspeakable horrors of police brutality.

We can never be satisifed as long as our bodies, heavy with fatigue of travel, cannot gain lodging in the motels of the highways and the hotels of the cities. We cannot be satisfied as long as the Negro's basic mobility is from a smaller ghetto to a larger one.

We can never be satisfied as long as our children are stripped of their selfhood and robbed of their dignity by signs stating "for whites only." We cannot be satisfied as long as a Negro in Mississippi cannot vote and a Negro in New York believes he has nothing for which to vote. No, we are not satisfied, and we will not be satisfied until justice rolls down like waters and righteousness like a mighty stream.

I am not unmindful that some of you have come here out of excessive trials and tribulation. Some of you have come fresh from narrow jail cells. Some of you have come from areas where your quest for freedom left you battered by the storms of persecution and staggered by the winds of police brutality. You have been the veterans of creative suffering. Continue to work with the faith that unearned suffering is redemptive.[6]

Go back to Mississippi; go back to Alabama; go back to South Carolina; go back to Georgia; go back to Louisiana; go back to the slums and ghettos of the northern cities, knowing that somehow this situation can, and will be changed. Let us not wallow in the valley of despair.

So I say to you, my friends, that even though we must face the difficulties of today and tomorrow, I still have a dream. It is a dream deeply rooted in the American dream that one day this nation will rise up and live out the true meaning of its creed—we hold these truths to be self-evident, that all men are created equal.

I have a dream that one day on the red hills of Georgia, sons of former slaves and sons of former slave-owners will be able to sit down together at the table of brotherhood.

I have a dream that one day, even the state of Mississippi, a state sweltering with the heat of injustice, sweltering with the heat of oppression, will be transformed into an oasis of freedom and justice.

I have a dream my four little children will one day live in a nation where they will not be judged by the color of their skin but by the content of their character. I have a dream today!

I have a dream that one day, down in Alabama, with its vicious racists, with its governor having his lips dripping with the words of interposition and nullification,[7] that one day, right there in Alabama, little black boys and black girls will be able to join hands with little white boys and white girls as sisters and brothers. I have a dream today!

6. **redemptive:** bringing about spiritual salvation.
7. **interposition and nullification:** two disputed doctrines that concern the rights of states to reject federal laws. States opposed to integration sometimes claimed these rights in order to keep local segregation laws in force despite the requirements of federal laws.

I have a dream that one day every valley shall be exalted, every hill and mountain shall be made low, the rough places shall be made plain, and the crooked places shall be made straight and the glory of the Lord will be revealed and all flesh shall see it together.

This is our hope. This is the faith that I go back to the South with.

With this faith we will be able to hew out of the mountain of despair a stone of hope. With this faith we will be able to transform the jangling discords of our nation into a beautiful symphony of brotherhood.

With this faith we will be able to work together, to pray together, to struggle together, to go to jail together, to stand up for freedom together, knowing that we will be free one day. This will be the day when all of God's children will be able to sing with new meaning—"my country 'tis of thee; sweet land of liberty; of thee I sing; land where my fathers died, land of the pilgrim's pride; from every mountain side, let freedom ring"— and if America is to be a great nation, this must become true.

So let freedom ring from the prodigious hilltops of New Hampshire.

Let freedom ring from the mighty mountains of New York.

Let freedom ring from the heightening Alleghenies of Pennsylvania.

Let freedom ring from the snow-capped Rockies of Colorado.

Let freedom ring from the curvaceous slopes of California.

But not only that.

Let freedom ring from Stone Mountain of Georgia.

Let freedom ring from Lookout Mountain of Tennessee.

Let freedom ring from every hill and molehill of Mississippi, from every mountainside, let freedom ring.

And when we allow freedom to ring, when we let it ring from every village and hamlet, from every state and city, we will be able to speed up that day when all of God's children—black men and white men, Jews and Gentiles, Catholics and Protestants—will be able to join hands and to sing in the words of the old Negro spiritual, "Free at last, free at last; thank God Almighty, we are free at last."

Reviewing the Selection

Answer each of the following questions without looking back at the selection.

Recalling Facts

1. King urged his audience to avoid
   - ☐ a. injustice.
   - ☐ b. dreaming.
   - ☐ c. white Americans.
   - ☐ d. wrongful deeds.

Understanding Main Ideas

2. Which phrase best summarizes King's dream?
   - ☐ a. increased economic aid for black Americans
   - ☐ b. an uprising against police brutality
   - ☐ c. equal treatment for black Americans
   - ☐ d. the end of violent protest

Placing Events in Order

3. Before King described his dream, he talked about
   - ☐ a. the civil rights bill in Congress.
   - ☐ b. the Civil War.
   - ☐ c. his family.
   - ☐ d. the debt that America owes to black people.

Finding Supporting Details

4. An example of discrimination that King mentioned is
   - ☐ a. "for whites only" signs.
   - ☐ b. job discrimination.
   - ☐ c. the Emancipation Proclamation.
   - ☐ d. lynchings.

5. "There will be neither rest nor <u>tranquility</u> in America until the Negro is granted his citizenship rights." In this context *tranquility* means
   - ☐ a. peace.
   - ☐ b. happiness.
   - ☐ c. freedom.
   - ☐ d. control.

Interpreting the Selection

Answer each of the following questions. You may look back at the selection if necessary.

6. King believed that the civil rights movement should be multiracial because
   - ☐ a. only whites could convince other whites to support equality.
   - ☐ b. the freedom of all people is interconnected.
   - ☐ c. blacks were not allowed to vote for members of Congress.
   - ☐ d. there were no black representatives in Congress.

7. When King described his dream for America, he
   - ☐ a. did not include white people.
   - ☐ b. was really talking about life in heaven and not on earth.
   - ☐ c. used mostly images of the southern states.
   - ☐ d. was talking mostly about his hopes for his own children.

8. One opinion that King gives in his speech
   is that
   - ☐ a. the March on Washington was the
     largest demonstration in United
     States history.
   - ☐ b. the Emancipation Proclamation did not
     free the slaves.
   - ☐ c. blacks in both northern and southern
     states are oppressed.
   - ☐ d. faith and nonviolence will win in
     the end.

*Identifying Cause
and Effect*

9. King feared that an effect of the new black
   militancy might be
   - ☐ a. police brutality against blacks.
   - ☐ b. distrust of all white people by
     black Americans.
   - ☐ c. the end of the civil rights movement.
   - ☐ d. retaliation by the Ku Klux Klan.

*Drawing
Conclusions*

10. When King said that America had "given
    the Negro people a bad check," he was
    referring mostly to the
    - ☐ a. black revolt against injustice.
    - ☐ b. Emancipation Proclamation.
    - ☐ c. jailing of civil rights workers.
    - ☐ d. discrimination against blacks.

Persuasion

In "I Have a Dream," Martin Luther King, Jr., was addressing two very different audiences. One audience was the crowd of 250,000 people gathered at the Lincoln Memorial. Those people had traveled to Washington, D.C., from all over the country to participate in the March on Washington for Jobs and Freedom. They believed in the same things that King believed in: equality for black Americans and nonviolent protest.

King's second audience was the rest of the United States. The march and rally were shown on national television and reported in newspapers across the country. Thus, King's second audience included people who agreed with him, people who strongly opposed his ideas, and those who were indifferent to his ideas.

King had different goals for his different audiences. For supporters of the civil rights movement, King wanted to deliver an inspirational message. He wanted to encourage his supporters to continue their work on behalf of the movement. For those who opposed or were indifferent to equal rights for black Americans, King wanted to deliver a persuasive speech. He wanted to convince them not only of the justice of the cause but also of its inevitable triumph. So King had two major goals: to inspire and to persuade.

In this lesson you will examine how Martin Luther King, Jr., used rational arguments and emotional appeals to accomplish both of his goals.

Using Rational Arguments

When you hear the word *argument,* you may think of a quarrel or an angry discussion. *Argument,* however, has another meaning. In a political speech or debate, an <u>argument</u> is one or more reasons presented by the speaker to lead the audience to a logical conclusion. Argumentation, you will recall, is one of the four main kinds of nonfiction writing.

As you learned in About the Selection, the March on Washington was planned to show support for a civil rights bill being debated in Congress. The purpose of the bill was to guarantee black Americans basic rights such as the right to use public facilities and the right to register to vote. In his speech Dr. King wanted to show that the bill was necessary and just.

1. Reread paragraphs 4 and 5 of King's speech. What argument does he give in support of the rights of black Americans?

King wanted to persuade people who were indifferent to the bill to support it. To do this, he had to convince them that blacks were entitled to equal rights and that they were currently being denied those rights. A convincing argument, however, must be built on concrete details rather than on general statements.

2. In the speech find a place in which King lists specific ways in which blacks were being denied equal rights through discrimination. Summarize the different types of discrimination he mentions.

Anticipating the Opposition

One technique of persuasive speaking and writing is called <u>anticipating the opposition</u>. That means addressing the arguments you think your opponents will use and answering those arguments effectively.

Martin Luther King, Jr., anticipated opposition from two separate groups. The first group included people who thought that the civil rights movement was growing too fast. That group believed that white people needed more time to get used to the idea of equality for black Americans. King calls this position "gradualism." He opposes the idea that integration should take place gradually. In his speech he says, "This is no time to engage in the luxury of cooling off or to take the tranquilizing drug of gradualism."

3. Read paragraph 8. In your own words explain King's answer to those who supported "gradualism." Do you think he gives an effective answer to the argument that integration should proceed more slowly? Why or why not?

King also expected opposition from those Americans who felt that King's philosophy of nonviolent protest was not effective. Those people said that the civil rights bill before Congress was too weak to improve conditions for black Americans. They called for more militant, or aggressive, action to achieve "black power."

King did not want to antagonize militants openly. After all, the march was a rally for freedom and justice for all blacks. So King worded his answer to the black militants carefully.

4. Read the paragraph on page 309 that begins, "The marvelous new militancy which has engulfed the Negro community. . . ." To whom do you think the paragraph is addressed? What do you think King was trying to accomplish with this statement? Was he trying to persuade the opposition to change its views, or was he trying to accomplish something else?

Emotional Appeal

Unlike rational arguments that try to change the way people think about an issue, emotional appeals try to influence an audience's feelings.

Suppose, for example, that you wanted to borrow five dollars from a friend. You might offer to repay the debt with interest in one week. You might also remind your friend that you have borrowed money before and repaid it on time. Both would be rational arguments in support of your request for a loan.

On the other hand, if you described how desperately you needed the money, you would be making an emotional appeal. You would be relying on your friend's kindness, rather than explaining why the loan would be a reasonable business arrangement.

Most persuasive writing mixes logical arguments with emotional appeals. People are influenced by their feelings as well as by their reason. In "I Have a Dream" Martin Luther King, Jr., appealed to his listeners' emotions.

Allusion. King used several techniques that affect people's feelings. One technique is called allusion. An <u>allusion</u> is a reference to something real or fictitious outside of a speech or a piece of writing. The speaker or writer expects the audience to recognize the allusion.

> Fivescore years ago, a great American, in whose symbolic shadow we stand today, signed the Emancipation Proclamation.

The "great American," of course, is Abraham Lincoln. The words "fivescore years ago" are an allusion to Lincoln's famous Gettysburg Address, which begins "Fourscore and seven years ago. . . ." In the Gettysburg Address Lincoln called on the nation to rededicate itself to "the proposition that all men are created equal." In "I Have a Dream" King makes the same proposition. The allusion makes the audience associate King's cause with Lincoln's cause.

5. How can King's allusion to the Gettysburg Address be considered an emotional appeal? What effect do you think it may have had on the audience?

6. Find the paragraph at the top of page 311 that begins, "I have a dream that one day every valley shall be exalted. . . ." The words "every valley shall be exalted" and the phrases that follow are taken from the Bible. What effect do you think that allusion might have had on King's audience?

Figurative Language. Another way for a speaker to appeal to an audience's emotions is by using figurative language. As you learned in Chapter 1, figurative language involves using words and phrases in unusual ways to create strong, vivid images. Such images are often intended to appeal to the emotions.

Throughout the speech, King includes metaphors to convey his meaning. Read the following metaphor: "One hundred years later, the Negro lives on a lonely island of poverty in the midst of a vast ocean of material prosperity."

King compares poverty to an island and prosperity to an ocean. He uses figurative language to suggest that poverty isolates blacks from American society just as the ocean isolates people on an island from those on the mainland. King could have said that poverty isolates blacks from the mainstream of American society. But that statement would have had less emotional appeal than the image of the island.

In paragraphs 4 and 5 of the speech, King compares the problems of black Americans to a person cashing a check. In those paragraphs he uses an <u>extended metaphor</u>, a special kind of metaphor that is longer and more involved than an ordinary metaphor. The smaller metaphors within an extended metaphor contribute to the overall meaning.

7. Review paragraphs 4 and 5 of the speech. What words in each paragraph are part of the extended metaphor? Summarize the meaning of the extended metaphor. Why does the metaphor have greater emotional appeal than its literal meaning?

Repetition. Another technique that can be used to sway an audience's emotions is repetition of words or phrases. Read paragraph 3 of King's speech. Notice that King repeats the phrase "one hundred years" three times. The meaning of the paragraph would have been clear without the repetition. But the repetition creates a rhythm that emphasizes King's point: It has been a long time since the Emancipation Proclamation, yet blacks are still not free.

8. Find at least two other examples of repetition in King's speech. Explain the point King was trying to emphasize in each case.

Emotional Appeal Through Delivery

As you have read, many people in the audience wept during Dr. King's speech. The effect of a speech is determined not only by *what* is said but also by *how* it is said. "I Have a Dream" is an emotional speech. Its effect, however, would have been much less powerful if it had been delivered in a monotone or in a cold, detached tone of voice.

9. You may have seen news clips showing King giving this speech. If not, imagine King speaking to the huge crowd. What tone of voice do you think he used? Do you think he spoke slowly or quickly? What words do you think he emphasized? How might his delivery of the speech have contributed to its appeal?

Questions for Thought and Discussion

The questions and activities that follow will help you explore "I Have a Dream" in more depth and at the same time develop your critical thinking skills.

1. **Interpreting Figurative Language.** King uses other metaphors in addition to the ones discussed in the lesson. Find at least one other metaphor. State what two things are being compared and explain how they are alike. What is the emotional effect of the metaphor?

2. **Making Inferences.** In his speech King makes the following statement: "Some of you have come fresh from narrow jail cells." Why do you think King assumed that some of the audience had recently been in jail?

3. **Recalling Facts.** What patriotic song does King quote in his speech? Why are the words especially appropriate for the occasion?

4. **Expressing an Opinion.** Dr. King delivered "I Have a Dream" in 1963. To what extent do you think his dream has been realized? Support your opinion with specific facts.

Writing About Literature

Several suggestions for writing projects follow. You may be asked to complete one or more of these projects. If you have any questions about

how to begin a writing assignment, review Using the Writing Process, beginning on page 341.

1. **Creating Metaphors.** Dr. King makes abstract ideas come alive by using metaphors. For example, he calls poverty a "lonely island . . . in the midst of a vast ocean of material prosperity." Create some original metaphors for such abstract ideas as loneliness, happiness, and peace. Write at least three metaphors.

2. **Describing a Dream.** What is your dream for the world? Imagine that you have been asked to speak before the General Assembly of the United Nations. Outline a speech that describes your dream. Include both the rational arguments and the emotional appeals that you might use to support your dream.

3. **Reporting on Research.** Find out more about some aspect of the civil rights movement and write a report based on your research. Be prepared to deliver your report orally. Possible topics include: the March on Washington for Jobs and Freedom; the Montgomery bus boycott; the integration of Central High School in Little Rock, Arkansas; the freedom riders; lunch counter sit-ins; any leader of the civil rights movement; or the Civil Rights Bill of 1964.

Chapter 14

Selection

Choice: A Tribute to
Dr. Martin Luther King, Jr.
ALICE WALKER

Lesson

Tone

About the Selection

Alice Walker delivered her tribute to Dr. King in 1972, four years after his death. The speech was made in a Jackson, Mississippi, restaurant. A few years earlier, the restaurant had refused to serve black people. Under pressure from the civil rights movement, the restaurant had changed its policy.

Walker's tribute is a style of speech called a eulogy. A <u>eulogy</u> is a speech or a piece of writing in praise of a person or thing. Eulogies are often given at funerals to praise a person who has recently died. A eulogy usually reflects how the speaker feels about the person being eulogized.

In her tribute Alice Walker assumes that her listeners are familiar with Dr. King's achievements. Instead of concentrating on his achievements, she focuses on her feelings about him. But to understand Walker's feelings about King, you need to know what Dr. King meant to black Americans during the 1950s and 1960s.

As you learned in Chapter 13, Dr. Martin Luther King, Jr., was a leader of the civil rights movement. He was committed to equal rights and to nonviolence.

Acting on the philosophy of nonviolence meant that protesters risked physical abuse, and they often faced jail for supporting their beliefs. Dr. King took these same risks. He, too, was physically attacked and spent time in jail.

In one famous campaign King led an effort to integrate public facilities in Birmingham, Alabama, such as waiting rooms, swimming pools, and bathrooms. During the demonstrations, police used fire hoses and dogs to frighten and hold back the demonstrators. When King ignored a local court order against the demonstrations, he was jailed.

In another widely publicized campaign, he worked to help blacks register to vote in Alabama. During the campaign, King became the first black to stay at the Hotel Albert in Selma. While signing in at the hotel, he was assaulted by a white man. Two months later, King led 3,200 blacks and whites from all over the country on a five-day march from Selma to Montgomery. The purpose of the march was to support efforts to register black voters. In the past many black voters were prevented by white officials from registering.

The Birmingham demonstrations and the Selma march, as well as many other nonviolent protests, helped black Americans win basic freedoms they had previously been denied. It also gave them pride in their accomplishments. Dr. King became a national symbol of that pride.

Like Dr. King, Alice Walker is a black American from Georgia. Walker was born in 1944, the youngest of eight children. Her father earned about three hundred dollars a year from sharecropping and dairy farming. Her mother worked in the fields and also worked as a maid to add to the family income. Of her mother Walker has said, "I grew up believing that there was nothing, literally nothing, my mother couldn't do once she set her mind to it. . . ."

Both of Walker's parents were storytellers. At an early age, Walker began to write down their stories and to create her own poems. When she was eight years old, she was accidentally shot in the eye with a BB gun by one of her brothers. Because the family did not have a car, it was a week before her parents could get her to a doctor. She lost the sight in that eye, and filmy white scar tissue grew over the eye. The disfigurement made Walker very shy, and she spent more and more time alone, reading and writing poetry.

In high school Alice Walker began to emerge from her shyness and was eventually voted the most popular girl in her class. Yet the years of solitude she spent reading and writing had opened a new world to her.

After graduating from college in 1965, Walker spent a summer in Mississippi to "be in the heart of the civil-rights movement." There she met and later married Melvin Leventhal, a white civil rights lawyer. They became the first legally married interracial couple in Jackson, Mississippi. They were divorced in 1976, and Walker now lives in San Francisco. She is still an activist and has recently been involved in the antinuclear movement.

Alice Walker has written essays, short stories, novels, and poetry. Her best-known work is a novel called *The Color Purple*. It won a Pulitzer Prize and was made into a popular movie. The book was praised for its loving portrait of Southern black women but criticized for its unsympathetic view of black men.

Whatever her fictional portrayal of black men might be, Walker clearly loved and respected Dr. Martin Luther King, Jr. In the speech you will read, she explains what Dr. King meant to her and to her family.

Lesson Preview

The lesson that follows "Choice: A Tribute to Dr. Martin Luther King, Jr.," focuses on the tone of Alice Walker's speech. Tone is a writer's attitude toward his or her subject or toward the audience. You might expect a eulogy to be full of praise for its subject. But writers and speakers do not always express their feelings directly. Sometimes a writer's attitude is implied, or suggested, rather than stated outright.

The questions that follow will help you discover Walker's tone. As you read, think about how you would answer these questions.

1 What does Alice Walker talk about in the first half of her speech? What are her feelings about this topic?

2 How is the first part of Walker's speech related to her feelings about Martin Luther King, Jr.?

3 What words does Walker use to describe King? What attitude do these words suggest?

4 According to Walker, what is the most important thing that Dr. King gave to black Americans?

Vocabulary

Here are some difficult words that appear in the selection that follows. Study the words and their definitions, as well as the sentences that show how the words are used. This will help you get the most from your reading.

ancestral inherited from one's forebears. *Although she had been away for many years, the woman finally returned to the ancestral home that she had inherited from her mother.*

dispossession the depriving of a person's belongings. *This homeless family suffered dispossession after a fire destroyed their apartment building.*

sensibility awareness; sensitiveness. *Her visual sensibility made her an excellent photographer.*

serene peaceful. *Despite many angry comments from the crowd, the speaker remained calm and serene.*

disinherit take away the rights of an heir. *The millionaire threatened to disinherit his children if they did not join the family business.*

Choice: A Tribute to
Dr. Martin Luther King, Jr.

ALICE WALKER

My great-great-great-grandmother walked as a slave from Virginia to Eatonton, Georgia—which passes for the Walker ancestral home—with two babies on her hips. She lived to be a hundred and twenty-five years old and my own father knew her as a boy. (It is in memory of this walk that I choose to keep and to embrace my "maiden" name, Walker.)

There is a cemetery near our family church where she is buried; but because her marker was made of wood and rotted years ago, it is impossible to tell exactly where her body lies. In the same cemetery are most of my mother's people, who have lived in Georgia for so long nobody even remembers when they came. And all of my great-aunts and -uncles are there, and my grandfather and grandmother, and, very recently, my own father.

If it is true that land does not belong to anyone until they have buried a body in it, then the land of my birthplace belongs to me, dozens of times over. Yet the history of my family, like that of all black Southerners, is a history of dispossession. We loved the land and worked the land, but we never owned it; and even if we bought land, as my great-grandfather did after the Civil War, it was always in danger of being taken away, as his was, during the period following Reconstruction.[1]

My father inherited nothing of material value from his father, and when I came of age in the early sixties I awoke to the bitter knowledge that in order just to continue to love the land of my birth, I was expected to leave it. For black people—including my parents—had learned a long time ago that to stay willingly in a beloved but brutal place is to risk losing the love and being forced to acknowledge only the brutality.

It is a part of the black Southern sensibility that we treasure memories; for such a long time, that is all of our homeland those of us who at one time or another were forced away from it have been allowed to have.

I watched my brothers, one by one, leave our home and leave the South. I watched my sisters do the same. This was not unusual; abandonment, except for memories, was the common thing, except for those who "could not do any better," or those whose strength or stubbornness was so colossal they took the risk that others could not bear.

In 1960, my mother and I bought a television set, and each day after school I watched Hamilton Holmes and Charlayne Hunter as they struggled to integrate—fair-skinned as they were—the University of Georgia. And then, one day, there appeared the face of Dr. Martin Luther King, Jr. What a funny name, I thought. At the moment I first saw him, he was being handcuffed and shoved into a police truck. He had dared to claim his rights as a native son, and had been arrested. He displayed no fear, but seemed calm and serene, unaware of his own extraordinary courage. His whole body, like his conscience, was at peace.

At the moment I saw his resistance I knew I would never be able

---

1. **Reconstruction:** the period from 1865 to 1877 following the Civil War. During that period, the states that had seceded from the union were reorganized. Blacks were encouraged to vote and to buy land. After Reconstruction ended, white Southerners again controlled state governments, and they passed laws limiting the rights of blacks.

to live in this country without resisting everything that sought to disinherit me, and I would never be forced away from the land of my birth without a fight.

He was The One, The Hero, The One Fearless Person for whom we had waited. I hadn't even realized before that we *had* been waiting for Martin Luther King, Jr., but we had. And I knew it for sure when my mother added his name to the list of people she prayed for every night.

I sometimes think that it was literally the prayers of people like my mother and father, who had bowed down in the struggle for such a long time, that kept Dr. King alive until five years ago. For years we went to bed praying for his life, and awoke with the question "Is the 'Lord' still here?"

The public acts of Dr. King you know. They are visible all around you. His voice you would recognize sooner than any other voice you have heard in this century—this in spite of the fact that certain municipal libraries, like the one in downtown Jackson, do not carry recordings of his speeches, and the librarians chuckle cruelly when asked why they do not.

You know, if you have read his books, that his is a complex and revolutionary philosophy[2] that few people are capable of understanding fully or have the patience to embody in themselves. Which is our weakness, which is our loss.

And if you know anything about good Baptist preaching, you can imagine what you missed if you never had a chance to hear Martin Luther King, Jr., preach at Ebenezer Baptist Church.

You know of the prizes and awards that he tended to think very little of. And you know of his concern for the disinherited: the American Indian, the Mexican-American, and the poor American white—for whom he cared much.

You know that this very room, in this very restaurant, was closed to people of color not more than five years ago. And that we eat here

---

2. **a complex and revolutionary philosophy:** Walker is referring to Dr. King's philosophy of passive resistance and nonviolence.

Tone

together tonight largely through his efforts and his blood. We accept the common pleasures of life, assuredly, in his name.

But add to all of these things the one thing that seems to me second to none in importance: He gave us back our heritage. He gave us back our homeland; the bones and dust of our ancestors, who may now sleep within our caring *and* our hearing. He gave us the blueness of the Georgia sky in autumn as in summer; the colors of the Southern winter as well as glimpses of the green of vacation-time spring. Those of our relatives we used to invite for a visit we now can ask to stay. . . . He gave us full-time use of our own woods, and restored our memories to those of us who were forced to run away, as realities we might each day enjoy and leave for our children.

He gave us continuity of place, without which community is ephemeral.[3] He gave us home.

3. **ephemeral:** short-lived.

Reviewing the Selection

Answer each of the following questions without looking back at the selection.

Recalling Facts

1. Alice Walker considers her ancestral home to be
   ☐ a. Alabama.
   ☐ b. Georgia.
   ☐ c. Africa.
   ☐ d. Mississippi.

Understanding Main Ideas

2. According to Walker, what did Dr. King give back to Southern blacks?
   ☐ a. their heritage
   ☐ b. their freedom
   ☐ c. their sense of history
   ☐ d. their voices

Placing Events in Order

3. Walker's great-grandfather bought his land
   ☐ a. during the American Revolution.
   ☐ b. after the Civil War.
   ☐ c. before Reconstruction.
   ☐ d. before the Civil War.

Finding Supporting Details

4. Walker became interested in the civil rights movement as a result of
   ☐ a. hearing Martin Luther King, Jr., preach.
   ☐ b. visiting the cemetery where her ancestors were buried.
   ☐ c. learning that the local library did not have recordings of Dr. King's speeches.
   ☐ d. watching television news stories about the integration of the University of Georgia.

5. "My father inherited nothing of <u>material</u> value from his father." In this context *material* means
   ☐ a. fabric.
   ☐ b. spiritual.
   ☐ c. necessary.
   ☐ d. worldly.

Interpreting the Selection

Answer each of the following questions. You may look back at the selection if necessary.

6. Alice Walker's brothers and sisters left the South to
   ☐ a. escape from segregation.
   ☐ b. make better lives for themselves.
   ☐ c. work in the civil rights movement.
   ☐ d. get a good education.

7. In her speech Walker shows
   ☐ a. more concern for her brothers than for her sisters.
   ☐ b. little feeling about her family.
   ☐ c. a strong sense of history.
   ☐ d. outrage at the University of Georgia.

8. Which of the following is a fact?
   - ☐ a. Walker's great-great-great-grandmother lived to be 125 years old.
   - ☐ b. Land does not belong to a family until they have buried a body in it.
   - ☐ c. The prayers of black Southerners kept Dr. King alive until 1968.
   - ☐ d. Dr. King was an outstanding preacher.

9. Alice Walker does not know when her mother's people came to Georgia because
   - ☐ a. they came so long ago.
   - ☐ b. all the family records were destroyed.
   - ☐ c. they are all dead now.
   - ☐ d. she is not interested in history.

10. Walker tells about seeing Martin Luther King, Jr., on television to
    - ☐ a. show what a famous man he was.
    - ☐ b. prove that his public acts were dangerous and violent.
    - ☐ c. portray his strength and courage.
    - ☐ d. explain that he wanted to be arrested.

Tone

After reading Alice Walker's speech, you understand how strongly she feels about Dr. Martin Luther King, Jr. Yet Walker never once states her feelings directly. She does not say, for example, that she loved, respected, or admired Dr. King. Instead, her feelings about Dr. King are suggested by the tone of her speech.

The tone of a piece of writing can be compared to the tone of voice that a person uses in speaking. When you speak, you communicate both by the words you use and by your tone of voice. Depending on your tone of voice, the same words can communicate very different ideas or feelings.

Suppose you get a phone call at home. After you hang up, someone in your family asks, "Who was that?" In response you say, "It was Amy." Without saying more, your tone of voice might suggest how you feel about Amy. You might convey the feeling that Amy is someone you dislike or someone you never expected to call. Your tone of voice might also reveal that you are delighted that Amy called.

1. Think of three other tones of voice you could use to say, "It was Amy." What feeling does each tone suggest?

In a piece of writing tone refers to the author's attitude toward his or her subject or toward the audience. Of course, you can't *hear* an author's tone of voice. But an author can use a number of techniques to let you know how he or she feels about a subject. In this lesson you will examine the tone of Alice Walker's tribute to Dr. Martin Luther King, Jr.

Tone and Emphasis

Reread the title of the selection. Then think about the content of Walker's speech. You may realize right away that at least half of Alice Walker's speech is about herself and her family. As you have learned, every writer and speaker must choose certain facts and ideas to emphasize. What a writer chooses to emphasize is one clue to his or her attitude toward a subject.

Alice Walker could have devoted her speech to a description of Martin Luther King's many accomplishments. Instead, she chose to talk about herself and her family. What does that emphasis show about her attitude toward Dr. King? It shows that, to Walker, King was not a remote public figure. Rather, he was someone who touched her life in a very personal way. Her attitude, then, is one of personal involvement with her subject.

2. What details about her family does Walker emphasize? How is that emphasis related to her feelings about Dr. King?

3. What details about Dr. King's public life does Walker include in her speech? What does that emphasis reveal about her attitude toward King?

Tone and Organization

Were you surprised by the way in which Alice Walker began her speech? Read the first paragraph:

My great-great-great-grandmother walked as a slave from Virginia to Eatonton, Georgia—which passes for the Walker ancestral home—with two babies on her hips. She lived to be

335

a hundred and twenty-five years old and my own father knew her as a boy. (It is in memory of this walk that I choose to keep and to embrace my "maiden" name, Walker.)

You might have expected Walker to begin her speech with words of praise for Dr. King. Instead, she begins with a fact from her family history. The way a speaker opens a speech is part of the speech's organization. Through organization, writers and speakers often reveal their attitudes toward their subjects.

The opening and closing parts of a speech are important because people tend to remember them. You usually pay close attention to the beginning of the speech. The opening words or phrases determine if the speech will catch your interest. You remember the end of a speech because it is the last thing you hear.

Walker's opening paragraph accomplishes two things. First, it offers an intriguing story about the speaker's past that catches her listeners' interest. Second, it reveals that history and heritage are important to Walker. The unusual beginning may leave you wondering what Walker's family history has to do with Martin Luther King, Jr. In fact, the story about her ancestors is the foundation for Walker's major point about Dr. King. She makes the point very clear at the end of her speech. Through her organization, Walker connects the whole speech.

4. Reread the last two paragraphs of Walker's speech. In your own words explain the statement, "He gave us back our heritage." How does the statement relate to the beginning of Walker's speech?

As you have noticed, Walker's speech has two main subjects. First, she talks about herself and her family. Second, she talks about Dr. King. How Walker moves from one subject to the other is an important element of the organization of her speech. As you learned in Chapter 6, a bridge from one idea to another is called a transition. A transition can be a few words or several sentences.

5. Skim the speech to find where Walker makes the transition from her first to her second topic. Notice where Martin Luther King's name is first mentioned. Briefly summarize what that transition says.

6. How does that transition contribute to the personal tone that Walker uses in her speech?

Tone and Language

As you learned in Chapter 1, the words a writer uses not only express ideas but also convey emotions. For this reason, the words a writer chooses contribute to the tone of a piece of writing. Sometimes a writer will choose one word over another because of the way the word sounds or because of its connotation. As you have learned, the connotation of a word refers to the emotions or associations that the word arouses or suggests.

> I watched my brothers, one by one, leave our home and leave the South. I watched my sisters do the same. This was not unusual; abandonment, except for memories, was the common thing, except for those who "could not do any better," or those whose strength or stubbornness was so colossal they took the risk that others could not bear.

Notice Walker's use of the word *abandonment*. She could have used the words *leaving* or *departure*. But *abandonment* suggests something mournful and lonely. It precisely describes the sadness Walker felt about the South before Martin Luther King, Jr., began to make changes.

7. Read the paragraph on page 328 that begins, "My father inherited nothing of material value from his father. . . ." What words in that paragraph have a strong emotional meaning? How do those words contribute to the tone in the first part of Walker's speech?

8. Find at least three other words or phrases that Walker uses to describe the South and the status of black people there. Explain how those words or phrases contribute to the tone of Walker's speech.

The tone of Walker's speech changes when she begins to talk about Martin Luther King, Jr. After the sadness and the anger of the first half of the speech, a note of hope and strength appears. Notice the names she gives to King: "The One," "The Hero," "The One Fearless Person," and "the 'Lord.'" They suggest a person of great strength, an extraordinary leader.

9. *Explain how the underlined words in each of the following sentences contribute to the positive tone that Walker uses when she discusses Dr. King.*

    a. *He displayed no fear, but seemed* <u>calm</u> *and* <u>serene</u>, *unaware of his own extraordinary* <u>courage</u>.
    b. *He gave us* <u>home</u>.

Words that Describe Tone

There are many words that can be used to describe a writer's attitude toward his or her subject. You can say a writer's tone is *serious, flippant, emotional, ironical, indifferent, reverent, objective,* or *reserved.* You have already seen the words *sad* and *angry* used to describe Walker's tone in the first part of her speech.

10. *What word or words would you use to describe Walker's tone when she talks about Dr. King? Give reasons for your answer.*

Tone and Delivery

When you read a speech, you experience only part of what the audience hearing the speech felt. When Walker gave her tribute in that Jackson, Mississippi, restaurant, what was the expression on her face? Did she smile? Did she gesture with her hands? What tone of voice did she use? Only the people who were present when Alice Walker gave her speech know what her delivery was like. But the tone of the written speech can help you make an educated guess about her delivery.

An exuberant tone might suggest that the author used gestures. A serious or angry tone might tell you that the speaker did not smile. A reverent tone might mean that the speaker spoke in a quiet voice.

11. *Think about the tone of Alice Walker's speech. How do you think she delivered the speech? Did she speak in a loud or a quiet voice? Did she gesture with her hands? What expression did she have on her face? Do you think she smiled at any point? Support your answers with evidence from the speech.*

Questions for Thought and Discussion

The questions and activities that follow will help you explore "Choice: A Tribute to Dr. Martin Luther King, Jr." in more depth and at the same time develop your critical thinking skills.

1. **Interpreting.** What do you think is the meaning of "Choice" in the title of Alice Walker's speech? In what way is the speech about choices?

2. **Understanding Cause and Effect.** According to Walker, why did blacks have to leave the South before Dr. Martin Luther King, Jr., began his campaign? How did King's work help to change conditions?

3. **Generalizing.** How was Alice Walker personally affected by Dr. King? What leader today do you think has a strong effect on people? Explain your answer.

4. **Paraphrasing.** In your own words explain the meaning of the last paragraph of Alice Walker's speech. What does she mean when she says "He gave us home"?

5. **Comparing.** Compare Alice Walker's speech to one of the speeches you read in Chapters 12 and 13. How are they similar? How are they different?

Writing About Literature

Several suggestions for writing projects follow. You may be asked to complete one or more of these projects. If you have any questions about how to begin a writing assignment, review Using the Writing Process, beginning on page 341.

Tone

1. **Writing a Eulogy.** Imagine that you have been asked to give a eulogy for someone who has had a positive effect on your life. Remember that a eulogy can be about someone who has died or someone who is still alive. You can use Alice Walker's speech as a model. Be sure to make clear how the person to whom you are paying tribute affected you.

2. **Describing a Place.** To Alice Walker, home is where her ancestors are buried. Write a short paper describing the place that is "home" to you. Tell why you consider it home. It might be the place where you now live, where you were born, or from where your ancestors came.

3. **Experimenting with Tone.** Choose a topic about which you have an opinion or a feeling. Possible topics might be a pet, camping out, a school trip, a food, or a popular song. Write two paragraphs about the same topic, each with a different tone. In your first paragraph use an enthusiastic, positive tone. Write your second paragraph using an objective or a negative tone.

Using the Writing Process

The lesson that follows is designed to help you with the writing assignments you will meet in this book. It explains the major steps in the writing process. Read the lesson carefully so that you understand the writing process thoroughly. On pages 351–352, following the lesson, is a checklist. Whenever you are asked to complete a writing assignment, you can just refer to the checklist as a reminder of the things you should consider as you're working on the assignment. The lesson can then serve as a reference—an information source. Turn to it whenever you feel that it would be helpful to review part or all of the process.

When presented with a writing assignment, many people's instant response is panic. What will I write about? Do I have anything to say? To ease the panic, remind yourself that writing is something that *no one* simply sits down and does with the words flowing freely and perfectly from first sentence to last. Rather, writing is a *process;* that is, it involves a number of steps. The writing process is not a straightforward, mechanical one, such as that involved in solving a mathematical problem. These pages give you a plan that you can follow to sensibly work through the complex task of presenting your ideas on paper.

341

Keep in mind that writing is not simply the act of filling a piece of paper with words. It is a sophisticated act of communication. The purpose of writing is to put *ideas* across to other people. Since ideas come from your mind, not your pen, the writing process begins with the work that takes place in your mind: the creation and organization of ideas. The process then proceeds to the expression of ideas—the actual setting down of words on paper. The final stage is the polishing of both the ideas and the words that express them.

As they work, writers engage in a variety of activities—thinking, planning, organizing, writing, revising, rethinking. For clarity, we label the various stages in the process prewriting, writing, and revising. However, the stages are not so straightforward and separate. One blends into the next, and sometimes a writer returns to a previous activity, moving back and forth through the process. When you write, your goal should be to produce a clear and lively work that expresses interesting ideas. The writing process can help you in that effort.

Stage 1: Prewriting

Define Your Task

The first stage in the writing process is prewriting. At this stage, your goal is to choose a topic, to figure out what you are going to say about it, and to decide what style and tone you are going to use. Making these decisions is essential if you are going to write something interesting and to express your ideas clearly and vividly. At this stage you jot down thoughts and ideas—the material that you will eventually organize and write about in detail. During the prewriting stage, you should search for answers to the following questions:

What Will I Write About? This question must be answered before you do anything else. You need to choose a topic. Then you need to *focus* the topic. A focused topic directs your thinking as you write. This is important whether you are writing a brief description, a short story, an essay, or a research paper. Deciding just what issues you want to address, what kind of character you want to develop, or what theme and events you want a story to revolve around will focus your thinking and help you create a bright, strong piece of writing.

A careful decision is called for here. A good topic is neither too broad nor too narrow. The length of what you are writing and your purpose for writing often dictate how broad your focus should be. In an essay or a research paper, for instance, you need to choose a topic that's defined enough to explore in depth. You don't want to choose a topic that's so broad that you can only touch on the main ideas. If your assignment is to write a short story, you'll want to focus on perhaps one main relationship between characters, one important conflict, just a few related events. You can then write in detail to create full, interesting characters and a well-developed story. When you need to focus a topic, think about what would be practical for the given task.

What Do I Want to Say? You need to think about what information you want or need to include, and what ideas you want to communicate.

What Is My Purpose for Writing? Will you try to persuade, to inform, to explain, or to entertain your readers?

What Style Will I Use? Do you want to write formally or in a casual, conversational style? Will you use the first person, I, or the third-person, he, she, or they? Will you write seriously or use jokes and humor? If you are writing a story, will you use dialogue?

How Will I Organize My Ideas? What will you start with? In what order will you present and develop your ideas?

Who Is My Audience? Who will be reading your work? Are you writing for other students? For people who already have some background in the subject? For people who know nothing about the subject? For children or for adults? Your audience will dictate the approach you take—whether you will write in a formal or an informal tone, whether you will provide a lot of background information or very little, what kind of words you will use.

Generate and Organize Ideas

Although most of the writing assignments in this book provide fairly specific directions about the type of writing to be done, they leave lots of room for imagination. By using your imagination, you can discover fresh and exciting ideas that are distinctly yours. How can you come up with those bright ideas? Below are some techniques that can help you tap your creative powers. They can help you at the prewriting stage and any time you need to generate new ideas. You might use them to come up with a topic for a research paper, an essay, or a short story. You might use them to focus a topic or to generate ideas about a topic you've already chosen. Techniques such as outlining and clustering are also useful for organizing ideas. Try each of the techniques, and eventually you'll find the ones that work best for you for a particular purpose.

Free Writing. Have you ever been given a writing assignment and found that you had no idea what to write? Free writing is an activity for getting started—for coming up with ideas to write about. To free write, write anything that comes to mind, no matter how far off the topic it seems. At first it may seem silly, but eventually your mind will start associating ideas. Soon you will be writing complete thoughts about the topic.

Suppose you were asked to write about winter. How to begin? Start writing. Put down the first thought that comes to mind and let ideas begin to flow. You might come up with something like this:

> I don't know what to write. Winter. What can I say that hasn't already been said about winter? It's cold, there's lots of snow . . . well, not in all places I guess. Actually when it's cold here, it's warm on the other side of the world. Do they call that winter then, or summer . . . ?

Can you see how you might go from thoughts that are totally off the track to thoughts that are intriguing? When you have finished, look at all the ideas you've written down. Perhaps there are whole sentences or paragraphs that can go into your story or essay. This exercise will have gotten you started.

Brainstorming. This also is an activity to generate ideas. It can be done alone or in a group. When brainstorming, you want to come up with as many ideas as possible. Each idea will spur a new idea. As you or others in a brainstorming group think of ideas, write them down. After you have come up with all the ideas you can, select several to develop for the assignment.

Clustering. This technique can be useful both to generate ideas and to organize them. In fact, you actually do both at the same time, for as you jot down ideas, you "cluster" the ones that go together.

Begin by putting your main idea—your focused topic—in the center of the page and circling it. As you think of ideas associated with the main idea, write them nearby, circle them, and connect them with a line to the main idea. Then, as you think of ideas related to each of those *subtopics*, attach the ideas to the word they relate to. You can take this process as far as you like. The farther you branch out, the more detailed you get. When you get to the point where you're ready to write your story or your essay, you can use such a diagram as a guide to grouping your ideas. A simple clustering diagram is shown below. The main idea is "symbols in a story."

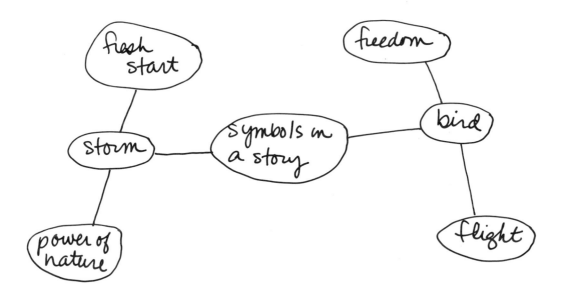

Using the Writing Process

Outlining. Outlining is usually thought of as an organizing tool, but it also provides a useful form in which to write down ideas as you think of them. It gives you a way to group ideas, just as clustering does. In addition, it helps you to organize those groups of ideas—to arrange them in the order in which you think you would like to write about them.

Start by writing down some main ideas that you want to include. Leave space after each one for listing related facts or thoughts—details— that you will want to include about the topic. Each idea you list will probably make you think of another idea. Look at the example below. Imagine that your assignment is to write a character sketch. You think you'd like to write about an old man. That's a main idea, so you write it down. One of the aspects of the man you want to talk about is his lifestyle. That, too, is a main idea, so you leave some space after your first idea and write it down. Okay, you ask yourself, what is the old man like? List each specific detail under the first main idea. Go on and do the same with lifestyle, and whatever other main ideas you may have.

Character Sketch

Old Man
    about 80 years old
    tall, thin, straight
    athletic
    friendly, outgoing
Man's Lifestyle
    lives in his own apartment in the city
    involved in theater
    many friends of all ages

You can work back and forth in an outline, adding and deleting, until you're satisfied with the ideas that are there. Your last step will be to arrange the outline in the order in which you think you want to present the ideas in your writing. Then the outline becomes a kind of map for writing. Remember, though, that it's a loose map—you can rearrange, drop, and add ideas even as you are writing.

Outlining is also a good way of organizing the ideas you generate through brainstorming and free writing. It helps you place those ideas in some kind of order.

Stage 2: Writing

The second stage in the writing process is the writing itself. At this stage, you write a first draft of your paper or story, using the notes or outline that you developed in the prewriting stage as a guide. This is the stage at which you turn those loose ideas into sentences and paragraphs that work together.

Get Your Thoughts on Paper. When you begin writing, the most important thing to focus on is saying what you want to say—getting all your ideas down on paper in sentences and paragraphs. Some people find it easiest to write their first drafts without worrying if they have chosen exactly the right words and without checking on spelling. Just put a question mark next to anything you aren't sure of and check it later. You can even put a blank in a sentence if you can't think of the right word to put there. Fill it in when you revise.

As you are writing, you may discover that you sometimes have to go back and do some more thinking and planning. You may need to gather more information or think through an idea again. You may also do some rearranging of ideas.

Develop a Tone. In the writing stage, you need to begin to develop a tone—an attitude toward your subject. How do you want to *sound* to the reader? What impression do you want the reader to have toward the subject? Do you want to sound authoritative, amusing, sad, pleased?

You'll want to establish your tone right away—in the first paragraph. The first paragraph is important because it must grab your reader's interest and show where you are headed.

Organize Your Writing. As you write, you will, of course, be following the basic rules of the language. Sentences should express complete thoughts. They should follow one another in logical order. Each paragraph should focus on one main idea, and it should contain details that support that idea.

As you move from one paragraph to the next, use transition words and phrases to link your ideas. Clearly connect ideas and thoughts that go together so the reader can follow your story, argument, or explanation.

Stage 3: Revising

The third stage in the writing process is revising. This is the point at which you look for ways to polish your writing. Revising is more than just fixing a few errors. It can involve both major and minor changes.

Rethink Ideas and Organization

The first goal in revising is to check for clear, logical expression. Does what I have written make sense? Have I clearly said everything I am trying to say? Have I arranged my ideas in the best order?

Reread the entire draft to see if paragraphs and sentences follow in a logical order. You may find that putting paragraphs in a different order makes your points clearer. Remember that each paragraph is part of a whole, and it should relate to your topic. Sometimes you may write an excellent paragraph, only to discover that it has very little to do with the topic. No matter how good you think a sentence or a paragraph is, drop it if it doesn't belong.

As you read what you have written, you may also want to rewrite sentences and paragraphs, or even add new material. At this stage, you may also want to go back to your prewriting notes to see that you included everything you wanted to include.

Look at Your Language

After you have checked the ideas and organization, review the style and form in which you have written. Think about the language—the words and phrases you have used. Do they say precisely what you mean? Do they create strong images?

If you want your writing to be lively and interesting, write with strong verbs and nouns. They make strong writing. If you find yourself piling on the adjectives and adverbs, you'll know that you're struggling to support weak verbs and nouns. What is a strong verb or noun? It is one that is precise, active, fresh. It paints a clear picture in the mind.

Use Strong Verbs. Some verbs, for instance, are tired, overused, dull. The verb *to be*, for example, is about the weakest verb in the language. It doesn't *do* anything. So look at the sentences in which you use the verbs *is, are, am, was, have been,* etc. Are there action words that you can use instead? Instead of saying "Sam was happy," might you describe an action that *shows* that Sam was happy? "Sam smiled shyly and nodded his head," "Sam beamed," "Sam grinned," "Sam jumped into the air, arms raised above his head, and shouted, YES!"

Use Precise Nouns. Your nouns too should be precise. Whenever possible, create a strong image for the reader. The word *thing*, for instance, is imprecise and overused. What kind of image does it create in your mind? None. Search for the word that *tells*. If you are describing a street scene, for instance, instead of saying that there is a building on the corner, can you tell what kind of building it is? Is it a bank? A three-story Victorian house? A gothic cathedral? An open-air vegetable market? Draw clear pictures with your nouns.

Don't Overuse Adjectives and Adverbs. Adjectives and adverbs have their place, but try not to overdo them. When you do find yourself in need of an adjective, choose one that creates a strong image. Avoid those that are overused and don't really describe. *Beautiful* and *nice*, for instance, are overused adjectives.

Toss Out Unnecessary Words. Have you used more words than you need to say something? This is known as being redundant. Saying that someone is "bright and intelligent," for instance, is redundant because the adjectives are synonyms. Use one or the other. Another example is the phrase "crucially important." Why not just say "crucial"?

As you examine your language, throw out any words that don't serve a purpose—that don't give information, paint a clear picture, or create atmosphere. By taking out unnecessary words, you will have "tight writing"—writing that moves along.

Check the Structure and Rhythm of Your Sentences. Read your work out loud and listen to the rhythm and sounds of the language. Do the sentences all sound the same? If they do, can you vary the structure of your sentences—making some simple, some complex, some long, some short? Correct any sentence fragments, and divide run-on sentences into two or more sentences.

After you've gone through that kind of thinking a few times at the revision stage, you'll find yourself automatically choosing livelier, clearer language as you write. You'll become a better writer. That, too, is a process.

Check for Errors

The final step in the revising process is the all-important "housekeeping" review—checking for correct spelling, grammar, and punctuation, and for readable handwriting. You don't, of course, have to wait until the end of the writing process to pay attention to those details. But before you write your final draft, check carefully for errors in those areas.

Checklist for the Writing Process

✓ What is my topic? Is it focused enough? Should I broaden or narrow it?

✓ What do I want to say about the topic? What are my thoughts, feelings, and ideas about it?

✓ Which prewriting activity or activities would most help me to gather ideas?

✓ Do I need to do some research? Some reading? Consult outside sources? What other materials, if any, do I need?

✓ What is the main point or idea that I want to communicate? What ideas are secondary? Which of those ideas are most important?

✓ What details will I include to support and expand on the main ideas?

✓ Should I include examples or anecdotes?

✓ How will I organize my ideas?

✓ What is my purpose for writing? Do I want to entertain? Inform? Explain? Persuade? Perhaps a combination?

✓ Who is my audience?

✓ What kind of language will I use? Will I be formal, informal, or casual? Will I use dialogue? Will I speak directly to the reader?

✓ What tone do I want to take—what feeling do I want to give the reader about the subject? How can I sustain that tone throughout my writing?

✓ How can I effectively begin my first paragraph? Should I use a question? A startling or unusual fact? An amazing statistic? Should I begin with an action or a description? Perhaps a piece of dialogue?

✓ How will I end? If writing nonfiction, should I summarize what I have already said, or should I offer a new thought or argument as my conclusion?

✓ Have I developed my ideas in the best order possible? Should I move some paragraphs around?

✓ Have I covered my topic adequately? Does the writing fulfill its purpose and get the main point across to my audience?

✓ Do I need to rewrite parts? Perhaps some ideas need to be clarified or explained further. Perhaps I could write a better description or account of an event?

✓ Do I want to add anything?

✓ Are there any unnecessary ideas or details that should be deleted?

✓ Is each paragraph well developed—are the facts and ideas presented in a good order?

✓ Do all the sentences in each paragraph relate to one idea?

✓ Are the ideas between sentences and between paragraphs connected with transition words and phrases that make the connections clear?

✓ Is the writing vivid? Have I used active, precise, colorful words that create strong images?

✓ Does the final paragraph provide a good ending?

✓ Are the sentences well constructed? Are there any run-ons or sentence fragments that need fixing? Do I vary the kinds of sentences—some long, some short, some active, some passive?

✓ Is the grammar correct?

✓ Are all the words spelled correctly?

✓ Is all the punctuation correct?

✓ Is the final draft clean and legible?

✓ Have I read the final draft over one last time to check for any errors that may have crept in as I was copying?

Glossary of Literary Terms

This glossary includes definitions for all the important literary terms introduced in this book. The first time they are defined and discussed in the text, the terms are underlined. Following each term in the glossary is a page reference (in parentheses) that tells the page on which the term is introduced.

Many terms are discussed in more than one chapter, especially as they apply to various selections. This glossary provides the fullest definition of each term. Boldfaced words within the definitions are other terms that appear in the glossary.

alliteration (page 25) the close repetition of the same first sounds in words. Writers use alliteration to add emphasis to an idea or to certain words. Although alliteration usually occurs at the beginnings of words, it can also occur within words.

allusion (page 318) a reference to something real or fictitious outside of a speech or a piece of writing. The speaker or writer expects the audience to recognize the allusion.

anecdote (page 113) a brief story about an interesting incident. Like a short story, an anecdote has characters, a setting, and a plot. Writers use anecdotes to support their opinions and to add interest to their work.

anticipating the opposition (page 316) a technique of persuasive writing or speaking in which a person addresses the arguments he or she thinks an opponent will use, and answers those arguments effectively.

argument (page 316) one or more reasons presented by a speaker or a writer to lead the audience to a logical conclusion.

Glossary of Literary Terms

argumentation (page 91) the kind of writing that tries to persuade readers to accept an author's opinions. Essayists, for example, use argumentation to convince readers that the essayist's opinions are correct. The other basic kinds of writing are **description, exposition,** and **narration.**

article (page 91) a written work that tries to give readers an unbiased, or balanced, view of a topic. Articles often appear in newspapers and magazines. Unlike **essays,** which contain opinions, articles usually focus on presenting factual information.

autobiography (page 3) the story of a person's life written by that person.

biography (page 3) the story of a person's life written by another person.

character development (page 80) the methods that writers use to show readers what a person is like. The four main techniques are (1) revealing a person's own words, (2) showing what others say or think about the person, (3) showing a person's actions, and (4) telling the reader through **description** and **interpretation** what the writer thinks of the person.

chronological order (page 177) the arrangement of events in the order in which they occur.

circumlocution (page 299) an indirect way of saying something. It often involves using many more words than necessary to express an idea. Writers sometimes use circumlocution as a method of adding humor to a work.

connotation (page 25) the emotion that a word arouses or the meanings that it suggests beyond its **denotation,** or dictionary meaning.

denotation (page 25) the dictionary meaning of a word.

description (page 82) the kind of writing that helps readers to picture a person, a place, or an event. The other basic kinds of nonfiction writing are **argumentation, exposition,** and **narration.**

dialogue (page 24) the actual conversation between the characters in a story.

diction (page 295) a writer's choice and arrangement of words.

digression (page 133) a wandering from the main point of a story. Some writers use digression as a method of adding humor to their work.

essay (page 91) a brief composition that expresses a person's opinions or views about a particular subject. An essayist usually tries to persuade readers to accept his or her views about that subject. *See* **formal essay** and **informal essay.**

eulogy (page 323) a speech or a piece of writing in praise of a person or a thing. A eulogy usually reflects the speaker's or writer's feelings about the person or thing being eulogized.

exaggeration (page 133) an intentional overstatement of facts or events so that their meanings are intensified. Exaggeration is not meant to trick the reader but to create humorous results.

exposition (page 91) the kind of writing that presents information. Exposition is sometimes called expository writing. The other basic kinds of writing are **argumentation, description,** and **narration.**

extended metaphor (page 319) a special kind of **metaphor** that is longer and more involved than an ordinary metaphor. The smaller metaphors within an extended metaphor contribute to the overall meaning.

figurative language (page 26) words and phrases used in unusual ways to create strong, vivid images, to focus attention on certain ideas, or to compare things that are basically different. When words or phrases are used figuratively, they have meanings other than their usual, or literal, meanings. *See* **figures of speech, hyperbole, metaphor, personification,** and **simile.**

figures of speech (page 26) words or phrases that create vivid images by contrasting unlike things. A figure of speech has meanings other than its ordinary meaning.

flashback (page 177) a scene, a conversation, or an event that interrupts the present action to show something that happened in the past. Writers use flashbacks to give readers information about past events and to add interest to the present action of the story.

formal essay (page 91) an **essay** that uses **formal language** and often sounds impersonal. Serious subjects such as philosophy and history are usually discussed in formal essays.

formal language (page 23) the language used by many writers of scholarly books. It usually has longer sentences and a greater variety of words than everyday speech.

frame of reference (page 240) the social and historical conditions in which a writer lives. An author's frame of reference influences his or her attitudes and opinions.

generalization (page 113) a broad, unspecific statement that is based on a number of facts.

hyperbole (page 27) a **figure of speech** which deliberately exaggerates the truth in order to express an idea or feeling. "I've told you that a million times" is an example of hyperbole. *See* **figurative language.**

inference (page 56) an educated guess based on limited facts. To draw a conclusion from an inference, a reader must decide what those limited facts imply, or suggest.

informal essay (page 91) an **essay** that uses **informal language** and often reveals the writer's personality. An informal essay is sometimes called a personal essay.

informal language (page 22) the language that people use in everyday conversation. It usually consists of fairly short sentences and simple vocabulary.

interpretation (page 53) one person's view of the meaning of certain words, events, or actions. Nonfiction writers are continually interpreting facts by explaining their meaning and evaluating their importance.

irony (page 27) the contrast between appearance and reality or what is expected and what actually happens.

lead paragraph (page 154) the opening paragraph of an article. The lead paragraph often catches the reader's attention.

metaphor (page 26) an imaginative implied comparison between two unlike things. A metaphor is a comparison that suggests one thing *is* another. The purpose of a metaphor is to give readers an unusual way of looking at one of the things. *See* **figurative language.**

monologue (page 81) a long, uninterrupted speech delivered by one person.

narration (page 24) the kind of writing that gives the events and actions of the story. The other basic kinds of writing are **argumentation, description,** and **exposition.**

nonfiction (page 3) prose writing that gives factual information about real people, places, and events.

objectivity (page 232) putting aside personal feelings and prejudices when looking at events.

order of importance (page 278) an ordering of topics or events based on the significance the writer places on each. For example, a writer may describe an unimportant idea first and work up to the most important, or the writer may do the reverse, moving from the most important topic to the least important one.

parallelism (page 25) the repetition of phrases or clauses that are similar in structure. Writers use parallelism to emphasize or to draw attention to certain ideas or feelings. An example of parallelism in the Bible is: Thou shall not kill. Thou shall not commit adultery.

personification (page 135) a **figure of speech** in which an animal, an object, or an idea is given human qualities. Personification can be used to add humor to a work or to describe abstract ideas. *See* **figurative language.**

Glossary of Literary Terms

perspective (page 232) examining things, people, or events in as general a way as possible to determine their true relationship to each other. Two ways of achieving perspective are allowing time to pass before judging a situation and examining a situation from another person's point of view.

primary information (page 175) information that comes directly from the author's own experience. In nonfiction writing primary information helps to make a scene lively and realistic. *See* **secondary information.**

profile (page 63) a short, concise **biography.**

secondary information (page 176) information that does not come from the author's own experience. *See* **primary information.**

simile (page 230) a direct comparison between two unlike things that are connected by *like, as,* or *resembles* or the verb *appears* or *seems.* The purpose of a simile is to give the reader a vivid new way of looking at one of the things. *See* **figurative language.**

spatial order (page 278) the order in which objects are arranged in space. Spatial order is often used to describe a scene, telling what is in the foreground and what is in the background, or what is at the left and what is at the right.

structure (page 295) a writer's arrangement or overall design of a work. Structure refers to the way words, sentences, and paragraphs are organized to create a complete work.

style (page 132) the way in which a piece of literature is written. How an author writes is part of his or her style. **Description, narration,** and **tone** are all elements of a writer's style.

subheads (page 204) short titles within an article that identify the beginning of each new topic.

subject (page 3) the person whose life story is being told in a biography or an autobiography.

synonym (page 157) a word or phrase having practically the same meaning as another word or phrase.

theme (page 54) the underlying message or the central idea of a piece of writing.

thesis statement (page 153) the way in which the main idea of an **article** is expressed. A thesis statement is usually worded as a **generalization** that a writer then supports with concrete, or specific, evidence. A thesis statement may be clearly stated or implied.

tone (page 114) a writer's attitude toward his or her subject or toward the audience.

topic sentence (page 155) a sentence that states the main idea of a paragraph.

transition (page 156) the connection between two or more ideas in a piece of writing. A transition may connect one sentence to the next or one paragraph to another. It may also connect a paragraph to a **thesis statement** in an **article.**

viewpoint (page 251) the feelings, opinions, and experiences that affect a writer's outlook on life. A writer's viewpoint affects not only how he or she understands the facts but also which facts he or she includes in a piece of writing.